Stable Nuclear Zero

This volume examines the conditions necessary for a stable nuclear-weapons-free world and the implications for nuclear disarmament policy.

The Nuclear Non-Proliferation Treaty (NPT) is a road map to nuclear zero, but it is a rudimentary one and it says nothing about the kind of zero to aim for. Preferably, this would be a world where the inhibitions against reversal are strong enough to make it stably non-nuclear. What then are the requirements of stable zero? The literature on nuclear disarmament has paid little attention to this question. By and large, the focus has been on the next steps, and discussions tend to stop where the NPT stops: with the elimination of the weapons. This book seeks to fill lacunae by examining the requirements of stable zero and their implications for the road map to that goal, starting from the vision to the present day. The volume highlights that a clear conception of the goal not only is important in itself, but can shed light on what kind of disarmament process to promote.

This book will be of much interest to students of nuclear proliferation, global governance, security studies and IR.

Sverre Lodgaard is Senior Research fellow and former Director of the Norwegian Institute of International Affairs (NUPI). He is author of *Nuclear Disarmament and Non-Proliferation* (Routledge, 2011) and co-editor of *Nuclear Proliferation and International Security* (with Bremer Maerli, Routledge, 2007).

Routledge Global Security Studies
Series Editors: Aaron Karp and Regina Karp

Global Security Studies emphasizes broad forces reshaping global security and the dilemmas facing decision-makers the world over. The series stresses issues relevant in many countries and regions, accessible to broad professional and academic audiences as well as to students, and enduring through explicit theoretical foundations.

Precision Strike Warfare and International Intervention
Strategic, ethico-legal, and decisional implications
Edited by Mike Aaronson, Wali Aslam, Tom Dyson and Regina Rauxloh

Nuclear Proliferation and the Psychology of Political Leadership
Beliefs, motivations and perceptions
K.P. O'Reilly

Nuclear Weapons and International Security
Collected essays
Ramesh Thakur

International Relations Theory and European Security
We thought we knew
Edited by Lorenzo Cladi and Andrea Locatelli

The Evolution of Military Power in the West and Asia
Security policy in the post-Cold War era
Edited by Pauline Eadie and Wyn Rees

Regional Peacemaking and Conflict Management
A comparative approach
Edited by Carmela Lutmar and Benjamin Miller

Nonproliferation Policy and Nuclear Posture
Causes and consequences for the spread of nuclear weapons
Edited by Neil Narang, Erik Gartzke and Matthew Kroenig

Global Nuclear Disarmament
Strategic, political, and regional perspectives
Edited by Nik Hynek and Michal Smetana

Nuclear Terrorism
Countering the threat
Edited by Brecht Volders and Tom Sauer

Stable Nuclear Zero
The vision and its implications for disarmament policy
Edited by Sverre Lodgaard

Stable Nuclear Zero
The vision and its implications for disarmament policy

Edited by Sverre Lodgaard

LONDON AND NEW YORK

First published 2017
by Routledge
2 Park Square, Milton Park, Abingdon, Oxon OX14 4RN

and by Routledge
711 Third Avenue, New York, NY 10017

Routledge is an imprint of the Taylor & Francis Group, an informa business

© 2017 selection and editorial matter, Sverre Lodgaard; individual chapters, the contributors

The right of the editor to be identified as the author of the editorial matter, and of the authors for their individual chapters, has been asserted in accordance with sections 77 and 78 of the Copyright, Designs and Patents Act 1988.

All rights reserved. No part of this book may be reprinted or reproduced or utilized in any form or by any electronic, mechanical, or other means, now known or hereafter invented, including photocopying and recording, or in any information storage or retrieval system, without permission in writing from the publishers.

Trademark notice: Product or corporate names may be trademarks or registered trademarks, and are used only for identification and explanation without intent to infringe.

British Library Cataloguing-in-Publication Data
A catalogue record for this book is available from the British Library

Library of Congress Cataloging-in-Publication Data
Names: Lodgaard, Sverre, editor.
Title: Stable nuclear zero : the visions and its implications for disarmament policy / edited by Sverre Lodgaard.
Description: Abingdon, Oxon ; New York, NY : Routledge, 2017. | Series: Routledge global security studies | Includes bibliographical references and index.
Identifiers: LCCN 2016012302| ISBN 9781138690608 (hardback) | ISBN 9781315536651 (ebook)
Subjects: LCSH: Nuclear disarmament. | Nuclear disarmament–International cooperation. | Nuclear nonproliferation. | Nuclear nonproliferation–International cooperation. | Nuclear arms control. | Nuclear arms control–International cooperation.
Classification: LCC JZ5675 .S74 2017 | DDC 327.1/747–dc23
LC record available at https://lccn.loc.gov/2016012302

ISBN: 978-1-138-69060-8 (hbk)
ISBN: 978-1-315-53665-1 (ebk)

Typeset in Times New Roman
by Wearset Ltd, Boldon, Tyne and Wear

Contents

Notes on contributors   vii

Introduction   1
SVERRE LODGAARD AND SATOKO TAKAHASHI

PART I
A nuclear-weapons-free world: desirable? Feasible?   5

1 **A world without nuclear weapons?**   7
   THOMAS C. SCHELLING

2 **Making NWFW attractive, stable and sustainable**   14
   MANPREET SETHI

3 **Icon off the mark: Schelling's nuclear disarmament scare**   30
   HARALD MÜLLER

4 **Towards a rigorous comparison of a pre-nuclear and a post-nuclear world**   40
   NIKOLAI SOKOV

PART II
The requirements and paths to stable nuclear zero   53

5 **Out of the box: nuclear disarmament and cultural change**   55
   HARALD MÜLLER

6 **Verification requirements**   73
   ANDREAS PERSBO

7 Missile defence as an alternative to nuclear deterrence? 95
TOM SAUER

8 Nuclear disarmament: a Chinese view 111
JINGDONG YUAN

9 Stable at zero: deterrence and verification 123
PATRICIA LEWIS

PART III
Summary and conclusions 131

10 The vision and its implications for disarmament policy 133
SVERRE LODGAARD

Index 157

Contributors

Thomas C. Schelling was Professor at Yale University (1953–8), Harvard University (1958–90) and the University of Maryland (1990–2003). In 2005, he was awarded the Nobel Prize for Economics (with Robert J. Aumann). He is the author of *The Strategy of Conflict* (1960), *Arms and Influence* (1966), *Micromotives and Macrobehavior* (1978), *Thinking Through the Energy Problem* (1979), *Incentives for Environmental Protection* (1983), *Choice and Consequence* (1984) and *Bargaining, Communication and Limited War* (1993).

Manpreet Sethi, Senior Fellow at the Centre for Air Power Studies, New Delhi, leads the project on nuclear security and is the recipient of the K. Subrahmanyam award, conferred for excellence in strategic and security studies. Her recent books include *Code of Conduct for Outer Space: Strategy for India* (Knowledge World, 2015), *Nuclear Power: In the Wake of Fukushima* (Knowledge World, 2012) and *Nuclear Strategy: India's March towards Credible Deterrence* (Knowledge World, 2009).

Harald Müller is Professor of International Relations at Goethe University Frankfurt. He has served on the UN Secretary-General's Advisory Board on Disarmament Matters (1999–2005), the IAEA Group of Experts on Multilateral Nuclear Arrangements (2004/5), and German delegations to NPT Review Conferences from 1995 to 2015. Recent books include *A New World Order* (House Publishing, 2008), *Norm Dynamics in Multilateral Arms Control* (University of Georgia Press, 2013) and *WMD Arms Control in the Middle East* (Ashgate, 2015).

Nikolai Sokov has been Senior Fellow in the Monterey office of the Center for Nonproliferation Studies (CNS) since 1996. He is an expert on Russian nuclear weapons policy. From 1987 to 1992, he worked at the Ministry for Foreign Affairs of the Soviet Union and later Russia, and participated in the START I and START II negotiations as well as in a number of summit and ministerial meetings. Sokov is the author or co-author of a dozen books and numerous articles on nuclear policies and postures, arms control and international security.

Andreas Persbo is the Executive Director of the London-based Verification Research, Training and Information Centre (VERTIC). His latest publications include 'Strengthening the IAEA Verification Capabilities' in Ida Caracciolo, Marco Pedrazzi and Talitha Vassalli Di Dachenhausen (eds) *Nuclear*

Weapons: Strengthening the International Legal Regime (Utrecht: Eleven International Publishing, 2016) and 'Verification and Nuclear Disarmament' in Nik Hynek and Michal Smetana (eds) *Global Nuclear Disarmament: Strategic, Political, and Regional Perspectives* (Routledge, 2016).

Tom Sauer is Associate Professor in International Politics at the Universiteit Antwerpen (Belgium). His most recent book is titled *Nuclear Terrorism: Countering the Threat* (Routledge, 2016), co-edited with Brecht Volders. In 2015, the Deep Cuts Commission asked him to write *The NPT and the Humanitarian Initiative*. Previously, he published *Eliminating Nuclear Weapons: The Role of Missile Defense* (Hurst, 2011), *Nuclear Inertia. US Nuclear Weapons Policy after the Cold War* (I.B. Tauris, 2005) and *Nuclear Arms Control* (Macmillan, 1998).

Satoko Takahashi is the Research Director at the Toda Institute for Global Peace and Policy Research, Honolulu Center (where she started as Program Manager in 1996). She graduated from Tokyo University of Education, and has an MA in Physiological Psychology and PhD in Cross Cultural Psychology from the University of Hawaii at Manoa. She has published several journal articles and done extensive translation work to and from English and Japanese for major Japanese newspapers, and for journals and book publications.

Jingdong Yuan is Associate Professor at the Centre for International Security Studies, University of Sydney. His publications include *A Low-Visibility Force Multiplier: Assessing China's Cruise Missile Ambitions* (National Defense University Press, 2014), *Australia and China at 40* (University of New South Wales Press, 2012) and *China and India: Cooperation or Conflict?* (Lynne Renner, 2013). He is currently preparing a book-length manuscript on China's relations with South Asia since the end of the Cold War.

Patricia Lewis is the Research Director, International Security at Chatham House in London. Her former posts include: Deputy Director and Scientist-in-Residence at the Center for Nonproliferation Studies at the Monterey Institute of International Studies; Director of the United Nations Institute for Disarmament Research (UNIDIR); and Director of VERTIC in London. Recent publications include 'Nuclear Winter-Safe and Sound in the Snow Globe', *Contemporary Security Policy*, 36(2): 378 (2015) and 'A Middle East Free of Nuclear Weapons: Possible, Probable or Pipe-dream?' *International Affairs*, 89(2):441 (March 2013).

Sverre Lodgaard is Senior Research Fellow and former Director (1997–2007) of the Norwegian Institute of International Affairs (NUPI). Before joining NUPI he directed the United Nations Institute for Disarmament Research (UNIDIR, 1992–6). He was a member of the UN Secretary-General's Advisory Board on Disarmament Matters (1992–9). Honoris causa, Soka University, Tokyo (2015). Latest books include *Nuclear Disarmament and Non-Proliferation* (Routledge, 2011) and *In the Wake of the Arab Spring* (Scandinavian Academic Press, 2013).

Introduction

Sverre Lodgaard and Satoko Takahashi

Is a nuclear-weapons-free world (NWFW) desirable – and, if so, is it feasible?[1]

The first resolution to be passed by the UN General Assembly answered the first of these questions in the affirmative, only to find that, with the advent of the Cold War, such a world was not to be.

Several years later, in the midst of intense arms-racing and spurred on by the Cuban missile crisis, arms control replaced the objective of nuclear disarmament. The aim was to reduce the risk of unintended war by enhancing stability. Arms limitation was part of this, but not necessarily disarmament: in principle, stability might be enhanced by arms acquisitions as well as by arms reductions.

The Non-Proliferation Treaty (NPT), which entered into force in 1970, committed all signatories – nuclear- and non-nuclear-weapon states – to work for the elimination of nuclear weapons. Legally speaking, a failure to take 'effective measures relating to cessation of the nuclear arms race at an early date and to nuclear disarmament' (Article VI) does not necessarily amount to non-compliance by any particular state. Progress depends on the seriousness of all negotiating parties, which is arguably beyond the power of any single participant. However, the political process that led to the NPT made it clear that Article VI was conceived as part of a dynamic bargain to be implemented over time, erasing – in due course – the distinction between nuclear-weapon states (NWS) and non-nuclear-weapon states (NNWS). Converging expectations were created and a review mechanism was set up to facilitate implementation of the treaty. Since then, all states save four (India, Israel, Pakistan and North Korea) have committed themselves to the goal of elimination by joining the NPT.

As the Cold War began to wind down, a spectacular attempt was made to rid the world of nuclear weapons. Mikhail Gorbachev and Ronald Reagan shared the objective of an NWFW, and had a go at it in Reykjavik in October 1986. They failed because of disagreement over the US Strategic Defense Initiative – but their meeting prepared the ground for the Intermediate-Range Nuclear Forces Treaty (INF), which eliminated all US and Soviet missiles in this category, and for the Strategic Arms Reduction Treaty (START I), which halved the number of their operational strategic weapons.

Two interrelated issues were glaringly absent from the 1986 Reykjavik negotiations agenda. First, in talking about an NWFW, the two superpowers seem to have taken the consent of the other NWS for granted, as if they were mere appendices to the dominant bilateral dimension of the Cold War order. Second, there was no mention of the NPT. The superpowers failed to recognize the legal obligation to disarm even as they were seeking to implement it.

By the time the four US statesmen (Shultz, Nunn, Kissinger and Perry) revived the vision of an NWFW on the twentieth anniversary of the Reykjavik summit, the world had undergone major changes. It had moved from being bipolar to becoming multipolar, and from six NWS (the five recognized by the NPT plus Israel) to nine (with India, Pakistan and North Korea). The world of nuclear weapons had become more dangerous and had better be replaced by a world without such arms.

Their call was followed up by Barack Obama. On his initiative, a UN Security Council summit was convened in the autumn of 2009, at which all member states reiterated their commitment to work for an NWFW. In the spring of 2010, a new strategic arms reduction agreement – New START – was concluded, limiting US and Russian strategic weapons to 1,550 each. A new US nuclear posture review extended unconditional security assurances to all non-nuclear signatories to the NPT in good standing and promised to work to establish the conditions for a transition to no-first-use doctrines.

But then progress came to a halt. There have been no disarmament negotiations for more than half a decade now. All NWS have set about modernizing their arsenals, and the Asian arsenals are growing. New nuclear weapon systems, which may be deployed in 10 to 15 years and which may last for 30 to 40, indicate potent arsenals up to 2070. The question is therefore not how best to continue disarmament, but whether and how it can be restarted.

The NPT is a road map to zero, but it is a rudimentary one and it says nothing about the kind of zero to aim for. Preferably, this would be a world where the inhibitions against reversal are strong enough to make it *stably* non-nuclear. What then are the requirements of such a stable zero? The question is not just hypothetical, of no practical consequence, for how we conceive of the goal has implications for the road map leading to it. The four statesmen hit the nail on the head when they emphasized the interrelationship between visions and measures: the vision is necessary to give full meaning to the measures, and the measures are necessary to make the vision realistic. The interplay is vital for the dynamism of any disarmament process.

The literature on nuclear disarmament has not paid much attention to this question. By and large, the focus has been on the next steps. Discussions tend to stop where the NPT stops: with the elimination of the weapons. Elimination is in itself a distant goal, and to plunge into a discussion of the conditions under which it could become a permanent feature of international security affairs may seem both unnecessary and presumptuous. Understandable as this may be, however, it is a major shortcoming: a reasonably clear conception of the goal is not only important in itself, but can shed light on what kind of disarmament process to promote. The vision can and should guide actions.

The book seeks to fill the lacunae by examining the requirements of stable zero and their implications for the road map to that goal. The focus is on the international dimensions of the problem. Strong interests in nuclear weapons are also woven into the domestic fabric of the NWS, and these obstacles may be as great as the international hurdles, but those issues are not the subject of this volume.

Part I features a chapter by Thomas Schelling, one of the founding fathers of arms control. In the face of renewed calls for elimination of the nuclear arsenals he remains a sceptic, concerned that the stability that has been achieved may be abandoned without any guarantee that a world without nuclear weapons will be a stable one. Schelling's chapter is followed by a contribution by Manpreet Sethi (India), who contests the assumption that the existing world order is secure enough not to require the elimination of nuclear weapons, especially in view of the nuclear dynamics in Asia. Sethi proposes a set of principles that should anchor an NWFW in order to make it stable and sustainable. These two chapters are commented upon by Harald Müller (Germany) and Nikolai Sokov (Russia).

In Part II, Harald Müller engages in thinking 'out of the box', where opponents – as well as many proponents – of an NWFW have difficulties liberating themselves from traditional security thinking, notably with regard to nuclear deterrence. Müller argues forcefully that deterrence – the virtual deterrence of a world where nuclear weapons have been eliminated but where not much else has changed – contradicts the principles on which an NWFW must be founded. He goes on to specify the elements that would help make such a world stably non-nuclear. In turn, Andreas Persbo (Sweden) examines the role of verification in a world that has attained nuclear-weapons-free status, and the verification requirements on the way to that status. He identifies three top-level tasks: during the transition to zero, dismantlement of the weapons must be verified; when this has been done, nuclear- and non-nuclear-weapon state compliance with the obligations must be verified; and at all times during the transition it must be possible to verify that nuclear weapons are not emerging elsewhere. These chapters are commented upon by Tom Sauer (Belgium), Jingdong Yuan (China) and Patricia Lewis (Ireland).

In the final summary and conclusions chapter, the editor – Sverre Lodgaard (Norway) – elaborates on the requirements of stable zero and their implications for the steps that may lead there, starting with the vision and going back to the present.

The book is a project of the Toda Institute for Global Peace and Policy Research (Tokyo/Hawaii). Sverre Lodgaard is a senior research fellow at the Norwegian Institute of International Affairs (NUPI) and a senior research fellow of the Toda Institute. We are grateful to the Vienna Center for Disarmament and Non-Proliferation for hosting the seminar that sparked off the work, and to Susan Høivik for applying her great professionalism and social science experience to the manuscript.

Note

1 A book with this title was issued by the Pugwash Conferences on Science and World Affairs: Joseph Rotblat, J. Steinberger and B.M. Udgaonkar (1993) *A Nuclear-Weapon-Free World: Desirable? Feasible?* Boulder, CO: Westview.

Part I

A nuclear-weapons-free world

Desirable? Feasible?

1 A world without nuclear weapons?[1]

Thomas C. Schelling

A new and popular disarmament movement was provoked by a completely unexpected combination of Henry A. Kissinger, William J. Perry, Sam Nunn, and George P. Shultz with their op-ed pieces in the *Wall Street Journal* from January 4, 2007, and January 15, 2008. For the first time since the demise of General and Complete Disarmament (GCD) in the 1960s, there is a serious discussion of the possibility of utterly removing nuclear weapons from the planet Earth. Furthermore, the discussion is taking place among nuclear policy professionals, the people who publish in *Foreign Affairs, International Security*, and other serious journals.

The International Institute for Strategic Studies, founded in London in 1958 and notable for its Adelphi papers, published in August 2008, Paper 396, *Abolishing Nuclear Weapons*, by George Perkovich and James Acton of the Carnegie Endowment for International Peace. It was central to a conference at the Carnegie Endowment that produced 17 response papers from around the world. Other meetings similarly motivated have been occurring, many under the sponsorship of the Nuclear Threat Initiative (NTI). The Stanley Foundation convened 25 officials, including diplomats from UN institutions, U.S. and foreign experts, and officials from other nations 'to examine the first steps toward a world free of nuclear weapons'. The rapporteur of that meeting noted, 'Participants were in general agreement that complete and eventual disarmament, or global zero, is the objective'.

The American Academy of Arts and Sciences, which publishes *Daedalus*, awarded the Rumford Prize to Perry, Nunn, Shultz, Kissinger, and Sidney Drell at its 1,929th Stated Meeting in October 2008, for 'their contribution to nuclear abolition'. President Obama's April 2009 Prague speech, in which he stated 'clearly and with conviction America's commitment to seek the peace and security of a world without nuclear weapons', was a sign that the disarmament debate was now a serious enterprise.

Some of the motivation, among the diverse respondents on the issue, is to fulfill, or appear to fulfill, the 'commitment' undertaken by the official nuclear-weapons states in the Non-Proliferation Treaty (NPT)

> to pursue negotiations in good faith on effective measures relating to cessation of the nuclear arms race at an early date and to nuclear disarmament,

and on a treaty on general and complete disarmament under strict and effective international control.

The underlying motive would be to renew and strengthen the Treaty itself, by removing an objection often voiced by non-nuclear governments about unacceptable discrimination. Some of the motivation is evidently to spur an overdue drastic reduction in Russian and American nuclear war-heads, especially those on high alert.

But hardly any of the analyses or policy statements that I have come across question overtly the ultimate goal of total nuclear disarmament.[2] Nearly all adduce the unequivocal language of the *Wall Street Journal* quadrumvirate.

None explicitly addresses the question, why should we expect a world without nuclear weapons to be safer than one with (some) nuclear weapons? That drastic reductions make sense, and that some measures to reduce alert status do, too, may require no extensive analysis. But considering how much intellectual effort in the past half-century went into the study of the 'stability' of a nuclear-deterrence world, it ought to be worthwhile to examine contingencies in a nuclear-free world to verify that it is superior to a world with (some) nuclear weapons.

I have not come across any mention of what would happen in the event of a major war. One might hope that major war could not happen in a world without nuclear weapons, but it always did. One can propose that another war on the scale of the 1940s is less to worry about than anything nuclear. But it might give pause to reflect that the world of 1939 was utterly free of nuclear weapons, yet they were not only produced, they were invented, during war itself and used with devastating effect. Why not expect that they could be produced – they've already been invented – and possibly used in some fashion?

In 1976, I published an article, 'Who Will Have the Bomb?' in which I asked, 'Does India have the bomb?' (Shelling, 1976: 77–91). India had exploded a nuclear device a couple of years earlier. I pursued the question, 'what do we mean by "having the bomb?"' I alleged that we didn't mean, or perhaps didn't even care, whether India actually possessed in inventory a nuclear explosive device, or an actual nuclear weapon. We meant, I argued, that India 'had' the potential: it had the expertise, the personnel, the laboratories and equipment to produce a weapon if it decided to. (At the time, India pretended that its only interest was in 'Peaceful Nuclear Explosives' [PNEs].) I proposed an analogy: does Switzerland have an army? I answered, not really, but it could have one tomorrow if it decided today.

The answer to the relevant question about nuclear weapons must be a schedule showing how many weapons (of what yield) a government could mobilize on what time schedule.

It took the United States about five years to build two weapons. It might take India – now that it has already produced nuclear weapons – a few weeks, or less, depending on how ready it kept its personnel and supplies for mobilization. If a 'world without nuclear weapons' means no mobilization bases, there can be no such world. Even starting in 1940 the mobilization base was built. And would minimizing mobilization potential serve the purpose? To answer this requires working through various scenarios involving the expectation of war, the outbreak of war, and the conduct of war. That is the kind of analysis I haven't seen.

A crucial question is whether a government could hide weapons-grade fissile material from any possible inspection-verification. Considering that enough plutonium to make a bomb could be hidden in the freezing compartment of my refrigerator, or to evade radiation detection could be hidden at the bottom of the water in a well, I think only the fear of a whistle-blower could possibly make success at all questionable. I believe that a 'responsible' government would make sure that fissile material would be available in an international crisis or war itself. A responsible government must at least assume that other responsible governments will do so.

We are so used to thinking in terms of thousands, or at least hundreds, of nuclear warheads that a few dozen may offer a sense of relief. But if, at the outset of what appears to be a major war, or the imminent possibility of major war, every responsible government must consider that other responsible governments will mobilize their nuclear weapons base as soon as war erupts, or as soon as war appears likely, there will be at least covert frantic efforts, or perhaps purposely conspicuous efforts, to acquire deliverable nuclear weapons as rapidly as possible. And what then?

I see a few possibilities. One is that the first to acquire weapons will use them, as best it knows how, to disrupt its enemy's or enemies' nuclear mobilization bases, while it continuing its frantic nuclear rearmament, along with a surrender demand backed up by its growing stockpile. Another possibility is to demand, under threat of nuclear attack, abandonment of any nuclear mobilization, with unopposed 'inspectors' or 'saboteurs' searching out the mobilization base of people, laboratories, fissile material stashes, or anything else threatening. A third possibility would be a 'decapitation' nuclear attack along with the surrender demand.

And I can think of worse. All of these, of course, would be in the interest of self-defense.

Still another strategy might, just might, be to propose a crash 'rearmament agreement', by which both sides (all sides) would develop 'minimum deterrent' arsenals, subject to all the inspection-verification procedures that had already been in place for 'disarmament'.

An interesting question is whether 'former nuclear powers' – I use quotation marks because they will still be latent nuclear powers – would seek ways to make it known that, despite 'disarmament', they had the potential for a rapid buildup. It has been suggested that Saddam Hussein may have wanted it believed that he had nuclear weapons, and Israel has made its nuclear capability a publicized secret. 'Mutual nuclear deterrence' could take the form of letting it be known that any evidence of nuclear rearmament would be promptly reciprocated. Reciprocation could take the form of hastening to have a weapon to use against the nuclear facilities of the 'enemy'.

But war is what I find most worrisome. In World War II there was some fear in the U.S. nuclear weapons community that Germany might acquire a nuclear capability and use it. There is still speculation whether, if Germany had not already surrendered, one of the bombs should have been used on Berlin, with a demand that inspection teams be admitted to locate and destroy the nuclear establishment. Would a government lose a war without resorting to nuclear weapons? Would a war include a race to produce weapons capable of coercing victory?

Could a major nation maintain 'conventional' forces ready for every contingency, without maintaining a nuclear backup? Just as today's intelligence agencies and their clandestine operators are devoted to discovering the location of terrorist organizations and their leaders, in a non-nuclear world the highest priority would attach to knowing the exact locations and readiness of enemy nuclear mobilization bases.

Would a political party, in the United States or anywhere else, be able to campaign for the abandonment of the zero-nuclears treaty, and what would be the response in other nations?

I hope there are favorable answers to these questions. I'm uncertain who in government or academia is working on them.

One can take the position that substantial nuclear disarmament makes sense, and that the abstract goal of a world without nuclear weapons helps motivate reduction as well as presents an appearance of fulfilling the NPT commitment. Maybe some leaders of the movement have no more than that in mind. But even as a purely intellectual enterprise the 'role of deterrence in total disarmament', to use the title of an article I published 47 years ago, deserves just as thoughtful analysis as mutual nuclear deterrence ever received (Shelling, 1962: 392–406).

In summary, a 'world without nuclear weapons' would be a world in which the United States, Russia, Israel, China, and half a dozen or a dozen other countries would have hair-trigger mobilization plans to rebuild nuclear weapons and mobilize or commandeer delivery systems, and would have prepared targets to preempt other nations' nuclear facilities, all in a high-alert status, with practice drills and secure emergency communications. Every crisis would be a nuclear crisis, any war could become a nuclear war. The urge to preempt would dominate; whoever gets the first few weapons will coerce or preempt. It would be a nervous world.

It took a couple of decades for the United States to work out a satisfactory theory of 'strategic readiness' of how to configure strategic nuclear forces to provide reasonably comfortable assurance against surprise or preemption, with appropriate command and control. Nothing is perfect: we never did solve the MX missile basing problem; we apotheosized a 'triad' that didn't really exist; we missed the early opportunity to restrain multiple independently targetable reentry vehicles (MIRV); we never had an agreed understanding of 'flexible response' or 'no-cities' and its relation to counterforce targeting; and we let a president carry us away with an expensive dream of active defense of the population. Still, we got away from soft, exposed, unready bombers and missiles; we

A world without nuclear weapons? 11

avoided the troubles that rival anti-ballistic-missile (ABM) systems would have brought: and we understood the MX problem, if we couldn't solve it.

There are now many proposals for radically reconfiguring the strategic offensive force. Possible reductions in numbers get plenty of attention. The composition of the force – undersea, airborne, and fixed; gravity, ballistic, and cruise; air and naval – gets less attention, but will receive it intensely when service rivalries become aroused. The proposals that to me sound hasty and in need of more thought than I can detect behind them are those that would drastically change the readiness status of the strategic force. These involve various proposals for reduced alert status. In particular, some propose physically separating warheads and vehicles. An extreme case is the idea of 'strategic escrow', warheads removed from vehicles, presumably at quite some distances, and stored under international supervision. I have heard proposals for keeping warheads nearby but separate from the bombers or the missiles themselves. There are also proposals, which I'm not able to judge, for electronic de-alert or failsafe retargeting.

What I think took those couple of decades I mentioned was really getting 'vulnerability' under control. It began seriously with the Gaither Committee in 1957, got incorporated into the surprise-attack negotiations in 1958, led to airborne alert for bombers and abandonment of Atlas and Titan, and gave the navy a strategic lease on life. One key to reduced vulnerability was dispersal. Minuteman was spread out so that no single enemy weapon could destroy more than one. (Decoys for the same purpose were considered during the MX predicament.)

What has me worried is a new kind of 'dispersal', a perverse kind: offering multiple disabling points for an enemy to target. If a missile or bomber can be rendered inactive by, alternatively, destroying it, destroying its warhead, or destroying the means of locomotion from warhead storage to vehicle, vulnerability has increased. If removed warheads are stored centrally, or in clusters, 'dispersal' has been reversed. (Subjecting warhead storage to inspection eliminates the possibility of keeping locations secret from potential targeting.) If there are limited transport routes by which warheads can join their vehicles, vulnerability is increased. And maybe not just vulnerability to strategic attack but to disruption or sabotage as well.

Another theme of strategic readiness that took pretty good hold during those decades was 'crisis stability'. The concept involved a couple of potentially contradictory ideas: that any urgent efforts to enhance readiness in a crisis should be unnoticeable, lest they alarm the enemy, and that any efforts should be so visible that, if they were not being taken, the enemy could see they were not! On balance I think the consensus was that the dynamics of mobilization should be minimized; that, of course, could depend on what kinds of actions we are talking about. And the actions depend on just what-mode of de-alert or separation of components is being considered.

I worry that the necessary scenario analyses to find the strengths and weaknesses, especially the weaknesses, of these proposals have not been done. I do not want to see many years – more than half a century now – of painfully acquired understanding of the requirements of 'safe readiness' be lost or ignored in a hurried effort to invent new configurations of readiness-unreadiness. In particular, just what can be done on what time schedule and with what visibility to the public or to the enemy (or to international referees) in various kinds of crises needs to be thoroughly worked out; the logistics need to be carefully simulated; and the range of choices needs to be identified.

I do not perceive that this analysis is being done before proposals are launched that would produce highly unfamiliar strategic-readiness situations. What we have developed and become acquainted with should be dismantled only when we are sure we understand what we may be getting into.

We have gone, as I write this, more than 63 years without any use of nuclear weapons in warfare. We have experienced, depending on how you count, some eight wars during that time in which one party to the war possessed nuclear weapons: United States vs. North Korea, United States vs. People's Republic of China, United States vs. Viet Cong, United States vs. North Vietnam, United States vs. Iraq twice, United States vs. Taliban in Afghanistan, Israel vs. Syria and Egypt, United Kingdom vs. Argentina, and USSR vs. Afghanistan. In no case was nuclear weapons introduced, probably not seriously considered.

The 'taboo', to use the term of Secretary of State John Foster Dulles in 1963 – he deplored the taboo – has apparently been powerful. The ability of the United States and the Soviet Union to collaborate, sometimes tacitly, sometimes explicitly, to 'stabilize' mutual deterrence despite crises over Berlin and Cuba, for the entire postwar era prior to the dissolution of the USSR, would not have been countenanced by experts or strategists during the first two decades after 1945.

These are two different phenomena, the taboo and mutual deterrence. We can hope that mutual deterrence will subdue Indian–Pakistani hostility; we can hope that the taboo will continue to caution Israel, and that it will affect other possessors of nuclear weapons, either through their apprehension of the curse on nuclear weapons or their recognition of the universal abhorrence of nuclear use (see Paul, 2008; Tannenwald, 2007; Schelling, 2006).

There is no sign that any kind of nuclear arms race is in the offing – not, anyway, among the current nuclear powers. Prospects are good for substantial reduction of nuclear arms among the two largest arsenals, Russian and American. That should contribute to nuclear quiescence.

Concern over North Korea, Iran, or possible non-state violent entities is justified, but denuclearization of Russia, the United States, China, France, and the United Kingdom is pretty tangential to those prospects. Except for some 'rogue' threats, there is little that could disturb the quiet nuclear relations among the recognized nuclear nations. This nuclear quiet should not be traded away for a world in which a brief race to reacquire nuclear weapons could become every former nuclear state's overriding preoccupation.

Notes

1 The article is a reprint of Thomas C. Schelling, 'A World Without Nuclear Weapons', *Daedalus*, 138: 4 (Fall, 2009), 124–129. © 2009 by the American Academy of Arts and Sciences. Reproduced with permission. It was one of the main background papers at the Vienna symposium on Stable Nuclear Zero, which inspired this book and where the author took part.
2 For exceptions, see Harold Brown and John Deutch, 'The Nuclear Disarmament Fantasy', *Wall Street Journal*, November 19, 2007, and Charles L. Glaser. 'The Instability of Small Numbers Revisited', in *Rebuilding the NPT Consensus*, ed. Michael May (Stanford, CA: Center for International Security and Cooperation. Stanford University, October 2008), http://iis-db.stanford.edu/pubs/2218/RebuildNPTConsensus.pdf

Bibliography

Brown, H. and Deutch, J. (2007) The Nuclear Disarmament Fantasy. *Wall Street Journal*, 19 November.
Glaser, C.L. (2008) The Instability of Small Numbers Revisited. In May, M. (ed.) *Rebuilding the NPT Consensus*. [Online] Stanford, CA: Center for International Security and Cooperation, Stanford University. Available from: http://iis-db.stanford.edu/pubs/2218/RebuildNPTConsensus.pdf.
Paul, T.V. (2008) *The Tradition of Nuclear Weapons*. Stanford, CA: Stanford University Press.
Schelling, T.C. (1962) The Role of Deterrence in Total Disarmament. *Foreign Affairs*, 40: 392–406.
Schelling, T.C. (1976) Who Will Have the Bomb? *International Security*, 1: 77–91.
Schelling, T.C. (2006) The Legacy of Hiroshima. In Schelling, T.C. (2007) *Strategies of Commitment and other Essays*. Cambridge, MA: Harvard University Press.
Tannenwald, N. (2007) *The Nuclear Taboo*. Cambridge: Cambridge University Press.

2 Making NWFW attractive, stable and sustainable

Manpreet Sethi

Over the past 70 years that nuclear weapons have been around, we have grown so attached to the 'balance of terror' and the 'stability' they are supposed to generate that we have actually become apprehensive of liberating ourselves. We believe that there is an inherent sense of stability in a nuclear dyad where two adversarial sides are facing the prospect not of the victory of one side or domination, but of mutual defeat and destruction. We even derive comfort from this belief.

This is reminiscent of the mind-set that existed at the time of slavery. When demands for the abolition of slavery were first made, there were those who argued that the economic and social system would not be able to survive the drastic change and would collapse. A similar nuclear dogma today appears to constrain us with the belief that the existing stability would be endangered in the absence of nuclear weapons. As with the situation nearly two centuries ago, we fear collapse – this time of the political and security system that has been built with much intellectual effort in the past half-century to ensure the 'stability' of a nuclear-deterrence world (Schelling 2009, 124–129).

Some even question whether the current state of the world, where the numbers of nuclear weapons in the superpower arsenals have been substantially reduced and there is a sense of 'nuclear quiescence', is not an attractive enough oasis. Why strive for a different kind of a world, which might not prove as 'stable' and comfortable as this one with our now seven-decades-old understanding of nuclear deterrence and strategic stability? What is there to guarantee that, having gone non-nuclear, countries capable of building nuclear weapons will not scurry back into the comfort of national nuclear arsenals at the slightest whiff of a crisis?

Such questions, which raise doubts about the stability of a nuclear-weapons-free world (NWFW), obviously cast a shadow on its desirability as well. Universal nuclear disarmament can be considered an attractive investment only if it can bring wholesome returns for the security of nations. As Thomas Schelling argues in his seminal article *A World Without Nuclear Weapons?*, 'it ought to be worthwhile to examine contingencies in a nuclear-free world to verify that it is superior to a world with (some) nuclear weapons' (ibid., 125). If, instead, the result is going to be more unstable interstate relations, then it might be better to remain where we are. If stability at zero is going to be elusive, then why venture into such a situation at all?

These are genuine concerns. If an NWFW is ever to be achieved, it must first be able to carry the conviction that it would be worth the effort. This chapter engages in the debate in two ways. First, it contests two specific assumptions that question the attractiveness of an NWFW. The first of these is *that the existing world order is stable and secure enough not to merit pursuit of an NWFW* – in other words, that we are happy and safe where we are. The second assumption is that a *race towards nuclear rearmament is inevitable in case of a crisis in an NWFW* – in other words, that in the event of a major war nuclear weapons would be re-produced and possibly even used.

Second, I address questions as to *how an NWFW could be sustained in a stable mode*. The retention of a small arsenal, or at least a remobilization capability, is an idea that has been mooted in this regard. This chapter explores this but finds it inadequate, and even counterproductive, for supporting a stable NWFW. Instead I suggest *a set of principles that must anchor the NWFW*. Only these are capable of providing a secure foundation as well as the essential scaffolding for maintaining a stable and sustainable NWFW.

Contesting the assumptions

Whither nuclear quiescence?

Compared to the tense years of the Cold War, when the superpowers were locked in a nuclear eyeball-to-eyeball confrontation, the post-Cold War years have been largely stress-free, at least as far nuclear relations between the USA and Russia are concerned. Consequently, the last US Nuclear Posture Review (US Department of Defense 2010) let the threats from nuclear Russia or other near-peers drop below those of nuclear terrorism and proliferation. For the moment, Washington envisages no possibility of a strategic nuclear exchange that could lead to mutual assured destruction. Therefore, for those who lived through the high drama of the first nuclear age, this may well appear to be a state of 'nuclear quiescence'. Threat perceptions of a nuclear war are down, and the numbers of warheads are steadily being reduced.

It is against the backdrop of this reality that Thomas Schelling argues in favour of staying with the current situation instead of stumbling into a new non-nuclear world possibly fraught with uncertainties and unanticipated dangers. He writes:

> there is little that could disturb the quiet nuclear relations among the recognized nuclear nations. This nuclear quiet should not be traded away for a world in which a brief race to reacquire nuclear weapons could become every former nuclear state's overriding preoccupation.
>
> (Ibid., 129)

Given that so much political, intellectual and arms control energies have been invested in crafting a sort of strategic stability with nuclear weapons, it is better not to rock the boat, unless the alternative can be a better world.

Unfortunately, it is impossible to guarantee that a non-nuclear world would be absolutely stable or free of insecurities and war. But, for the multitudes of people living in South Asia, the Middle East or even north-east Asia, where many more nations have joined the game of nuclear deterrence, there is little that is stable about the current nuclear situation either.

In fact, Asia is today the most active nuclear playground. Housing eight of the nine nuclear-armed states, it has become the 'most nuclearized of all continents' (Roberts 2009, S–1). This includes all the nuclear-weapon states (NWS) except the UK, which has no territorial or nuclear weapon holdings in Asia at present. Nuclear-armed states that are not signatories to the NPT – Israel, Pakistan, India and North Korea – are also to be found here. Several states that might develop nuclear weapons as a result of a domino effect (Japan, South Korea and Taiwan in response to North Korean nuclear weapons, and Saudi Arabia and Turkey in response to Iran) are in Asia. The now well-documented proliferation networks that once operated potent supply chains were also active to and from the region, and may still be around. Meanwhile, all of the five nuclear-weapons states physically located in Asia – Russia, China, India, Pakistan and North Korea – are currently engaged in honing their strategic capabilities. Modernization of existing strategic systems in Russia and China is progressing, along with the activities of the other three in building 'credible' nuclear arsenals. To complicate matters further, the relations of these nations overlap with one another in both positive and negative ways. Ideally, every nuclear dyad must seek strategic stability so that existential risks accompanying nuclear weapons can be minimized and the chances of deliberate or – more importantly, inadvertent – nuclear exchange can be virtually obviated. That is not how the situation is today. Rather, the reality of multipolar deterrence has created nuclear dyads that impinge upon each other. So the strategic stability that India might possibly establish with China does not appear reassuring enough for Pakistan, just as the strategic stability between the USA and China has security implications for India.

All of this has 'given way to something far messier', as Roberts (2009, S–2) notes, than the rather tame game of bilateral deterrence during the Cold War. For the majority of nations, the current state of affairs is not particularly stable. In fact, the risks to stability are greater because, today:

- The nuclear-armed states are geographically closer, even contiguous.
- The nuclear-armed states are suffering from territorial conflicts, which raises the risk of war.
- The nuclear-armed states are not equally convinced about the value of establishing and maintaining strategic stability – for example, countries like North Korea or Pakistan believe that they reap greater dividends from maintaining a state of strategic instability or through a policy of nuclear brinkmanship, so they have little interest in taking bilateral or multilateral measures that could bring a modicum of stability into the nuclear dyad. Such a policy, however, raises the risks of inadvertent escalation or nuclear war as a result of miscalculation.

- The nuclear-armed states are currently expanding their fissile material stockpiles and modernizing their nuclear arsenals. None of the nuclear dyads in Asia currently appears interested in nuclear arms control.
- The new nuclear dyads are located in areas of dense and increasing populations. While this should deter nuclear use owing to the huge humanitarian and environmental impacts that a nuclear exchange could have, it could also raise the appetite for war. For instance, populous nations may have higher thresholds for damage acceptance, or nations with overwhelmingly young populations could be prone to be more excitable or 'hot-headed' about war.
- At least one nuclear-armed nation in the region is also widely acknowledged as a sponsor of terrorism. While Pakistan claims that it has secured all of its nuclear weapons and infrastructure, terrorist attacks have occurred on sensitive military and nuclear establishments which cause concern. In a politically unstable situation, where terrorist groups are as anti-India/USA as anti-own establishment, the dangers of nuclear terrorism cannot be lightly dismissed. Nor can the concern over state complicity in nuclear terrorism be easily wished away.

Thus, the status quo is dangerous, vulnerable to the existential risks that inevitably accompany nuclear weapons. Nuclear quiescence may be visible as seen from Washington, but certainly not so from the other nuclear capitals of the world. In fact, from the Indian perspective, there is no nuclear quiet – Pakistan is rapidly expanding its nuclear capabilities and moving into ever-riskier domains with the development of tactical nuclear weapons. It effectively uses its nuclear arsenal to conduct sub-conventional conflict against India and also as an effective tool for economic bargaining with the USA. Both of these realities validate the utility of nuclear weapons as a useful asymmetric tool.

In February 2013, North Korea displayed dangerous nuclear brinkmanship when it responded to the UN-imposed sanctions by conducting a third nuclear test. Tense weeks in March and April brought the risks of nuclear weapons into sharp focus as North Korea 'declared war' after two USF-22 stealth fighter jets took part in ongoing US–South Korean military exercises for the first time. South Korea pledged a response to any provocation, and the USA moved its USS *John S. McCain*, which can intercept missiles, and the SBX-1 radar to the region. China, too, moved its troops and jets close to Korea. The situation appeared to contain all of the ingredients that could have made it spin into an escalatory spiral leading all the way up to a nuclear crisis on account of a mistake or a miscalculation by any of the players. More such episodes cannot be ruled out if some possessors of these weapons believe in the philosophy of nuclear instability as a means of deterrence.

Another outcome of this episode has been the rising nuclear disquiet in South Korea and Japan. Despite the existence of the US nuclear umbrella, a new sense of vulnerability has led some in South Korea to openly recommend bringing back US tactical nuclear weapons or breaking a decades-old taboo by developing the country's own nuclear arsenal. Two opinion polls in 2013 found support for the idea from no less than two-thirds of South Koreans (Asian Institute for Policy Studies 2013).[1] Japan, too, has been engaged in an internal debate on the need to develop its own nuclear weapons (see, e.g. McNeill 2011; Mochizuki 2007; *Japan Times* 2013). The recent claim by North Korea on its having tested a miniaturized hydrogen bomb on 6 January 2016 is only going to add fuel to this debate.

Washington has responded to this by doubling its efforts to reassure allies, especially by increasing its ballistic missile defence (BMD) capabilities. This, however, has its own ramifications for China's nuclear deterrent and its equations with the region and the USA.[2] Beijing has expressed concern, and its strategic modernization now focuses on countering the BMD's perceived degradation of the Chinese nuclear deterrent. This has downstream effects on India's nuclear build-up, and in turn on that of Pakistan.

Asia today is a complex web of diverse strategic relationships with no shared understanding of strategic stability as it once existed between the superpowers. The situation is certainly nowhere near nuclear quiescence.

Inevitability of nuclear rearmament?

A second aspersion cast on an NWFW is by arguing that, since the knowledge of making nuclear weapons can never be removed from nations that once had them, there is likely to be a race among nations to get back to these weapons in the event of a crisis. Thomas Schelling has argued in his article that, if war were to break out in a state of zero nuclear weapons, nuclear rearmament through 'covert frantic efforts' or 'purposely conspicuous efforts', and use of the weapon by the first achiever would be inevitable (Schelling 2009).

There are two assumptions here in case of a crisis – first, that efforts towards nuclear rearmament would be almost reflexive and hence inevitable; and, second, that the use of the weapon by the first achiever would also be reflexive and inevitable. Both of these suppositions are premised on the US experience and behaviour in the run-up to and during World War II. While this is understandable, it nevertheless merits further exploration, given that mankind has already cohabited with nuclear weapons for over seven decades now and should understand their nature well.

In 1939, information that German physicists had made a breakthrough in nuclear fission, and fear that the Axis powers might get the atomic bomb before the Allies could, led Albert Einstein (who had fled from Germany) and Enrico Fermi (who had fled from Italy) to appeal to the US president to start a *secret* project to this effect in 1942. The occurrence of this race in those unique circumstances has come to colour views today as well, leading to the conclusion that a similar race for rearmament could recur.

However, this assumption tends to overlook many new realities. Covert efforts at nuclear rearmament have been rendered increasingly difficult by the quantum jump in space-based surveillance capabilities, making nations far more transparent. Meanwhile, during the long period of the existence of nuclear weapons in national arsenals, countries have become aware of the horrors of the use of the weapon. In fact, it is the extremely high destructive potential of the weapon that has acted as a limiting factor on its own use, and this fact is well understood today. Experience has also taught us that nuclear monopoly cannot be maintained. Even in the past, it took the Soviet Union only four years to demonstrate its own nuclear prowess. In the future, it would take even less time for determined nuclear challengers, since the technology and engineering involved in bomb-making is no secret.

In such a situation, with the destructive potential of the weapon, its environmental and humanitarian consequences and the inability to escape retaliation (because there could be no monopoly over the weapon) all well known, why would nations want to rearm themselves with the same weapon? Surely, having understood that the weapon is of such little military utility but of such high political liability, it is unlikely that countries will find it tempting to return to these weapons. On the contrary, mindful of the struggle that it has been to get rid of them and their accompanying dangers, it is not totally believable that countries will want to reacquire them.

The possibility of nuclear rearmament, in fact, would be even less likely if the journey to becoming nuclear-free could include the conclusion of two essential UN-mandated Conventions – one *banning the use or threat of use of nuclear weapons* and another *mandating a universal no-first-use (NFU) agreement*.[3] Many road maps for nuclear disarmament have recommended these two steps as important milestones for getting to an NWFW. Indeed, doing so would enable not only getting to an NWFW, but also sustaining it. The race to rearmament would be rendered meaningless by the existence of legal commitments of nations not to use nuclear weapons. Of course, an NFU would seem to have no meaning or role in a world that has already been disarmed. But such a Convention, crafted on the way to disarmament, could serve to *keep* nuclear weapons useless even in the case of rearmament, thereby making rearmament a worthless exercise – and contributing to keeping the world non-nuclear.

It could still be argued that if nations find themselves staring war in the face they would pay little attention to legal hindrances to using a weapon that they might deem necessary for national security. However, two things could hold them back. First, the use of nuclear weapons when faced with the prospect of retaliation, even if delayed, hardly upholds the cause of national security. Second, it is not that easy to violate international laws (or, indeed, breach widely held norms). Nations must take into consideration issues of reputation and values, and these combine with calculations of self-interest to stay the hands of nations from straying into taboo territory.

This can be illustrated with the experience of the international community with chemical weapons (CW). The use of CW was banned in 1925 by the Geneva Convention. So, in 1939, when World War II broke out, there was nothing more than a decade-old agreement on the non-use of CW. Countries still had the knowledge and the wherewithal to develop these weapons. And, yet, they did not automatically do so. The Chemical Weapons Convention was finally concluded in 1996, but the instances of the use of such weapons during the 71-year period were very few, even though many countries possessed stockpiles of chemical weapons.

There is a lesson to be learnt here for nuclear weapons as well. Given that there has been no use of the nuclear weapon after Hiroshima and Nagasaki, a norm of sorts concerning the non-use of the weapon is in place. True, some nations continue to hold doctrines that project a readiness to use the weapon, since that is considered necessary for credible deterrence. But even those that profess 'first-use' are nevertheless inclined to accept that the use of the weapon can be sanely envisaged only as a last resort in the most unthinkable situation where the survival of the state is at stake. Widespread popular revulsion against nuclear weapons and widely held inhibitions on their use do influence nuclear decision-making. Here we might recall an interesting statement made by John Foster Dulles in 1953. In a discussion on the use of the weapon, he stated that 'since in the present state of the world opinion we could not use an A-bomb, we should make every effort now to dissipate this feeling....'

Apparently then, within less than a decade of the first (and only) use of nuclear weapons, the US administration was factoring in public sentiment and actually feeling constrained by it. At about the same time, an officer in the US Department of State's Bureau of Far East Affairs warned, 'The A-bomb has the status of a peculiar monster conceived by American cunning and its use by us in whatever situation would be exploited to our serious detriment' (Tannenwald 1999, 433–468). The ensuing six decades without the use of the weapon have only strengthened the taboo. Now, in order to further reinforce it, its codification into law through a Convention is imperative.

A universally adopted Convention banning the use and threat of use of nuclear weapons it would make these weapons of mass destruction (WMD) impotent and useless. It would even deter 'rogue' states if it carried a specific provision on how the international community should deal with such use.[4] Unity of action by the international community can be a major deterrent in modern times, when economic interdependence and the power of the information revolution add to the vulnerabilities of nations.

However, for the threat of united action to be credibly conveyed, it is necessary that there be a common understanding of the danger and mutual trust and confidence, at least among the major powers. Of course, good relations between all nations are important, but relations between major powers have a way of spilling into the equations of these nations with others – hence the need for amicable and non-confrontationist relations between major nations. For instance, a change in relations between the USA and Russia or the USA and China would have huge impacts on international security as a whole.

One move that could ease threat perceptions is a universal commitment to NFU among the nuclear-armed states. An NFU has the potential to lessen interstate tensions, increase mutual confidence and thus reinforce a cycle of positives. Also, given that an NWFW requires a sense of understanding and bonding between major states, an NFU Convention, as the first agreement of its kind among all NWS, would have great symbolic political value.

Above all, an NWFW in which nations have committed themselves to no-first-use as well as the non-use of nuclear weapons, whether through individual agreements or as part of one nuclear weapons convention, would obviate the need for rearmament. After all, even if a country had the knowledge and capability to do so, what would be the sense in acquiring weapons that were unusable?

Sustaining a stable NWFW

We should bear in mind that, in the process of getting to an NWFW, nations would have undergone a significant transformation in security perceptions. They would have consensually arrived at the elimination of their nuclear warheads, fissile material and weapons infrastructure. The very act of arriving at such agreements and of coordinating steps to move towards verifiable disarmament would have influenced the ways in which states relate to each other. As noted by Ken Booth, 'a world of near zero nuclear weapons cannot possibly be "like" the world of today. World politics would have moved far beyond the post-Cold War into a condition of an anti-nuclear non-violent conflict culture' (Booth and Wheeler 1992, 44).

Of course, we cannot expect that in such a world all states would have somehow miraculously acquired a shared sense of security and would have resolved all threat perceptions. But we can nevertheless expect that at least a majority of states would be enjoying relatively peaceful relations. In the very journey to becoming non-nuclear, an interlocking of security mechanisms, verification processes would have introduced a new paradigm of interstate relations more conducive to stability. As Harald Müller (1992, 17) points out, 'Regimes aimed at achieving non-nuclear security would thus build upon the shared interests of states with their effect on security perceptions cumulative over time.'

In the following two subsections, the article explores ways of maintaining stability at zero.

Stability through knowledge of rearmament?

In searching for stability at nuclear zero, at least two strategic scholars have advocated the need for nuclear rearmament. Schelling suggests that in a non-nuclear world, '"mutual nuclear deterrence" could take the form of letting it be known that any evidence of nuclear rearmament would be promptly reciprocated' (Schelling 2009). Jonathan Schell, too, has maintained 'if all states know that aggression will lead – albeit with a time lag – to crippling counter-retaliation, then deterrence will be as firmly in force as it is believed to be today' (Schell 2000, 118). Therefore, for him, one of the provisions for nuclear abolition should be 'to permit nations to hold themselves in a particular, defined state of readiness for nuclear rearmament' (ibid., 118), so he suggests underpinning the NWFW on the mutual threat of nuclear rearmament. He called it a 'condition of weaponless deterrence' in which each state well realizes that any attempt to rearm will carry the risk of provoking others too, and this itself would serve as a deterrent. This, he argued, would suffice to maintain stability in a world of zero nuclear weapons by pitting factory against factory and blueprint against blueprint rather than missile against missile or bomber against bomber. 'Just as the potential for nuclear aggression flows from the knowledge, menacing the stability of the agreement, so does the potential for retaliation, restoring the stability of the agreement' (ibid.). Thus he turned one of the major criticisms from nuclear realists – that 'nuclear weapons cannot be disinvented' – into the key to nuclear abolition. 'War would not become any more attractive since the mutual threat of nuclear rearmament will induce a healthy caution.' Stability in such a world would lie in a state of 'rearmament parity' (Schelling 1966).

Though well intentioned, this argument could actually prove to be a retrograde step. If every country decides to remain at the threshold of capability of quick rearmament, then the world will certainly be even more nervous than it now is. Moreover, the rearmament capacities of various states would be different based on their domestic capacities. Also, some might be better at concealing nuclear weapons than others, thus fostering mistrust and fear. Stability can hardly be robust in such a situation. On the contrary, for interstate relations to be stable it is essential that they be built on mutual trust, which requires confidence in verification mechanisms that can ensure irreversibility.[5] Nations must have the assurance that facilities capable of building weapons have been verifiably shut down and will remain so, also during crisis situations.

It is in this context that the two Conventions suggested in an earlier section of this chapter become even more relevant and important. Together, the two would obviate the need for nuclear rearmament and thus make an NWFW more stable. Even if verification were to fail in some remote instance, irreversibility would be strengthened by the universal commitment to not using the nuclear weapons – whether first-use or at all. Stability at global zero would be better sustained through these two measures than if it were premised on the threat of rearmament.

Stability through anchoring the NWFW on principles

A need for some kind of a 'world government' in order to realize nuclear disarmament has often been advocated. Schell even pinned down the inability of nation-states to agree on the abolition of nuclear weapons because 'the requirement for world government as the inevitable price for nuclear disarmament is at the heart of the impasse that the world has been unable to break through ...'. Further: 'until we find some way of ridding ourselves of nuclear weapons without having to establish world government, or something like it – major relief from the nuclear peril seems unlikely'.

Laudable as it is, the idea of a world government is not easy to implement as long as sovereign nations exist as the building blocks of the international order. Instead, it might be more worthwhile to try to establish a system of world governance built on an accepted set of principles and processes that honour cooperative security based on the rule of law. It is in this context that I hold that an NWFW based on a set of widely accepted principles can be both stable and sustainable. This is especially pertinent in the case of nuclear weapons, which, more than any other weapons that mankind has had or renounced, have the potential to change the nature of power play or interstate dynamics. Nuclear disarmament will have to be conceived as being equally beneficial to all, individually and collectively, in order for nations to move in that direction and continue to invest in the enterprise. Only when anchored in these principles can an NWFW exist in a positive overall atmosphere in which threat perceptions have dissipated sufficiently to create a constructive framework within which countries can find it easy to enter into meaningful engagements and negotiations.

In my view, there are five principles that must undergird a world free of nuclear weapons.

Non-discrimination

Uniformity of commitments is critical for the success of an NWFW. A uniform yardstick to measure compliance with equally applicable verification procedures should be the bedrock of an NWFW. This would be drastically different from the case of the NPT, which has created two classes of states, with varying levels of verification and compliance standards. In fact, by doing so, it has inadvertently created an adversarial relationship between non-proliferation and disarmament. For all countries to be subject to the same rigour for the implementation of obligations to which they uniformly commit themselves, it is necessary to premise disarmament on a *single* standard of compliance which is non-discriminatory. This would also go a long way towards addressing the sense of unfairness that currently bedevils the relationship between the nuclear- and non-nuclear-weapon states. Therefore, a lack of discrimination and a presence of uniform standards must be the first pillar of an NWFW.

Verifiability

Given the current lack of trust among nations, and in order to foster greater confidence among them in the future, measures towards nuclear disarmament must be underpinned by treaties and institutions which ensure against nuclear delinquency. This will require the establishment of an integrated multilateral verification system, perhaps under the aegis of the UN or a newly created body tasked specifically with this responsibility.[6] While it is true that the scope of verification measures may need to be different for possessors and non-possessors of nuclear weapons, intrusiveness and stringency must be equal in principle and practice. Only if disarmament is premised on this value can there be enough transparency in the process to foster confidence among states to stick to their commitments and remain steadfast in the long term, especially during crises. A credible and robust verification system must be the second essential pillar of a stable NWFW.

Simultaneous collateral measures

Nations have perceived nuclear weapons as contributing to meet their security needs. In giving them up, there could be a natural tendency to lean on other types of crutches – conventional forces, space-based weaponry, new offensive technologies etc. – to make up for a perceived security deficit. Such moves would not only be counterproductive; they would also jeopardize the stability of the NWFW. Therefore, there must be a multi-pronged strategy for sustaining a world without nuclear weapons, which would also address wider security perceptions through adequate confidence-building in such areas as reducing conventional military capabilities to minimum levels required for defensive purposes, prohibiting the weaponization of outer space and precluding the development of new weapon systems. In his address to the UN Third Special Session on Disarmament in 1988, Indian Prime Minister Rajiv Gandhi presented an Action Plan for a Nuclear Weapon Free and a Non-violent World Order. He had particularly emphasized this point: 'While nuclear disarmament constitutes the centrepiece of each stage of the plan, this is buttressed by collateral and other measures to further the process of disarmament' (Gandhi 1988, cited in Sethi 2009, 146).

Given that conventional arms control and nuclear disarmament could be mutually reinforcing, a restructuring of conventional forces so that they can be employed only in defence of national territory can have positive influences on interstate relations. The mandate for the Treaty on Conventional Armed Forces in Europe (CFE) negotiations reflected such a consensus about the need 'to limit, as a matter of priority, capabilities for surprise attack and large-scale offensive action'. The CFE holds many lessons in this regard and is worth exploring in the individual contexts of the many nuclear dyads that exist today.

This, of course, will not be easy in the contemporary context. The answer may lie in the nature of collateral measures taken along with moving towards nuclear elimination. For one thing, if nuclear disarmament is *either the result of or results in more cooperative and secure interstate relations, then countries will not feel the need to move towards the further build-up of conventional capabilities*. For instance, US and Russian convergence of views on universal nuclear disarmament seems most likely to arise from a cooperative approach to ballistic missile defence. In such a scenario, the nature of interstate security automatically changes. This serves to underscore the importance of a broad, consensually agreed process of disarmament consisting of a multitude of simultaneous steps. Collectively, these would act to generate greater confidence and have a benign effect on the international security climate.

Acceptance and tolerance

An emphasis on a culture of non-violence, with a de-emphasis on the military dimension of international relations, is a sound principle for the conduct of international relations in a world free of nuclear weapons. The new world order will have to be based on 'respect for various ideologies, on the right to pursue different socio-economic systems, and the celebration of diversity' (ibid., 148). It is the threat of regime change or the non-acceptance of a particular political or economic system that gives rise to insecurities. As long as basic humanitarian values are respected, the new world order must show greater respect for the principles of coexistence, the non-use of force, non-intervention in the internal affairs of other countries and the right of every state to pursue its own path of development, all of which are enshrined in the UN Charter.

India's first prime minister frequently emphasized the goal of peace over security. The reason behind this is well explained by India's foremost strategic analyst, Jasjit Singh (2009, xvi):

> An environment of peace would naturally provide security, whereas mere security may or may not bring peace. For example, security in Europe during the Cold War was ensured for 45 years by something like 60,000 nuclear weapons, 94,000 combat airplanes, about 110,000 tanks and massive quantities of other weapons and military systems.

And yet, with all those security measures in place, peace proved elusive. The acquisition of nuclear weapons, whether as a national possession or through extended deterrence, brought security – but not peace. Therefore, as Singh points out, 'Peace has to be given a chance in shaping future paradigms' (ibid., xvi).

For peace to prevail, interstate relations must shift from the current competitive security paradigm to one of cooperative security. This is needed to meet not only the requirement of nuclear disarmament but also the many other challenges of the twenty-first century. Globalization has brought into focus the economic linkages between nations, and the ongoing economic recession has made these even clearer. Climate change, too, has been a great – if dubious – equalizer across continents and nation boundaries. Security-related issues also have similar cross-border linkages. Seeking security at an adversary's expense ultimately proves counterproductive, since it triggers an arms race and raises crisis instability. In some small measures, admission of this understanding can be found in UN Security Council Resolution 1887,[7] adopted on 24 September 2009 under the chairmanship of US President Obama. It established a linkage between nuclear disarmament and the promotion of international stability, peace and security premised on 'the principle of increased and undiminished security for all'.

Can nations bring themselves to rise above existing paradigms of security to envision a different world order premised on cooperation and the objective of peace rather than security? Can we at least begin to talk, write and debate about the contours of a post-nuclear world so that its appeal and advantages can begin to pervade wider spaces – geographically, and of the mind? As mind-sets change, so will the reality of the day. This is a fact proven in history – and the abolition of once-well-entrenched systems such as slavery and apartheid bear testimony to this.

Greater credibility of the rule of law

Cooperative security based on acceptance and tolerance may provide the philosophical underpinning for an NWFW. But its legal anchor must lie in the rule of law. Indeed, the essential difference between common and cooperative security lies in this aspect. While common security looks at the whole issue of security in its entirety, cooperative security places greater emphasis on intentional and institutionalized cooperation. This requires the existence of multilateral institutions whose functioning upholds the rule of law. It is in this context that we can argue for the reformation of the United Nations to reflect not just the wider membership of its Security Council but also its ability to enforce the rule of law.

Recognition of the prevalence of the rule of law must extend beyond the narrow realm of nuclear issues. As noted by Ken Booth,

> If progress in an anti-nuclear direction is conceived as a cultural problem rather than one of disarmament, it becomes apparent that such issues as the spread of democracy, the promotion of human rights, the search for economic justice, the research into and application of conflict resolution techniques and the growth of non-offensive defence schemes are all crucial anti-nuclear strategies.
>
> (Booth and Wheeler 1992, 46)

The acceptance and implementation of strategies that promote the concept of non-offensive defence will be critical to ensure stability in an NWFW. Schell has argued in favour of this by suggesting that the adoption of a non-provocative defence posture could rule out a conventional arms race and even tone down the possibility of aggression. In his schema, conventional weapons would be deployed in such a way that 'they could repel an invasion by another country, yet ... they could not themselves invade another country' (Schell 2000, 138). This could involve, for instance, having a large number of anti-tank weapons but not enough tanks, or enough anti-aircraft guns but not enough aircraft that could mount an offence.

Another author whose work is worthy of greater exploration in the contemporary context is Bjørn Møller, who has conducted extensive examination of the concept of non-offensive defence as it emerged in Europe as a means of defusing the East–West conflict. The concept of non-offensive defence, which underlies cooperative security, is premised on the assumption that individual states are better off pursuing polices of common security, since such policies make the international system more stable and peaceful.[8] Further work on this could provide valuable pointers for enhancing the prospects for stability in an NWFW.

Conclusions

It is certainly important that we take steps into an NWFW with open eyes. But, as André Gide (1925) so perceptively noted, it is equally true that '*One doesn't discover new lands without consenting to lose sight of the shore for a very long time.*'[9] The problem with visualizing a 'stable zero' from the world we currently inhabit lies in the fact that our thinking is shackled by the reality of an anarchic international system. This constrains us into believing that 'nuclear disarmament under conditions of international anarchy is impossible and, should it ever become possible, would be dangerously destabilizing' (Karp 1992, 19). In other words, since anarchy made nuclear weapons necessary, these weapons cannot be discarded until anarchy goes away. That is a dangerous argument. Some level of anarchy will always remain in interstate interaction, because that is how human nature is. But, just as the creation of society, with certain acceptable norms and mores, laws and enforcement mechanisms have enabled mankind to rise above the Hobbesian reality of a 'nasty, brutish and short' life at the individual level, so can it be done at the interstate level in a non-nuclear world.

Actually, the more attached the realists are to the 'inevitability' of an anarchic world order, the more should they desire a non-nuclear world in which the danger of nuclear annihilation as a result of a deliberate nuclear exchange or an inadvertent nuclear war is reduced, thanks to the elimination of such weapons. To accept anarchy as the sole reality of the world is to submit to the inevitability of the end of history and the end of exercising choice in the fate of our future. Mankind has a responsibility to make intelligent, informed choices in a constant process of learning. As Regina Owen Karp points out, 'Learning is not about accumulating information but about choice within the context of an existing civilization framework. Our capacity for choice does not depend on our ability to pin down the last consequential detail' (Karp 1992, 19).

Life requires taking calculated risks. A state of nuclear zero, which might not be perfectly stable but which will be free of the risk of nuclear use, versus a state of continuing nuclear dangers – these are the dimensions of nuclear weapons that have to be contended with. We have a choice. Do we want to keep the known dangers, which can only become exacerbated with time, or can we muster the courage to conceive of international security in a new way?

Notes

1 Poll conducted by the Seoul-based Asian Institute for Policy Studies in February 2013. Results available on the website of the Institute, www.en.asaninst.org.
2 Russia has been a strident critic of the ongoing development and deployment of elements of the USA's BMD architecture in its close vicinity. Many writings coming out of Russian think tanks voice their country's alarm at the 'advancements of NATO's BMD, given the technological characteristics and geographical positioning of the system'. For instance, see Zamanskaya (2013).
3 A draft resolution on a 'Convention on the Prohibition of the Use of Nuclear Weapons' has been tabled by India at the UNGA every year since 1982.
4 Syria has been alleged of having used chemical weapons in the civil war in the country. If the international community could respond to this through a collective show of abhorrence and force, that would serve as a powerful deterrent against future use of all WMD.
5 Harald Müller elaborates on this point in his chapter in this volume.

6 For more on verification, see the chapter by Andreas Presbo in this volume.
7 The full text of the UNSCR is available at www.un.org/en/sc/documents/resolutions/2009.shtml.
8 For more on the concept of non-offensive defence see Møller and Wiberg (1994).
9 In *Les faux-monnayeurs* [*The Counterfeiters*] (1925). The original reads: 'On ne découvre pas de terre nouvelle sans consentir à perdre de vue, d'abord et longtemps, tout rivage.'

Bibliography

Asian Institute of Policy Studies (2013) *The Fallout: South Korean Public Opinion Following North Korea's Third Nuclear Test*. Issue Brief, Asian Institute of Policy Studies. [Online] available from: http://en.asaninst.org/contents/issue-brief-no-46-the-fallout-south-korean-public-opinion-following-north-koreas-third-nuclear-test/

Booth, K. and Wheeler, N.J. (1992) Beyond Nuclearism. In Karp, R.C. (ed.) *Security without Nuclear Weapons? Different Perspectives on Non-Nuclear Security*. Oxford: Oxford University Press.

Gandhi, R. (1988) *A World Free of Nuclear Weapons*. Speech delivered at the UN Third Special Session on Disarmament, June 1988. In Sethi, M. (ed.) (2009) *Towards a Nuclear Weapon Free World*. New Delhi: Knowledge World.

Gide, A. (1925) *Les faux-monnayeurs* [*The Counterfeiters*] (first ed., 12 June 1973). London: Vintage.

Japan Times (2013) Nuclear Arms Card for Japan. [Online] 29 April. Available from: www.japantimes.co.jp/opinion/2013/04/29/commentary/japan-commentary/nuclear-arms-card-for-japan/ [accessed 28 January 2016].

Karp, R.C. (1992) Introduction. In Karp, R.C. (ed.) *Security without Nuclear Weapons? Different Perspectives on Non-Nuclear Security*. Oxford: Oxford University Press.

McNeill, D. (2011) Japan Must Develop Nuclear Weapons, Warns Tokyo Governor. *Independent*. [Online] Available from: www.independent.co.uk/news/world/asia/japan-must-develop-nuclear-weapons-warns-tokyo-governor-2235186.html [accessed 23 June 2014].

Mochizuki, M.M. (2007) Japan Tests the Nuclear Taboo. *Non-proliferation Review*, 14(2) (July): 303–328.

Møller, B. and Wiberg, H. (eds) (1994) *Non-offensive Defence for the Twenty First Century*. Boulder, CO: Westview.

Müller, H. (1992) The Role of Hegemonies and Alliances. In Karp, R.C. (ed.) *Security without Nuclear Weapons? Different Perspectives on Non-Nuclear Security*. Oxford: Oxford University Press.

Roberts, B. (2009) Asia's Major Powers and the Emerging Challenges to Nuclear Stability Among Them. *Institute for Defence Analyses*, Paper no. P-4423:S-1. [Online] available from: www.dtic.mil/cgi-bin/GetTRDoc?AD=ADA530036 [accessed 28 January 2016].

Schell, J. (2000) *The Abolition*. Stanford, CA: Stanford University Press.

Schelling, T.C. (1966) *Arms and Influence*. New Haven, CT: Yale University Press.

Shelling, T.C. (2009) A World Without Nuclear Weapons? *Daedalus*, Fall 2009: 124–129.

Singh, J. (2009) Introductory Remarks to the New Delhi Conference. In Sethi, M. (ed.) *Towards a Nuclear Weapon Free World*. New Delhi: Knowledge World.

Tannenwald, N. (1999) The Nuclear Taboo: The United States and the Normative Basis of Nuclear Non-use. *International Organizations*, 53(3): 433–468.

US Department of Defense (2010) *Nuclear Posture Review Report, April 2010*. [Online] available from: www.defense.gov/Portals/1/features/defenseReviews/NPR/2010_Nuclear_Posture_Review_Report.pdf

Zamanskaya, Y. (2013) *Moscow Has Every Reason to Believe that NATO's BMD is Targeted Against Russia*. [Online] Available from: https://rickrozoff.wordpress.com/2013/01/15/russia-has-every-reason-to-fear-nato-missile-system/ [accessed 28 January 2016].

3 Icon off the mark
Schelling's nuclear disarmament scare[1]

Harald Müller

Schelling's analysis is based on assumptions that are epistemologically implausible, inconsistent measured by his own ontological assumptions and marred with distorted empirical assessments.

Thinking about constellations in a nuclear-weapons-free world is a complicated epistemological operation. We are trying to construct knowledge about a non-existing context. Principally, there are two methods available for doing so, both working with counterfactual methodology.[2] Counterfactual forward induction starts from where we are and changes a variable, then constructs the world with this changed variable at time $t+1$, changes the next variable, constructs the world in $t+2$ and so on, until a plausible path to the chosen final state of the world is completed. Backwards induction starts with the final state f, constructs the state $f-1$ in which all the preconditions are present to move towards f, and eliminates, in a logical sequence, these conditions one by one until we are back to our present world. It is obvious that either process is fraught with speculations, but it is the only plausible method to go from here to there.

Schelling, however, uses a rough, even brutish counterfactual operation: he starts from the assumption that the parameters of a non-nuclear world remain unchanged compared to the present one but for one single element, the existence of nuclear weapons. However, the scenario in which all parameters remain the same while nuclear weapons disappear is epistemologically a non-starter. It is inconceivable that governments would move beyond minimum nuclear deterrence when they believe a war probable enough to make their security ultimately contingent on having nuclear weapons (if not immediately available, then at least quickly reconstitutable). Such governments would stop at perhaps 50, 100 or several hundred deliverable nuclear weapons and leave it at that, while something would be 'left to chance'.[3] It is obvious that states are not willing to renounce nuclear weapons under current political and military circumstances. What would drive them to do so if nothing changes?

Schelling makes the same mistake as many other pundits of nuclear deterrence: assuming that everything can remain equal in the process of disarmament and that zero can still be achieved (funnily enough, those who ask for immediate nuclear disarmament start from the same assumption). Nuclear disarmament with the aim of reaching a real zero is a large-scale effort at political re-engineering. It is bound to progress in small steps that states undertake because they believe these steps enhance their security or, at a minimum, do not diminish it. Successful steps may enhance mutual trust and thus encourage the parties to go further, and may lead to new requirements (e.g. in transparency and verification) whose implementation leads to even more trust accumulated. The major powers would also undertake efforts to sort out the problems they have with each other. In addition, the lower they go in terms of overall nuclear weapons holdings the more common interest they develop in keeping third parties from crossing the nuclear threshold; at some point, the joint security interest in keeping the nuclear door closed will surpass the interest to steal a geostrategic march on their peers by offering protection to a would-be proliferator. Going down to low numbers and envisaging the possibility of zero enhances their stakes in order and stability. This moves them in the direction of a great-power concert which might provide an indispensable structure for a zero-nuclear world, as has been argued elsewhere (Müller 2010, 33–66).

It is particularly implausible that it should be so easy to hide away fissile material for a small arsenal of nuclear weapons. It might sound credible at first but not on further consideration. No government would store weapons-grade material 'in a refrigerator' or 'in a well' and leave it at that, as Schelling appears to insinuate. Bomb-usable fissile material would be thoroughly guarded and fenced in order to prevent unauthorized actors from obtaining it. These security measures would have signatures that could be picked up by verification agencies who would enjoy greater authority and access rights than in the present world (because otherwise states would not lay down their nuclear arms). In order to ensure true reconstitution capabilities, governments would also have to maintain many technical experts, who would have to practise their reconstitution job lest they risk failing in the hour of truth. Such clusters of expert people practising their future breach of the rules in appropriate facilities would also leave a significant detectable signature. And that brings us back to the unrealistic assumptions – the verification system of a nuclear-weapons-free world would be geared towards picking up such signatures in order to fulfil its early-warning mission.[4]

As for the persistent high risk of a great-power war motivating the perpetual reliance on nuclear weapons, John Mueller (1989), Richard Ned Lebow (2010b) and Steven Pinker (2011) have argued in book-length studies that the value of war for great powers is in decline, and for developed middle powers war is already in disrepute. Major wars might still be possible, but would be much more likely to occur between developing middle powers (such as the Iraq–Iran or the Ethiopia–Eritrea wars). The interests of the great powers, once they reach the level of very low nuclear numbers or even a final zero, would be to contain these wars and terminate them at an early point. The scenario envisioned by Schelling, then – a desperate race into nuclear pre-emption – is an out-of-the-blue catastrophe that has never had great plausibility or probability even though it informed paranoid war games on both the US and Soviet sides during the Cold War. It would be utterly implausible once nuclear arms have been abolished, because nuclear-armed nations would not have taken this step if the risk of major war still loomed large in their minds. The simple counterfactual operation Schelling undertakes to construct a nuclear-weapons-free world compares unfavourably with the more complex and multifaceted counterfactual construction presented here, even if that is still far from a complete forwards – or backwards – induced counterfactual method.

Responsible or irresponsible: inconsistency in the rationalist assumptions

Schelling's nightmare scenario of a high-speed competition for successful pre-emptive nuclear war should surprise no one, given this assumption. Nevertheless, it is unconvincing. As he insists, 'responsible' governments have to take a cautionary approach towards security in that world. They have to mistrust their peers and, for that reason, take a prudential attitude towards the complete elimination of their reconstitution capabilities (it is important to note that this reliance on prudence is essential for Schelling's deterrence theory to work): in case of a major conflict, they must keep the preconditions for the prompt reconstitution of a military nuclear capability, including material, equipment, parts, technology and manpower. From there, he develops a scenario in which the first state to acquire a few nuclear weapons would use them pre-emptively to ensure a monopoly and would then be in a position to erect a blackmail-based nuclear tyranny – not a prospect anyone would welcome with enthusiasm; here I agree with him.

However, a 'responsible' government would also anticipate that other governments in a position to do so would pursue similar policies. Schelling dismisses the possibility of establishing a complete inventory of relevant materials and sites for all nuclear-weapon-capable powers. At the same time, he predicts that national intelligence services would be tasked to identify all relevant sites in potentially hostile states, which is the only circumstance under which a 'responsible government' could ever consider a disarming first strike. It is not explained how secret services, which do not enjoy the access privileges of an international inspectorate, would do better than inspectors in uncovering everything that a state tries to hide. A state that has successfully reconstituted a small nuclear arsenal thus could never be confident in his agents' omniscience concerning enemies' capabilities. With the failure of US intelligence to identify India's preparations for a nuclear test in 1998, or the botched reporting of Iraq's nuclear activities (or lack thereof) in 2003, which 'responsible' leader would ever trust so completely in their spies? The leader – if he or she were both rational and responsible, as Schelling presumes – would have to assume that others may be as quick if not quicker than their own state in the reconstitution race. A government participating in such a race must thus assume that, while it might be possible that its state would be the first to succeed, this is by no means assured. It would be possible as well that others had also procured a few nuclear weapons that they had not employed and would not employ prematurely. Not using one's few nuclear weapons prematurely would be prudentially justified for two reasons: first, since the probability of eliminating all the enemy's nuclear assets would never be 1 (owing to a failure of the attack or the failure of intelligence to uncover all relevant sites on the enemy's territory), a nuclear attack might trigger nuclear retaliation and thus the worst case. Second, because the state breaching the nuclear taboo might be seen as rogue – and a significant future threat – by other parties not involved in the war in question, a nuclear first strike might provoke the formation of a hostile alliance determined to destroy the rogue threat before it becomes overwhelming. Together, these two considerations make it likely that a rational ('responsible') government would abstain from attacking first with nuclear weapons. Once we assume that prudence guides governmental decisions, the idea of a disarming first strike in a reconstitution race can be ruled out.

Even if we accept for a moment that a reconstitution race – including a drive towards pre-emption – might be irresistible (and I will explain shortly why it is not), the rational way of pre-emption would be with conventional weapons. An enemy posture of a few nuclear weapons, hastily assembled and mated to delivery vehicles capable of carrying them, might indeed be thought to be vulnerable; likewise, the decapitation of a powerful enemy might look attractive – let us buy the argument for the sake of it. But the instrument of choice would have to be conventional weapons – conventionally armed intercontinental ballistic missiles, submarine-launched ballistic missiles, cruise missiles and long-range nuclear-capable bombers. They might do the job without precipitating nuclear retaliation, and one's own limited nuclear assets could be held back for intra-war deterrence against the enemy's crossing of the nuclear threshold. In addition, the attacking state would not acquire the opprobrium of being the first to breach the 'nuclear taboo' in place since Nagasaki.

Conventional pre-emption in a reconstitution race is also not a future to celebrate. A major war with an early, horrible exchange of conventional ordinance is not what developed societies need. It is also not what governments of developed societies want. Since the vast majority of the states that could clash in the way Schelling hypothesizes consists of developed societies (and China and India may be there once nuclear disarmament happens), a war would thus bring a very unwanted result early on. Responsible governments applying prudential calculations and projections would develop a clear idea of this most-likely scenario and feel compelled to avoid it. They would also know that the sword of Damocles of 'something left to chance', which Schelling (picking up legendary British admiral Horatio Nelson's quote) had so aptly depicted as the essence of nuclear deterrence, would fully apply in this situation (Schelling 1980, 187–203; see also Schelling 1965, 92–125). I submit that the double expectation of a high probability of outrageous conventional devastation, combined with an above-zero probability of unwanted nuclear escalation, would serve as a mighty deterrent against starting a war and as a powerful incentive to take all possible preventive diplomatic measures to avoid war in the first place. One may remark that the spectre of unwanted nuclear war would then still hang over the world, and this is true when one accepts this whole scenario, but this situation is not largely different from today. If one believes in a world in which nothing has changed but the physical existence of nuclear weapons, deterrence would still hold in a similar way that it holds today, with the same risk of an above-zero probability that it might fail. It is not logically consistent to believe in the stability of the present world of nuclear deterrence and to deny it to the future world in which deterrence, including its nuclear aspect, would be present in a different form but the same substance. But this means that, contrary to Schelling's sombre predictions, the world would not be worse off than today.

Framing the record: four empirical objections

Schelling's arguments contain four empirical claims that are not tenable: his account of wars among nuclear powers is incomplete; his denial of a present-day nuclear arms race is ill-informed; his negation of the influence that current nuclear arsenals have on the motivation of proliferators overlooks contrary evidence; and his assessment of the disarmament discourse is heavily biased.

Wars involving nuclear powers

Schelling provides a list of eight wars in the last 60 years in which one of the parties was a nuclear-weapon state. The list is significantly incomplete. There was the war between Israel and Lebanon/Hezbollah and Syria in 1982 (importantly, as it pitted a nuclear-armed state against a chemically armed state), two wars between China and Vietnam (1979 and 1987) and a war in which both parties had nuclear weapons (India–Pakistan in 1999). The latter is particularly relevant: a shooting war with a strategically important prize (the strategic road through northern Kashmir that would connect Pakistan with China) should not occur, according to Cold War-informed deterrence theory. Even more importantly, the one war which comes closest to being a template for Schelling's scenario (war between 'latent nuclear powers' in a world without nuclear weapons) is not mentioned: the war between Iran and Iraq in the 1980s. Both Iran and Iraq had incipient nuclear technology capabilities at the outset of the war. The Shah of Iran, Mohammad Reza Pahlavi, left behind a broad nuclear research programme established with the goal of developing a military nuclear option if and when necessary; Iraq had launched its own nuclear programme centred on the Osirak reactor, which was destroyed by an Israeli air strike in 1981. The war between Iran and Iraq was long, cruel and bitter. Both restarted nuclear activities during the fighting. But neither embarked on a crash programme as should be expected on the basis of Schelling's projections for a nuclear-weapons-free world. Even after being repeatedly attacked with chemical weapons, Iran did not race towards acquiring a nuclear capability. The pace of the programme was slow and investment was limited; it was not a top priority (Hymans 2012, 79–123, 255–259). This alone should be motivation enough to reconsider Schelling's scenario.

No nuclear arms race

Schelling states that today no nuclear arms race is 'in the offing'. It might not be 'in the offing', but the precursor elements are present and it is difficult to understand how they can be overlooked (Kile *et al.* 2012; Delpech 2012, 115–140).[5] US plans and activities for national and regional missile defences, together with US superiority in long-range strike options, are creating worries in Russia and China about the survivability of their second-strike forces. Consequently, Russia is modernizing its arsenal even as its overall size decreases, seeking to introduce a new, more-capable multiple warhead missile with increasing evasion and deception capabilities. China is slowly but steadily enhancing its small nuclear arsenal. In turn, India is deploying nuclear weapons on air-, land- and sea-based platforms and has not put a cap on the growth of its own arsenal as long as China's is increasing. Pakistan does not want to fall behind and is pursuing weapons-grade plutonium production to complement its use of highly enriched uranium. Islamabad has also blocked any negotiations on a fissile material cut-off treaty at the Conference on Disarmament in Geneva in order to avoid pressure to halt production. The whole process is deeply worrisome, given that we know little about the dynamics of multipolar nuclear arms races and even less about how to stop them. This need not obviate, for the time being, further quantitative reductions of US and Russian warheads, but is far from the 'nuclear quiet' which Schelling claims with a view to contrast the status quo positively against the horrors of a world without nuclear weapons.

No impact of existing nuclear arsenals on proliferators

Schelling accepts the well-known position that the nuclear arsenals of the 'official' nuclear-weapon states (those recognized as such by the Treaty on the Non-Proliferation of Nuclear Weapons) have nothing to do with those of 'rogues' like North Korea or Iran. But the security motivations for the North Korean and Iranian nuclear programmes centre on a confrontation with the United States, which is both conventionally superior and nuclear-armed. The threat emerging from the United States as a conventional power can hardly be disentangled from its nuclear capability. North Korea has been a target of nuclear threats during the Korean War, by Presidential Decision Directive 60 in 1997, and by its inclusion in the 'axis of evil' in 2002 (Arms Control Association 2012). Iran has shared the latter fate. As for the 'status' motive of the two states, this would diminish if nuclear weapons were devalued as symbols of standing in the process of disarmament. Instead, they are embraced (notably by Russia, France and the United Kingdom), enhancing their political value for status-conscious elites in Tehran and Pyongyang. And, as argued above, sharp reductions in all presently existing arsenals would create a much more urgent joint interest of the established nuclear-weapon states to prevent others from joining their club. Pressure on both Tehran and Pyongyang would consequently increase, and the prospects of dissuading them from further pursuing their present course might thus rise.

The nuclear disarmament discourse

Schelling complains about the lack of defence of the status against the disarmament juggernaut and quotes two lonely 'exceptions'. This is an amazing under-representation of the pro-nuclear deterrence literature: there is, inter alia, an entire special issue of *International Affairs* in which a crowd of pro-nuclear pundits beats up a lone moderate defender of nuclear disarmament, William Walker (*International Affairs* 2007). There is former Secretary of Defense Harold Brown's 2007 article in the Washington Quarterly (Brown, 2007). There are the widely read, witty and well-written blogs of former US Special Representative for Nuclear Nonproliferation Christopher Ford.[6] There is NATO Energy Security Section head Michael Rühle's polemical book against nuclear disarmament, and Bruno Tertrais's (senior research fellow at the Fondation pour la Recherche Stratégique) treatise in defence of deterrence (in English and French), to name a few (Rühle 2009; see also Tertrais 2011, 39). On the other hand, Schelling's proposition that serious disarmament discourse started only in 2007 with the *Wall Street Journal* op-ed by George Shultz, William Perry, Henry Kissinger and Sam Nunn is mistaken. The 1990s and early 2000s witnessed multiple proposals in this direction, from the Stockholm International Peace Research Institute's project 'Security without Nuclear Weapons', to the reports and studies of the Canberra Commission and those of the Weapons of Mass Destruction Commission. Contributors to the debate – in addition to people, like me, whom Schelling would possibly condemn as 'not serious' – also encompassed 'serious' people such as General Charles Horner, the former commander of Allied air forces during the Gulf War, General Lee Butler, the former commander of the Strategic Air Command, and General Andrew Goodpaster, the former NATO Supreme Allied Commander Europe, together with former French prime minister Michel Rocard.[7] Seen in this light, the 2007 op-ed by the 'four horsemen' elevated a long-standing debate to a new level, thanks to the high political rank and bipartisan distinction of the four elder statesmen. And there is no denying that their call was an important factor in President Barack Obama's decision to make nuclear disarmament a centrepiece of his foreign policy.

In sum, Schelling's comments on the empirical world overrate the risks existing in a nuclear-weapons-free world, understate the risks of a new arms race and the impact that current nuclear arsenals might have on proliferation and overlook the continuity, depth and breadth of the disarmament discourse, including serious work on how nuclear disarmament might be achieved, as well as the operational and practical aspects of eliminating nuclear weapons. All of these omissions make nuclear disarmament appear more difficult and improbable than it may actually be.

Conclusion

The basic flaw in Schelling's argument is the misrepresentation of nuclear disarmament as a jump from today's world to a very similar, but nuclear-weapons-free one, one where the future will resemble the past. But nuclear disarmament – if it occurs – can only develop as a slow and incremental process that combines various measures related to nuclear weapons with changes in conventional postures, arms control practices and broader political relations and their institutional and normative anchoring. The notion of change, which has been much more the pattern of history than stasis, is largely absent (Lebow 2008, 567–570).

To be sure, I understand that people might be sceptical as to whether a process of nuclear disarmament as briefly alluded to above would be possible and lead to its pronounced end-state. Personally, I believe in its possibility because nothing in the physical world stands in its way, and thus it is within our grasp. Measured optimism is not the least encouraged by the process that finished the Cold War, the ensuing relative devaluation of the role of nuclear weapons in Western national security policies, nuclear reductions and further measures in the US–Russian relationship, and the long-term trend in the reduction of interstate war. However, I am far from certain that the process will eventually reach its desired end. Nevertheless, even if it does not, there will be achievements on the road that would be worthwhile having in order to enhance international security. The pivotal task for today is thus to think through this process and the steps it entails, rather than to invent far-fetched and methodologically questionable scenarios that have little relevance other than to serve as the bogeyman to scare people away from even thinking about the possibility of a nuclear-weapons-free world.

Acknowledgements

For their very useful comments, I thank Thomas Schelling, Sverre Lodgaard and all the participants at the November 2012 Vienna workshop at which I presented my thoughts for the first time, two anonymous reviewers and my colleague, Marco Fey, who read and commented on both the first and the final drafts.

Notes

1 A first draft of this chapter was presented at the Vienna symposium on Stable Zero and later included in 'Icons Off the Mark', *The Nonproliferation Review*, Issue 3, 2013. The comment is an extract of that article. Reprinted with permission.
2 Counterfactual analysis has been largely applied with regard to the empirical analysis of the past. For example, see Lebow (2010a), Capoccia and Kelemen (2007), Tetlock and Belkin (1996), Sylvan and Majeski (1998) and Fearon (1991). But it is worthwhile noting that when we try to develop well-founded assessments of the future (like in prognoses or scenario analysis), we are working with counterfactuals as well and should do so methodologically. See Weber (1996).
3 This is a famous expression of Schelling's deterrence theory. It is because of the inherent uncertainties of crisis interaction between two nuclear-armed states that their governments will work to avoid, or at least to terminate early, such crises in the first place.
4 There is a growing literature about such steps, and about elements granting security in a nuclear-weapons-free world. For a few examples, see Kelleher and Reppy (2011), Hinderstein, C. (ed.) *Cultivating Confidence: Verification, Monitoring, and Enforcement for*

a World Free of Nuclear Weapons (Washington, DC: Nuclear Threat Initiative), Blechman and Bollfrass (2010), Perkovich and Acton (2009, 2008) and WMDC (2006).
5 Delpech underrates the role of the United States in this race, but establishes convincingly that it is under way.
6 See 'New Paradigms Forum', www.newparadigmsforum.com/NPFtestsite/.
7 General Goodpaster was chairman of a nuclear abolition project run by the Atlantic Council. See Goodpaster (1997). For analyses and proposals, see Karp (1992), the Canberra Commission of the Elimination of Nuclear Weapons (1998) and WMDC (2012).

Bibliography

Arms Control Association (2012) Clinton Issues New Guidelines on U.S. Nuclear Weapons Doctrine. [Online] available from: www.armscontrol.org/act/1997_11-12/pdd.
Blechman, B.B. and Bollfrass, A.K. (eds) (2010) *Elements of a Nuclear Disarmament Treaty: Unblocking the Road to Zero*. Washington, DC: Henry L. Stimson Center.
Brown, H. (2007) New Nuclear Realities. *Washington Quarterly*, 31 (Winter 2007–8): 7–22.
The Canberra Commission of the Elimination of Nuclear Weapons (1998) *Statement*, 2 July. [Online] available from: www.ccnr.org/canberra.html.
Capoccia, G. and Kelemen, R.D. (2007) The Study of Critical Junctures Theory, Narrative, and Counterfactuals in Historical Institutionalism. *World Politics*, 59: 341–369.
Delpech, T. (2012) *Nuclear Deterrence in the 21st Century: Lessons from the Cold War for a New Era of Strategic Piracy*. Rand Corporation. Available at www.rand.org
Fearon, J.D. (1991) Counterfactuals and Hypothesis Testing in Political Science. *World Politics*, 43: 169–195.
Goodpaster, A.J. (1997) *An American Legacy: Building a Nuclear-Weapon-Free World. The Final Report of the Steering Committee of the Project on Eliminating Weapons of Mass Destructions*. Washington, DC: Henry L. Stimson Center.
Hymans, J.E.C. (2012) *Achieving Nuclear Ambitions: Scientists, Politicians and Proliferation*. Cambridge: Cambridge University Press.
International Affairs (2007), 83: 427–574.
Karp, R.C. (1992) *Security Without Nuclear Weapons? Different Perspectives on Non-Nuclear Security*. Oxford: Oxford University Press.
Kelleher, C.M. and Reppy, J. (eds) (2011) *Getting to Zero: The Path to Nuclear Disarmament*. Stanford, CA: Stanford University Press.
Kile, S.N. with Fedchenko, V., Schell, P., Kristensen, H.M., Glaser, A. and Mian, Z. (2012) World Nuclear Forces. In Stockholm International Peace Research Institute (ed.) *SIPRI Yearbook 2012*. Oxford: Oxford University Press.
Lebow, R.N. (2008) *A Cultural Theory of International Relations*. New York: Cambridge University Press.
Lebow, R.N. (2010a) Forbidden Fruit: Counterfactuals and International Relations, Princeton, NJ: Princeton University Press.
Lebow, R.N. (2010b) *Why Nations Fight*. Cambridge: Cambridge University Press.
Mueller, J.E (1989) *Retreat from Doomsday: The Obsolescence of Major War*. New York: Basic Books.
Müller, H. (2010) Enforcement of the Rules in a Nuclear Weapon-Free World. In Hinderstein, C. (ed.) *Cultivating Confidence: Verification, Monitoring, and Enforcement for a World Free of Nuclear Weapons* (pp. 33–66). Washington, DC: Nuclear Threat Initiative.

New Paradigms Forum. Available from: www.newparadigmsforum.com/NPFtestsite/
Perkovich, G. and Acton, J.M. (2008) *Abolishing Nuclear Weapons*, Adelphi Paper 396. London: Routledge.
Perkovich, G. and Acton, J.M. (2009) *Abolishing Nuclear Weapons: A Debate*. Washington, DC: Carnegie Endowment for International Peace.
Pinker, S. (2011) *The Better Angels of Our Nature: Why Violence Has Declined*. New York: Viking.
Rühle, M. (2009) *Good and Bad Atomic Bombs*. Hamburg: Körber-Stiftung.
Schelling, T.C. (1965) *Arms and Influence*. New Haven and London: Yale University Press.
Schelling, T.C. (1980) *The Strategy of Conflict*. Cambridge, MA, and London: Harvard University Press.
Sylvan, D. and Majeski, S. (1998) A Methodology for the Study of Historical Counterfactuals. *International Studies Quarterly*, 42: 79–108.
Tertrais, B. (2011) *In Defense of Deterrence: The Relevance, Morality and Costeffectiveness of Nuclear Weapons*. Paris: IFRI Security Studies Department.
Tetlock, P.E. and Belkin, A. (eds) (1996) *Counterfactual Thought Experiments in World Politics: Logical, Methodological, and Psychological Perspectives*. Princeton: Princeton University Press.
Weber, S. (1996) Counterfactuals, Past and Future. In Tetlock, P.E. and Belkin, A. (eds) *Counterfactual Thought Experiments in World Politics: Logical, Methodological, and Psychological Perspectives* (pp. 268–288). Princeton: Princeton University Press.
WMDC [The Weapons of Mass Destruction Commission] (2006) *Weapons of Terror: Freeing the World of Nuclear, Biological and Chemical Arms*. Stockholm: WMDC.
WMDC [The Weapons of Mass Destruction Commission] (2012) *The WMDC Concludes Its Collective Work*. [Online] available from: www.un.org/disarmament/education/wmdcommission.

4 Towards a rigorous comparison of a pre-nuclear and a post-nuclear world

Nikolai Sokov

The first two chapters of this volume share two main concerns about the elimination of nuclear weapons. The first is that, while the existing world is not perfect, we know the risks, the potential instabilities and the ways of minimizing them. In contrast, the nuclear-free world is potentially unstable and entails risks that we do not know and requires solutions that we cannot develop without knowing the risks. It all boils down, in other words, to whether we know what to expect from the nuclear-free world.

The second concern is equally powerful – the risk of re-nuclearization in the event of conflict. If, as they suggest, the world without nuclear weapons can be unstable, there will remain a risk of a rush to nuclear weapons in the event of a large-scale conflict. The reacquisition of nuclear weapons in the midst of war would produce assets intended to be used in fighting instead of their current role – that of preventing war. It is a common point of nuclear disarmament sceptics that technology cannot be disinvented; hence, nuclear weapons will always remain with us, whether overtly or potentially.

The authors reach conclusions that appear opposed. Thomas Schelling believes that the existing system is reasonably stable, if not perfect, and 'this nuclear quiet should not be traded away for a world in which a brief race to reacquire nuclear weapons could become every former nuclear state's overriding preoccupation'. In contrast, Manpreet Sethi insists that the choice is between 'a state of nuclear zero, which might not be perfectly stable but which will be free of the risk of nuclear use, versus a state of continuing nuclear dangers'. She believes that the root cause of the continued existence of nuclear weapons is the state of anarchy, which still defines the international system, and offers a range of recommendations for enhancing the role of international regimes that would allow nuclear disarmament.

These two arguments reveal, first and foremost, the shallowness of our knowledge about the world we seek – the world without nuclear weapons. One must admit that concentration on achieving nuclear disarmament has led its proponents to turn a blind eye to the simple fact that the elimination of nuclear weapons is not – and cannot be – the ultimate goal: the ultimate goal is a safer world while disarmament is only an instrument towards it. While it might be psychologically difficult to admit the seriousness of these challenges, the arguments discussed by

Thomas Schelling and Manpreet Sethi are powerful and should stimulate further research.

Challenges of building a nuclear-free world

About nuclear-free world we know everything – and nothing. Humankind lived in a nuclear-free world for almost the entirety of its history except for the last seven decades. Knowledge about the 'pre-nuclear' world does not generate optimism. At any given moment, humankind was either preparing for war, or fighting, or recovering from war – only to begin preparation for the next one. Thomas Schelling makes a valid point when he expresses concern about returning to the status quo ante.

On the other hand, fighting did not end with the advent of nuclear weapons: wars at 'sub-nuclear' level continued and perhaps even intensified. The only new feature that nuclear weapons (perhaps) have introduced – given that we do not have tools to conclusively determine that this new feature is, indeed, causally related to the emergence of this new variable – is the absence of a global war or, more precisely, wars between major powers.

The widespread belief that the presence of nuclear weapons helped to prevent World War III is not difficult to explain: after two world wars, which took place in relatively quick succession (some may even claim that this was one world war with a long interval between two parts), the third was a logical expectation, especially given the intensity of the East–West conflict. That a new major war did not happen had to be attributed to a cause. The intuitively assumed causal chain was straightforward and, in a sense, unavoidable given the state of international relations theory, which until the 1980s was largely dominated by realism with its emphasis on the role of power. The most visible parameter that differentiated the world before and after 1945 is the presence of nuclear weapons; hence, they were attributed the key role in the maintenance of the 'long peace'. Obviously, the correlation can be – and most likely was – spurious. It is well known that several times during the Cold War the world came close to major war as a result of accidents or miscalculations. Wars practically never stopped during the post-World War II period either, although they were limited to the periphery – Korea, Vietnam and Afghanistan are only the more visible ones. On the other hand, it is known that the spectre of large-scale nuclear use weighed heavily on the minds of policy-makers and could have facilitated greater caution on the part of decision-makers, for example, during the Cuban missile crisis.

In the end, the propensity to assign a 'peace-maintenance' property to nuclear weapons is an attitude that can be expected on the part of those who had lived through two world wars. Seen within this framework, nuclear disarmament involves the choice between the dangers stemming from the presence of nuclear weapons and the dangers stemming from the risk of sliding into a new conventional world war. Proponents of nuclear disarmament believe things cannot be worse than they are today; opponents say that things could be much worse. There is no rational solution if the choice is framed in these terms.

The mechanism through which nuclear weapons are supposed to play that role is simple and, by virtue of its simplicity, persuasive. Since nuclear weapons are associated with large-scale devastation, their mere presence makes decision-makers more cautious regardless of all other stakes or plans. Caution is exercised both in 'normal' policy planning and especially during crises, when the prospect of nuclear devastation dictates risk avoidance. Of course, in real-life decision-makers on both sides, the East and the West have often displayed a propensity to initiate crises or escalate low-level conflict situations to the level when it was easy to slip into war; on the other hand, in each case decision-makers eventually stopped and sought a peaceful resolution.

The belief in the special role of nuclear weapons in preventing a major new war has two corollaries, which make opposite assumptions but lead in the end to the same pessimistic view of the chances of elimination of nuclear weapons. The first posits high requirements for the reliability of nuclear disarmament, while the other places equally high – if not higher – conditions on the change of the international system.

The first corollary that follows from the assumption about the role of nuclear weapons in preventing major war is the need for a guarantee against the speedy reintroduction of nuclear weapons in time of crisis. Thomas Schelling discusses that risk in detail, pointing out that if serious conflict ensues among major powers, especially those that used to have nuclear weapons, parties to that conflict will be tempted to quickly and secretly manufacture a small number of nuclear weapons in hope to 'win' the conflict. This (or even just an expectation of such behaviour) would greatly destabilize the situation and prompt a race by many states – not necessarily limited to those involved in the conflict – to follow suit. The result would be a major destabilization of the international system and an elevated risk of nuclear use as a result of uncontrolled proliferation.

To avoid this scenario, requirements for the depth of disarmament measures, for verification and for the nuclear non-proliferation regime should be very high. Scepticism about the ability of the international community to agree on necessary measures makes Thomas Schelling and many others doubt the wisdom of nuclear disarmament – while the existing situation is far from perfect, they say, the alternative could be more dangerous and unstable.

In fact, the challenge is hardly insolvable. There are plenty of reasons to believe that irreversibility can be ensured with a sufficient degree of reliability. Some characterize the target regime as 'disarmament plus' – a state of affairs that goes beyond the mere elimination of nuclear weapons and includes the in-depth dismantlement of nuclear weapons complexes coupled with an intrusive verification regime capable of detecting activities aimed at a clandestine restoration of the ability to produce nuclear weapons. The International Atomic Energy Agency's (IAEA) system of safeguards, complemented with recommendations of the Trilateral Initiative (a joint US–Russia–IAEA study on safeguarding plutonium removed from nuclear weapons) (Shea 2001), as well as other studies (such as the UK–Norway experiment and the ongoing US–UK programme) – all suggest that the task is achievable. Of course, more studies, experiments and negotiations will be needed, but there is no reason to be pessimistic.

There will probably remain a residual chance that a small number of nuclear weapons could still be manufactured in secret, but that eventuality can hardly have a decisive impact on future international relations. At a minimum, the 'disarmament plus' regime would significantly increase the time needed to re-nuclearize. Moreover, since the verification system would be international, it would likely operate even under conditions of a low-level conflict – at least at the initial level prior to dangerous escalation. An attempt to shut out inspectors and a monitoring system would thus represent a signal that would elicit an appropriate response by other states. This response could include collective action – a joint response by the international community (including states that would otherwise have remained neutral to the ongoing conflict) or a re-nuclearization programme by the state's opponent(s). In this situation, an attempt to restore the nuclear weapons complex and produce nuclear weapons in the course of a conflict would entail costs so high that the likelihood of that course of action should remain low (Lewis 2010).

Furthermore, one should not overestimate the potential benefits of the reacquisition of a small number of nuclear weapons. Available evidence suggests that the benefits associated with monopoly of a small nuclear arsenal are hardly decisive. The four years when the United States held nuclear monopoly and a longer period of overwhelming superiority over the Soviet Union yielded remarkably few tangible gains. A small number of nuclear weapons, if used, can inflict great destruction, but can hardly win a war, especially a war against a large power such as the United States, China, Russia or India. Instead of giving the violator an overwhelming preponderance, a crash secret programme to acquire nuclear weapons will likely saddle it with massive problems, such as making it an outcast in the international system and triggering the emergence of a broad coalition to punish the violator. That is, a small number of nuclear weapons in an otherwise non-nuclear world would likely be a liability rather than an advantage.

The other, perhaps even more challenging corollary of the view that postulates the special role of nuclear weapons in preventing major war is the assumption that nuclear disarmament requires, as a precondition, a fundamental change in the way that the international system is organized and functions. If nuclear weapons were the main reason why a global war did not start in the past seven decades, then to ensure the continuing absence of such a war without the presence of nuclear weapons the international system should be changed so that at least wars at the scale of World Wars I and II would not happen. In other words, this view postulates that the post-nuclear world should not be a simple return to the pre-nuclear stage.

While the logic itself appears valid, at least at the first glance, there are three problems associated with the proposal that the international system needs an overhaul:

- What exactly needs to be done to radically reduce the probability of large-scale wars?

- Can the leading powers agree on such changes and, moreover, will they, in fact, implement them without major conflicts (caused by misinterpretation, timing, etc.)?
- Will it will be possible to reduce the probability of 'other' wars – those that are not systemic but are nonetheless sufficiently serious to involve the risk of escalation to a global war? After all, nuclear weapons are supposed to prevent not just direct conflict among major powers, but also the escalation of lower-level wars to a global one.

At a minimum, the behaviour of the great powers needs to change, which entails a change in the domestic politics of these states. Major powers will have to learn to reign in their aspirations, resist temptations, become much more restrained in wielding their economic and political weight and become more tolerant of the interests of smaller states. Even more important is restraint in crisis situations, whether in bilateral relations or during regional crises, otherwise there would remain a risk of slipping into an escalatory trajectory, which could result in a major war.

All of this seems only theoretically possible, and even then only in a distant future, meaning that nuclear disarmament should be postponed indefinitely – 'not in my lifetime', as President Obama said in his 2009 speech in Prague. Such a proposition would be quite acceptable to the opponents of nuclear disarmament. According to their logic, nuclear weapons have not been used for seven decades, and based on that experience the likelihood of their use from today's perspective would appear distant. Within that framework, nuclear weapons could be classified as a known evil; we know how to control it – a lesson learnt from a difficult and dangerous sequence of crises in the midst of the Cold War – and thus should be by definition preferable to the unknown dangers of the non-nuclear world.

On the other hand, it is well known that straightforward extrapolation is not a sufficiently reliable predictor: circumstances can change and causal chains that seemed to work in the past will no longer produce the same result as before. Thus, on top of the uncertainty about the causality between nuclear weapons and the absence of global war, which was mentioned above, there is no reason to believe that, even if the hypothesis about causality is valid, the same relationship will remain unchanged.

Moreover, the proposition that fundamental change in the ways the international system is organized and functions represents a necessary condition for elimination of nuclear weapons is hardly a foregone conclusion either. The bill might simply be unnecessarily high and one wonders whether the same result could be achieved through much more modest (and thus more feasible in the near future) measures.

The shape of the world free of nuclear weapons

The prospects of nuclear disarmament depend, to a large extent, on our ability to balance two requirements. On the one hand, we need to construct a plan of a

Pre- and post-nuclear world 45

nuclear-free world that would be sufficiently stable (i.e. the probability of major war will be low). On the other, it is necessary to minimize the scale of changes to make the task feasible – only changes that are necessary and fall short of ideal.

When tackling these tasks, we need to contend with the fact that nuclear weapons do not necessarily ensure stability and the prevention of major war. Manpreet Sethi points out in her chapter that nuclear balance(s) in Asia lack the key stability characteristics of the US–Soviet balance during the Cold War; the system is inherently unstable and thus a status quo can hardly be sustained.

Indeed, South Asia demonstrates all or nearly all sources of destabilization in a nuclear relationship: numerical imbalance; close proximity (resulting in extremely short warning times); challenges of command and control (full-scale centralization can deprive parties of the ability to respond while delegation of authority can result in unsanctioned escalation); territorial disputes; and a high role of groups outside government control, which can trigger conflict. A close look at this situation reveals that the US–Soviet nuclear relationship, which continues to serve as the main (often the only) case study for proponents of the 'nuclear stability' hypothesis, has serious limitations and can hardly be applied to many other cases, existing or potential future ones.

There are, indeed, indications that the presence of nuclear weapons has made governments more cautious, but solid proof is not available – only personal reflections and conjecture. While India and Pakistan have agreed on a set of confidence-building measures to reduce the risk of nuclear confrontation, these measures have not removed the risk of conflict itself or mitigated the inherent instabilities of the nuclear balance. This only proves that these weapons, in and of themselves, cannot ensure the stability of the overall relationship – instead, they make such a conflict potentially more devastating.

A more recent example of the (non-)role of nuclear weapons in preventing major conflicts is the unfolding crisis over Ukraine, or, more specifically, the dynamic of the relationship between the West and Russia (Pomper 2016). Moscow invoked its nuclear status very early during that crisis – in the spring of 2014. This included a range of signals, such as a stream of public statements at all levels that reminded the West about Russian nuclear capability, multiple launches of delivery vehicles that are primarily used to carry nuclear weapons, and the description of new research and development programmes for new types of nuclear-capable delivery vehicles. Together, these signals were clearly intended to prevent the West from escalating the conflict through, for example, major arms supplies to Ukraine, sending troops or other steps that could leverage the military power of the United States and NATO.

One might be tempted to say that the plan worked: the West has (at least at the time of writing) consistently refrained from the use of force and concentrated instead on a broad range of economic and political sanctions. The absence of escalation does not, however, prove that such escalation was prevented by Russian references to nuclear weapons. There is no evidence whatsoever that NATO seriously contemplated the escalation of the crisis to a military confrontation; from the very beginning it concentrated on economic and political measures that exploited the economic and financial weaknesses of Russia. There is little reason to expect that this overall orientation could change.

What is even more interesting, the Russian 'nuclear bravado' appeared pretty hollow. Statements are tangible, but do not require the commitment of resources; rhetoric can be escalated or reduced at will; it only matters in the long term if supported by actions, such as production, deployment and modernization programmes. The latter, however, remained in short supply except for more active overflights of aircraft, including nuclear-capable aircraft, in areas adjacent to NATO (the intensity of training, however, can also be increased relatively 'on the cheap'). Otherwise, little has changed in the Russian nuclear posture policy. For example, the number and the nature of launches of nuclear-capable delivery vehicles, although widely touted in the spring and autumn of 2014, remained fundamentally the same as in 2013; no new R&D programmes were launched and there is no indication that existing programmes were accelerated. (Sokov 2015)

Of course, there remains a possibility that resource-intense commitments will be made at a later date. Yet even that seems unlikely: Russia launched a considerable (some would say excessive) number of R&D programmes in the relatively stable years since the mid-2000s and there is simply no apparent need to do something extra. It is, however, possible – and the Kremlin has been doing just that – to talk more and more threateningly about the same programmes.

In fact, the enhanced talk about nuclear weapons was apparently directed to a large extent (if not primarily) to the domestic audience. The message resonates well with the consistent support for nuclear status among the Russian public. It can also help to mitigate concerns about confrontation with the West and feeds well into the narrative about external threat.

A similar trend can be detected in Europe. The debate about the possible withdrawal of American tactical nuclear weapons from the continent, which was not fully closed even after the Defense and Deterrence Posture Review and the new Strategic Concept, was terminated by the Russian annexation of Crimea. Proposals about weapons withdrawal are simply no longer tenable in the current political climate. Yet, the crisis conditions have not added any tangible military mission to these weapons: they retain the same role of the psychological prop for a handful of members of the Alliance. The security situation does not warrant a 'return' to nuclear deterrence; rather, the political atmosphere helps to freeze the 'nuclear status quo'.

A more recent – and more dangerous – chain of events that could have resulted in a major conflict took place at the very end of 2015. When the Turkish Air Force shot down a Russian Su-24 aircraft on 24 November, Russian President Vladimir Putin was under strong pressure to respond in kind and order a shooting down of a Turkish aircraft. Such a step could almost unfailingly have led to an escalation well beyond the bilateral Russian–Turkish context: NATO, even if reluctantly, felt it needed to support Turkey (after all, the credibility of

NATO security guarantees to members of the Alliance in east-central Europe was at stake) and thus would have been, willingly or not, embroiled in the conflict. The situation was terrifyingly similar to the summer of 1914, when the assassination of Archduke Franz Ferdinand in Sarajevo triggered an escalation that resulted in World War I. One is tempted to say that major war was averted only because Putin decided to respond in a non-military manner. It remains, however, a fact that Turkish leaders were not fazed by the Russian nuclear status when they chose the manner in which they wanted to signal displeasure with the Russian military operation in Syria.

In the end, recent events demonstrate that the role of nuclear weapons in the post-Cold War period has been very limited, perhaps smaller than during the Cold War. This might be seen as an encouraging sign in terms of implications for the prospects of moving towards a nuclear-weapons-free world. It suggests, in particular, that the chances of conflict will probably not increase and thus the changes in the international system required for the elimination of nuclear weapons might be rather limited. Perhaps we need to talk about adjustments rather than a major reform.

On the other hand, their presence did not make conflict less likely, which should be regarded as troubling sign – the absence of nuclear weapons will not necessarily bring peace in and of itself. In fact, in the autumn of 2015 Russia demonstrated that is has usable long-range conventional high-precision weapons, over which the United States and its allies had had the monopoly for almost 25 years. While this new development does not contradict the elimination of nuclear weapons (which have demonstrated a low ability to prevent conflict), it certainly points to the urgent need to relaunch efforts to limit, regulate and reduce conventional forces.

In this regard, Manpreet Sethi's reference to the Chemical Weapons Convention (CWC) deserves close attention. These weapons were eliminated after a protracted period of non-use and a de facto injunction against their use or threat of use. The effort did not require any changes in the international system whatsoever. The end of the Cold War, seen from that perspective, was not a condition, but rather an enabler that helped to codify a decision for which the vast majority of states, including the major holders of chemical weapons, were ready. One of the key impediments to the CWC was the details of the verification system; the more positive atmosphere generated by the end of the Cold War helped to overcome the deadlock.

The downside of this analogy is the time it took to finally agree to the elimination of weapons, whose use was banned in the 1920s and proved militarily unusable during World War II. As happened with chemical weapons, it might turn out to be necessary to wait until the elimination of nuclear weapons becomes politically feasible – a constellation of circumstances that makes more-constructive, result-oriented dialogue between nuclear-weapon states possible or a major crisis of the nuclear non-proliferation regime that energizes nuclear-weapon states towards the same goal (Tannenwald 2008). Of course, it is always possible to count on rational analysis of the threats associated with nuclear weapons, but rationality in decision-making is a remote possibility.

Considering all of the above, we can perhaps conclude that the end of the Cold War has represented a change in the international system nearly sufficient to seriously consider the elimination of nuclear weapons. Whereas in a tight bipolar structure of the international system, which was characteristic for the Cold War period, nuclear weapons could have played a stabilizing role between the United States and the Soviet Union (whether they did, in fact, play that role can be contested, but this is beyond the scope of this argument at the moment), the post-Cold War period has ushered in a looser and more flexible – but also much less regulated – structure. The potential 'nuclear instability' in South Asia, about which Manpreet Sethi writes, clearly demonstrates that even if nuclear weapons had a war-prevention role in the past, their impact today is far less certain; at least, the dangers stemming from their existence have increased.

Proceeding from a 'minimalistic' assessment of the changes needed in the international system to make nuclear disarmament possible and from the assumption that the end of the Cold War has taken us long way towards that goal, what else needs to be done?

Manpreet Sethi makes a range of suggestions in her chapter. These suggestions, at first glance, sound too general and a bit idealistic, but, in fact, can be operationalized in sufficiently practical terms.

A ban on nuclear weapons, she writes, should be *non-discriminatory*. This is without doubt self-evident, at least from a legal and political point of view. One wild card that remains is North Korea, but if all other nuclear-weapon states agree on nuclear disarmament, it is difficult to imagine that North Korea will be able to remain a holdout for too long.

The *nuclear-weapons-free world should be verifiable*. While this might seem a high barrier, in fact it is not. Significant work has been done in that area by many experts and think tanks; this author would particularly like to point to a joint VERTIC–VCDNP programme that explores the applicability of past experiences in verification to the task of the complete elimination of nuclear weapons. In a summary, there is every reason to believe that, with appropriate adjustments, additions and strengthening, the existing nuclear safeguards regime fulfils most of the requirements for guarding against the possible clandestine resumption of nuclear weapons programmes. If there are serious gaps in our combined verification experience, it is with the elimination (dismantlement) of nuclear weapons; with most other aspects and especially the requirements for the 'post-nuclear' world the international community already has considerable experience to build upon. No one can say the task of completing the system will be easy, but it is certainly within the realm of the possible.

The verifiability requirement is closely linked to the criterion of inclusiveness (non-discrimination). Any reasonable verification system for a non-nuclear world has to engage all states, both those that possess nuclear weapons today and those that do not. The regime could be fashioned on the same basic principles as the Comprehensive Test Ban Treaty (CTBT): it includes as equal parties all countries – not only those that have conducted tests or have a theoretical ability to conduct them, but also states that have never possessed that capability in the first place.

The same applies to the CWC – the Organisation for the Prohibition of Chemical Weapons (OPCW) is global and does not accord any preferential treatment in terms of verification to states that possessed chemical weapons at the time of its conclusion.

Sethi also proposed a *range of 'collateral measures'* in adjacent areas, such as conventional weapons, space and others. Indeed, her warning about the danger of shifting to alternative military tools as a precondition for nuclear disarmament is very valid. The 'revolution in military affairs' (RMA) appears dangerous in many ways because it leads to the emergence of military tools that are *usable*, unlike (or at least much more than) nuclear weapons. A host of regimes that limit and/or regulate the new generations of military capabilities can facilitate the elimination of nuclear weapons.

This task is by no means simple: the US–Russian dialogue on nuclear reductions remains deadlocked precisely over Russian demands that, simultaneously or in a single package, such reductions also address missile defence, long-range conventional strike assets and the weaponization of space; similar conditions are advanced by China. The United States continues to oppose these conditions. It should be noted, however, that US resistance stems from its domestic politics – first and foremost, the political commitment of significant parts of the elite and the public to relevant military programmes. And, while domestic politics is always very difficult to deal with, it should not be conflated with systemic impediments, which are usually put forwards as the main justification for keeping nuclear weapons. Now that Russia has demonstrated the capability that the United States was bent on safeguarding against, and now that China is not far behind Russia, perhaps politics in Washington could turn a more favourable eye to arms control measures with regard to modern conventional weapons.

The *rule of law* requirement is also more practical and operational than it might seem at first glance. Essentially, it is about giving greater weight to existing international regimes and organizations, the United Nations and its Security Council first of all. These regimes and organizations are not perfect and might need reform, but they appear a solid foundation that could be built upon. Interestingly, this requirement resonates very closely with what Russia and China have been saying for a long time. Moscow in particular has traditionally insisted that all important international decisions should be made within the UNSC and has accorded preference to well-established and institutionalized regimes (embodied, for example, in legally binding treaties, conventions and other similar instruments) over *ad hoc* 'coalitions of the willing'. The latter might be more practical for immediate tasks; they take much less time to form and can operate more flexibly and with greater efficiency. Yet, in international affairs 'slow' sometimes also means less opposition and greater durability.

All of this suggests that a nuclear-weapons-free world is somewhat more attainable than common wisdom might suggest. If arguments about the war-prevention role of these weapons are reassessed under the conditions of the post-Cold War world, they would appear primarily psychological – a natural human fear about jumping into the unknown. Caution is a laudable characteristic, but it should not overwhelm all else. Nuclear weapons do not generate stability in all situations (and the range of such situations has narrowed since the end of the Cold War), while the crisis over Ukraine has demonstrated that these weapons' primary role is psychological rather than operational military and the crisis between Russia and Turkey has showed that nuclear weapons do not prevent conflict.

To a large extent, impediments lie in the realm of domestic politics, it appears. For the United States, it is the reluctance to subject modern non-nuclear assets to regulation; for Russia, it is the tendency to invoke nuclear weapons to address concerns of the public. As happened with chemical weapons, such a situation could theoretically continue for a long time until domestic conditions are ripe for action. There is, however, one caveat that needs to be taken into account. Russia, China and India pursue similar non-nuclear weapons programmes (both strike and the defence varieties); the question is not whether they can succeed, but rather when. Now that Russia has succeeded, we could, unfortunately, see other countries (the United States and their allies first of all) accord new prominence to nuclear weapons to balance the new Russian and, in the future, Chinese and Indian capabilities.

This scenario, which appears uncomfortably likely, reinforces the above-referenced warning that nuclear disarmament should not come as a result of the unrestricted development of alternative military tools. Unfortunately, the courageous Prague speech of Barak Obama owes its support in the United States in part to the 25-year-old near-monopoly on modern conventional weapons; without that monopoly, part of the domestic support in the United States for further nuclear arms reductions and eventual nuclear disarmament could disappear as well.

This really brings this author to perhaps the central conclusion of this review piece, namely that the greatest obstacle to nuclear disarmament comes from domestic politics in nuclear-weapon states and partially in states under the 'nuclear umbrella', rather than from properties of the international system or from properties of nuclear weapons. The latter appears far from insurmountable, although it will require a serious and focused commitment of effort over an extended period of time. The former is much more difficult to address.

Bibliography

Lewis, P. (2010) Delegitimizing Nuclear Weapons: Examining the Validity of Nuclear Deterrence. In Lewis, P., Berry, K., Pélopidas, B., Sokov, N. and Wilson, W. *CNS Occasional Paper in Association with the Swiss Confederation.*

Pomper, M. with Egle Murauskaite, Nikolai Sokov, and Jessica Varnum (2016) *Ensuring Deterrence Against Russia: The View from NATO States.* Center for Nonproliferation Studies Occasional Paper.

Shea, T. (2001) *Report on the Trilateral Initiative: IAEA Verification of Weapons-Origin Materials in the Russian Federation & the United States.* IAEA Bulletin, 43/4/2001: 49–53.

Sokov, N. (2015) Russian Perspective on Nuclear Disarmament and the Post-Nuclear World. In Hynek, N. and Smetana, M. (eds) *Global Nuclear Disarmament: Strategic, Political, and Regional Perspectives*. London: Routledge Global Security Studies.

Tannenwald, N. (2008) *The Nuclear Taboo: The United States and the Non-Use of Nuclear Weapons Since 1945*. Cambridge: Cambridge Studies in International Relations.

Part II
The requirements and paths to stable nuclear zero

5 Out of the box
Nuclear disarmament and cultural change

Harald Müller

Introduction

The debate about nuclear disarmament is plagued by the hegemony of existing mentalities. Opponents as well as many proponents of a nuclear-weapons-free world face difficulties in liberating themselves from the traditional thinking about national security, notably with regard to deterrence. Nuclearism has become so much a part of everyday thinking on security that breaking out of this frame faces formidable barriers, not least the inability of many pundits to 'think out of the box'.

Deterrence remains the sturdy child of the nuclear era. Acceptance of deterrence as the mainstay of nuclear security tends to lead people back to the assumptions and remedies that were elaborated for the nuclear age, overlooking possible alternative paths to national security that are more compatible with a world without nuclear weapons. The main point of a nuclear-weapons-free world (NWFW) is to leave the nuclear age behind, for good. On the road to this new and highly desirable state of affairs, many fallacies of the nuclear age must be discarded. To start with the worst one: 'nuclear weapons cannot be disinvented'. This statement, put forwards in good faith many times over by nuclear proponents in the debate, totally ignores the myriad things that were once thought necessary, that 'could not be disinvented' – from slavery through DDT to CFCs. Again and again in history, the impossibility of disinventing eventually failed to impress political decision-makers who had become determined to get rid of something they had come to recognize as undesirable. And so they invested the effort and political capital necessary to create normative and institutional contexts that could make bans both possible and effective.

I do not pretend that this will be easy to achieve concerning nuclear weapons – nor do I feel sure it will be eventually done. However, allegations of impossibility are simply unfounded. Nuclear weapons are the creation of humans: a social construct that can also be deconstructed. And, given the increasing dangers of a nuclear-armed world, we should certainly try.

This chapter marks a serious attempt at thinking out of the box. First, I address the issue of deterrence and its role in the security system of an NWFW. Next, I examine why virtual deterrence, a popular solution for security in such a world, contradicts the very principles on which such a world will have to be founded. I then turn to five elements that could help make that world stable. The first is embedded in the transformative character of the disarmament process itself. The second is an institutional innovation, a concert of major powers. The third is conventional deterrence against breakout and the institutional arrangements on which it is based. The fourth – optional – is collective (rather than national) missile defence. And the fifth is the creation of a true nuclear taboo, and not merely a metaphorical one.

Deterrence as a social relationship

Let us think for a moment about the last 10 years before the time comes when all nuclear weapons are dismantled, and the 10 years afterwards, when, as I propose in this chapter, all weapons-grade fissile material is diluted, transmuted, introduced into the civilian nuclear fuel cycle and/or disposed of in an irretrievable state, while the related facilities are dismantled, nuclear weapons research phased out and nuclear command organizations dissolved. During this phase of 20 years, residual, and, in the end, virtual (see below) nuclear deterrence among the great powers will remain the default option in the event of cooperation failure and breakout. The possibility of falling back on this option to ensure national security if disarmament fails to produce the desired security gains is probably an initial prerequisite for the great powers to try nuclear disarmament in the first place. At the same time, however, the participants must take steps – and determined steps at that – to leave the nuclear deterrence age for good. They will have to push the default option of nuclear deterrence more and more into the background, building down its physical basis and eliminating the reasons for it. As a consequence, decision-makers in security policy will perceive less and less cogent reasons to stick to nuclear deterrence even in virtual form. Here we are speaking about a protracted process that will probably require the time of a full generational change.

The benchmark of this phase is the reversal of preferences for nuclear deterrence on the one hand and cooperative/collective security on the other hand. Today, nuclear deterrence is the default option, with cooperative security the add-on. Nuclear deterrence has come to represent normality, whereas cooperative security is still an anomaly in national security policies. The confidence-building process as proposed here aims to reverse this relation. Only through such a process of reversal will we be in a position to build the 'mental springboard' from which the daring leap into the spirit governing a world without nuclear weapons can become possible.

In order to understand the need for this basic reversal, we must start from a basic insight: even when nuclear deterrence is already perceived as an anomaly, it still remains a stumbling block for nuclear disarmament, from a mental as well as political perspective. It impacts on the chances for disarmament in the mental perspective because the nuclear security dilemma continues, albeit in a weakened form: although deterrence policy always implies that nuclear war may become increasingly improbable through measures jointly taken, a bit of its residual probability lingers on. And thus there will remain some remnant of the inclination to ascribe to one's partner(s) the potential intention of provoking or starting a nuclear war. Enemy images might have shrunk to a shadow of their strength today, but they would not have disappeared completely. Of course, they would diminish to an absolute minimum before final disappearance if all nuclear possessors could adopt credible no-first-use doctrines in line with their respective nuclear postures. This consideration suggests that the 'symbolic politics' of changing doctrines will have to play their role in the transformation process. What we might call 'empathic doctrinal change' is a necessary interim stage on the way to enhanced mutual confidence.

Politically and institutionally, the survival of the nuclear weapons complexes needed to maintain the nuclear deterrence apparatus in today's nuclear-weapon states (NWS) represents a major stumbling block for going to zero. These bureaucratic formations preserve their vested interest in their own immortality and thus in the continuation of their military nuclear core mission. Therefore, the fertile ground for continuing lobby work will be still there. Their allies in the security policy decision-making apparatus will receive both pressure and support for sticking to the status quo. The influence of the nuclear weapons complex will weaken over time, but it will still provide considerable obstacles also in the final phase of the nuclear disarmament process. Here we may recall the success of the US nuclear bureaucracy during the 1994 nuclear posture review, when it overcame the preferences of the disarmament-friendly Secretary of Defence Les Aspin, who would have gone for a new doctrine more compatible with disarmament (Nolan 1999).

This constellation is unavoidable, as the complexes cannot be completely dissolved until the very last weapon has been dismantled and the very last grams of fissile material transferred to non-weapons use. Nevertheless, it is possible to establish counterweights that can serve to marginalize or neutralize the influence of the nuclear weapons lobby. Promising in this regard is the road taken by Austria, Switzerland and other non-nuclear-weapon states during the 2010 and 2015 NPT Review Conference: efforts for the further de-legitimizing of nuclear weapons by emphasizing their fundamental incompatibility with humanitarianism, including humanitarian law (Berry *et al.* 2010). This implies an incremental outlawing of nuclear weapons, following the model of chemical and biological weapons (Price 1997). Such a process of outlawing is a Siamese twin of the process that can lead to a world without nuclear weapons. The stronger the roots of the norm become, the harder it will be for nuclear weapons proponents to find receptive audiences, and the more dominant the coalition of supporters of nuclear disarmament will become in political institutions.

In order to weaken the lobbying frenzy of the nuclear complexes, they should increasingly be entrusted with disarmament missions, and their budgets must be restructured accordingly. This move will create significant bureaucratic counterweight within the institutions, in turn making it harder to maintain a unified policy line for sabotaging the disarmament process. Useful templates here can be the international science centres established in Moscow and Kiev after the demise of the Soviet Union in order to create new and interesting jobs for former WMD experts. Another case in point has been the British nuclear weapons establishment at Aldermaston, which has been instructed to do research on verification options for a world free of nuclear weapons (Milne and Wilson 1998).

All of the above has concerned the problems of deterrence among the great powers. We must not forget the additional problem of the smaller NWS with their own concerns and agendas (as well as those possessing chemical or biological weapons) that also have to be 'deterred' while disarmament is under way (Hagerty 2012; Ogilvie-White and Santoro 2012). This point is highly relevant, as the policies of the great powers towards these states have varied widely in the past; this disunity creates a quasi-natural drift to fall back on national deterrence policies 'just in case' as the default option, in the absence of a collective security understanding among the great powers. There are two possible responses here. First, a move to no-first-use – an important stepping-stone in the nuclear disarmament process and at least envisaged in the 2010 US Nuclear Posture Review – includes combating biological and chemical weapons not in kind or by nuclear weapons, but by advanced conventional means. Second, and more essentially, there is a political dynamic which disarmament sceptics usually neglect: the necessary change in vital great-power interests during and through the disarmament process. The closer their nuclear arsenals approach zero, the more sensitive will governments become to the significance of nuclear weapons of smaller parties for their security and even more for their international status. Their interests in non-proliferation and in the rollback of the nuclear armaments of smaller nations will become a shared concern among all established nuclear powers.

Today, their already-existing interests in preventing new entries into the nuclear club are weighed by NWS governments against geopolitical and geostrategic interests. In contrast, once we are on the way to zero, the scales will give more weight to the convergent interest of preventing status gains by third parties compared with today's nuclear powers. The pressures on small NWS and potential proliferators will grow correspondingly. This will affect the China/DPRK, China/Pakistan and China–Russia/Iran dyads, but also USA/Israel. The resulting diplomatic cooperation among the great powers with a view to persuading their (presumably reluctant) clients to renounce nuclear weapons could prove particularly effective in giving massive traction to the idea of cooperative security. In the negotiation process that led to the agreement with Iran in 2015, a sense of this convergence could be felt.

This strengthening of motivations to pursue cooperative security as a matter of national interest is likely to become a powerful element of collective deterrence against the possessors of chemical and biological weapons. In the process, deterrence is transformed from the normal core of *national* security policy at the centre of international relations into the exceptional instrument of *collective* security policy at the periphery of international relations (Müller 2010).

The fatal proposition of virtual deterrence

The decisive question for any transformation strategy reads as follows: what will happen to deterrence in a world without nuclear weapons? Today, the most prominent answer is to maintain nuclear deterrence in 'virtual' form once the last weapon has been dismantled (Drell and Goodby 2009). Instead of physical nuclear arsenals, this new form of nuclear deterrence is based on 'virtual arsenals', consisting of a combination of residual technical/material assets, like the resource material, consisting of fissile material, non-nuclear building blocks for nuclear weapons and nuclear weapons facilities, and an organized reconstitution capability of skilled manpower and stored information (Mazarr 1997). It is obvious that virtual arsenals will be an inevitable transition stage in the phase in which the last weapons and then the related facilities are dismantled and the fissile material extracted from warheads is either transferred to the civilian fuel cycle or transmuted or finally disposed of. This phase is dictated by the nature of the disarmament process and its technical parameters. During this period, the possibility of reconstitution will hang like a sword of Damocles over the non-nuclear world. But it is a fallacy to see in virtual arsenals the final state of nuclear disarmament (Schell 1998). That view is incoherent and untenable for several reasons.

Nuclear weapons complexes are prone to exert continual political pressure in order to maintain or reconstitute their cherished nuclear arsenals. Keeping alive a sub-organization in the state apparatus whose only mission is to prepare for breaching the non-nuclear weapons norm perpetuates this pressure into the future and prevents the development of the most important cultural counterweight: the outlawing of nuclear weapons through a complete taboo (explored below). In this way, the nuclear security dilemma will be extended *ad kalendas Graecas* as well. Each great power would be aware that the others maintain such an institution endowed with the potential for rapid reconstitution. Each great power will thus see to have at its disposal such an institution itself and to bring it as much to perfection is possible. To believe that a world could be stable where as possible a few states – and certainly not only those that have nuclear weapons today – are just a few turns of the screw away from a bomb overtaxes even the most daring fantasy. Thomas Schelling has called such a 'non-nuclear' configuration more dangerous than that of today, since a conflict would trigger a headlong race to reconstitute the physical arsenals (Schelling 2009). Certainly, it does not meet common-sense requirements for crisis stability.

The gravest objection, however, is the logical impossibility of ever arriving at a deterrence system based on virtual arsenals. It is simply not plausible that governments that believe that national security is in need of a rapid reconstitution capability, and therefore eventually dependent on nuclear deterrence, would even consider taking that final step from a few nuclear weapons to zero. Those governments believe in nuclear deterrence. They have to decide between the option of having a small physical arsenal – the devil they know – and virtual arsenals – the devil they don't. In that situation, the comparison of the security insurance provided by, say, 120 deployable warheads as compared to a virtual arsenal will tilt the scales towards the physical alternative *as long as* governments believe in the indispensability of nuclear-tinged deterrence for purely prudential reasons. Achieving a world conditional on virtual deterrence will fail on the rational order of preference emerging from the deterrence paradigm which ranks the deterrence value of physical above that of virtual arsenals.

Advocates of virtual deterrence commit the same fallacy as the defenders of nuclear deterrence who dismiss the vision of an NWFW as impossible because it would not meet the security requirements of today's world: They construct the world in which nuclear disarmament will be realized as today's world, simply minus nuclear weapons: all other parameters remain unchanged. But that is not possible. An NWFW will require changes in many of the parameters that make up the political context of security as well as the mentalities of security decision-makers. And, if these changes take place, virtual deterrence will become neither necessary nor possible as the end-state of nuclear disarmament. If they do not take place, we will not achieve even the state of virtual arsenals.

Pursuing the objective of an NWFW requires therefore liberating not only our physical world, but also our mentalities from the infection with the idea of nuclear deterrence. 'Nuclear-weapons-free' not only designates a physical state of affairs, but extends to cultural and psychological components. The best comparison is perhaps how the thinking that war among the core states of the EU is possible has disappeared, now that they have come to form a security community (Adler and Barnett 1998). Only through a similar shift in mentality can we imagine achieving a world free of nuclear weapons in the long term, since only then will nuclear disarmament play its transformative role in breaking down hostility and rivalry among the great powers.

Remedies

The transformative function of the disarmament process

Ascribing a transformative potential to arms control and disarmament might seem counter-intuitive at first glance, because 'stability' is the central objective of arms control (Müller and Schörnig 2006, 124–125). However, closer conceptual analysis reveals that, paradoxically, successful arms control will almost automatically destabilize a system of hostility that has been frozen by the permanent security dilemma. This stability/destabilization paradox could only be overlooked because the US mainstream has regarded arms control and disarmament largely as a material/technical issue, ignoring the fact that it is in the first place a social relationship with significant psychological dimensions.[1]

The security dilemma in which both deterrence and arms control are sited is a perceptual construction which ascribes to the 'other' the potential intention of attack with a variable probability assessment and makes countermeasures look necessary; these measures will then evoke and/or enhance identical negative perceptions, assessments and measures on the other side (Booth and Wheeler 2007,

1–18). Arms control seeks to stop this spiral movement – which tends towards pre-emptive strategies – by measures aimed at the removal of attack potentials, notably those with surprise and disarming effects. Because successful arms control among equals can come about only on the basis of agreement, the measures agreed will have to satisfy the security interests of each side. This, in turns signals that both partners do not harbour malign intentions of preparing to attack. The mutual perception of such positive signals, then, affects the whole structure of the relationship: the relationship was so far based on the ascription of the potentially intended aggression by the 'other'. What was believed with near certainty about the supposed enemy will be put to new scrutiny. New, more positive hypotheses about the nature of the rival/partner appear suddenly possible. This, in turn, creates the incentive to test these hypotheses through additional, more daring measures. Their success then deconstructs further the former enemy image and the system relying thereon. This opens the chances for far-reaching rapprochement. Successful arms control transforms into genuine disarmament if not the forces of the status quo – like the often-referred-to 'military-industrial complexes' (Homolar 2015) – manage to halt and reverse the process before it becomes irresistible, as happened during the late 1970s and again in the late 1990s.

The historical model that shows how arms control and disarmament steps help constitute, and in turn are enabled by, a comprehensive transformation process is the final phase of the Cold War. Neo-conservative myth will have it that Ronald Reagan had arms-raced the Soviet Union to death. That was not the case (Lebow and Stein 1994). To the contrary, without the US (and German) readiness to respond positively to Mikhail Gorbachev's cooperative offers, what would have ended was not the Cold War, but the Gorbachev experiment.[2] In this interaction of mutual steps, which transformed the conflict into a spiral of cooperation, arms control and disarmament played a key role (Evangelista 2004).

Obviously, arms control and disarmament have not carried the transformation of this powerful structural confrontation alone. They interacted with political steps that the parties pursued, such as the successive loosening of the Soviet grip on Eastern Europe, the joint efforts at conflict termination in Latin America, Southern Africa and South East Asia and the incremental convergence of policies in the UN Security Council. Nevertheless, in the course of this interactive process, arms control and disarmament made an enormous contribution to the permanent build-up of mutual trust and the permanent build-down of the previous security dilemma. This contribution started with the signal given by Gorbachev's surprising 1986 suspension of the restrictions which had governed the Western observation of Warsaw Treaty exercises in the framework of the Helsinki Process. It developed further through the historical 1986 Reykjavik summit, the 1987 INF Treaty, the halting of SDI in the US Senate (1987), the announced withdrawal of 500,000 Soviet soldiers from Eastern Europe (1988), which was then duly implemented, and culminated in the CFE and START I negotiations (1989–90). In this process, the arms control/disarmament progress moved in parallel with steps like the renouncement of the Brezhnev doctrine, the cooperation of the Soviet Union in conflict management and resolution around the world and the Soviet withdrawal from Afghanistan (1988). The dynamic process led to elections in Poland, Hungary's opening of the Iron Curtain with Soviet consent, the fall of the Berlin Wall, the democratization of Eastern Europe and the Paris Charter (Evangelista 1999).

Walter Stützle summarized well and very early this close interrelationship and positive feedback circle of arms control and broader policy steps:

> the longstanding East–West experience, namely, that the solution of regional conflicts may be an easier task if the Washington–Moscow relationship is buttressed by a favorable arms control atmosphere, but it is equally true that arms control can easily be damaged by major events in the overall political environment.
>
> (Stützle 1988, 3)

The nuclear disarmament process may play a comparable catalytic role for the present relationships among the four leading great powers. Or, without such catalyst, it may be doubtful whether these relationships will improve sufficiently for nuclear disarmament to find the political environment to proceed to its true end. Instead, we would probably witness a hardening of conflict fronts and a multipolar nuclear arms race with an incalculable trajectory, full of high risks.

A concert of powers

How can we overcome the felt need for virtual arsenals once the last warhead is dismantled into its conventional and physical package parts? The true key to an NWFW lies in an intentional and strategic approach towards using the disarmament process systematically to change great-power relations and to construct an institutional structure that can substitute for institutionalized cooperation among them for the present open or hidden power competition. The model for such a structure can be found in further back European history: the European Concert of the early nineteenth century (Holbrad 1970; Schulz 2009).

Such a 'concert' builds on the mutual reassurance of recognition as equals, with mutual respect for vital interests, and the granting of equal participation in governance. The unilateral use of force is excluded, as is intervention in the internal affairs of others. This set of principles and norms can create and maintain the interest of all major powers in the stability of the system – a healthy 'shadow of the future' of non-threatening and cooperative security relations.

Nuclear disarmament, including the dismantlement of the infrastructure of deterrence, enhances the common interest in global stability considerably: any attempts at breakout become massive threats to both security and status of all, once the cheap option of fallback to nuclear deterrence has been eliminated. Today, if an ally breaks the rules, that is seen by the great powers as minor irritant, if not even a geostrategic asset to be put in position against one's main great power rival. However, in a world without nuclear weapons, that would be seen as imperilling the system that serves one's interests in national security, perpetual great-power status and a stable environment for economic prosperity. Such an ally would thus turn into a rogue enemy, not just for one annoyed power, but for the whole community.

A great-power concert is the key precondition for achieving and maintaining an NWFW in four aspects:

- It helps to get to zero in the first place – as it mitigates the threat environment and enhances mutual confidence by each (well-verified) step the NWS are taking together towards the final objective of complete nuclear disarmament.
- It provides the prerequisite for collective action to manage regional crises and conflicts, which may motivate third actors to go nuclear. Once jointly managed stability is the name of the game, the attraction of playing proxy geostrategic games in critical regions plummets drastically, as the gains to be expected are dwarfed by the risks entailed.
- It thus shapes interests in such a way as to give priority to enforcement over playing regional geopolitical games. Not only are such games risky in themselves, but if they assume a nuclear tinge by a proxy or client going nuclear, they may shatter the whole system in which each great power, at this stage, has already invested considerable energy and political capital.
- It minimizes temptations for the great powers themselves to consider breaking out. With power rivalry reduced to low-key friendly competition, and high security and economic stakes in the stability of the whole set-up, shattering the system is simply not a rational option for any of them.

The challenge facing the international community, then, is to phase out the deterrence system while phasing in this kind of concert system. It is vital to note that this does not mean a sequence in which the 'conditions' of a world without nuclear weapons are created first, with moves in the direction of that world coming later. The French are quite right in maintaining that nuclear weapons cannot be reduced to zero out of the blue: the conditions for zero must be worked out carefully. However, it would be wrong to believe that the 'infeasibility' of creating such conditions would keep the move towards zero on hold forever. While the disarmament process must be accompanied and strengthened by additional measures in other areas (notably in regional conflict management and political efforts to improve great-power relations) it is itself a key instrument for changing the character of these relations by diminishing the level of perceived mutual threats.

Conventional and political deterrence

In a non-nuclear world, military response to 'cheating' would have to be achieved by conventional means (Nitze 1997). There is a trade-off between keeping open the option of unilateral action and the possibility of creating the necessary motivation among the major powers to abolish their arsenals completely. A conventional response requires, at a minimum, the destruction of the facilities designed to produce weapons material, the weapons themselves and, possibly, the delivery systems. Here it is assumed that verification and intelligence will enable the outside world to locate such sites. Successful prevention of attempts at cheating, then, presupposes the availability of long-range, precise power projection capabilities with a reliable destructive potential by ballistic missiles, air forces, or cruise missiles launched from forward-deployed naval or air platforms; even space-based weaponry might appear useful for that mission. Today, the USA has at its disposal such capabilities (with the exception of space-based strike assets).

However, the extensive availability of such power projection capabilities in *national* hands might be a serious barrier to achieving nuclear abolition, notably if they remain as asymmetrically distributed as they are today. Unilateral capabilities of this kind might create exactly the kind of anxiety about being helplessly subjected to conventional aggression that might caution governments against giving up a minimum deterrence nuclear posture (White, Pendley and Garrity 1992). Curbing offensive potentials – e.g. prohibiting, or minimizing the number of, long-range ballistic missiles (Feiveson *et al.* 1999, 299) – could help to assuage these anxieties, but would also curb the capability of the more powerful states, the USA in particular, to act promptly and successfully against a would-be violator of the abolition treaty.

For a transition period, when necessary capabilities would continue to rest in the hands of a few, military action against a rule-breaker could be coupled to two multilaterally determined contingencies. First, it could be permitted through the time-honoured authorization by the UN Security Council under Chapter VII. Second, it could be made contingent on a finding by the IAEA or a successor verification agency that a country had embarked on a nuclear weapon programme which was close to completion (say, within 100 days or six months). The nuclear weapons convention constituting the NWFW could define such a finding as permitting self-defence under Article 51 of the UN Charter unless and until the Security Council should take action. The double risk of provoking the Council or facing unilateral action by a superior power should provide food for thought to governments considering a policy of breakout (Müller 2010).

At a later stage, if and when sufficient trust in effective collective action has been developed, national conventional capabilities could be shaped so as to permit no state to take offensive action alone, only in combination with other states. This would require having, in parallel to nuclear disarmament, a well-designed conventional arms control process. Ideally, security cooperation among major powers could reach a quality in the evolution of nuclear disarmament that such an agreement, today unthinkable, could be seriously considered (Feiveson *et al.* 1999, 297–298). From today's vantage point, though, it is an open question whether major states would muster the will to embark on either path simultaneously; maintaining strong conventional capabilities might be seen as the indispensable compensation for relinquishing nuclear arms.

There might be a compromise line to devise conventional structures capable of promptly destroying a limited number of targets but not suitable for a large-scale offensive to conquer and subdue a major enemy. This could suffice for taking out the key installations of a nuclear weapons programme without creating fears of a total conventional onslaught that only a nuclear deterrent might be seen capable of preventing.

In any event, this is a critical question that should be noted and revisited repeatedly throughout the process of nuclear disarmament, to uncover new solutions that might become possible as the character of world politics undergoes fundamental change. Further, we should note that, if a few nuclear weapons were built and actually used, the major powers would have available the conventional capabilities for retaliating in a devastating way (Generals Charles Horner and Lee Butler in conversation with Jonathan Schell, in Schell 1998, 23, 56).

The (possible) role of cooperative missile defence

Missile defences in a denuclearized world would engender quite different consequences than today. Under present circumstances, they aggravate fears among numerically and/or technologically inferior NWS that their deterrent might be compromised. The construction of nationwide missile defences thus almost automatically triggers responses that enhance the offensive capabilities (numbers or penetration technology, or both) of strategic nuclear forces. Inexorably, national missile defences have a destabilizing and arms-race driving effect (Krepon 2003, 9–10).

The unconstrained, unilateral build-up of national ballistic missile defence (BMD) is thus likely to prevent nuclear disarmament, by creating and bolstering fears in missile-laggard NWS that such defences, erected by their rivals, are meant to build the option of a first disarming strike at lower levels of nuclear weapons. In contrast, agreed missile defence configurations might serve to support the process and stability, once a world free of nuclear weapons is achieved (see Sauer 2011).

Two configurations for concerted BMD systems are conceivable:

- National systems strong enough to deny ballistic missile aggression by single actors, but not strong enough to avoid saturation by collective action. This would require the negotiation of well-devised numerical limits on national systems, backed up by a solid verification system.
- An international system that can be put out of function by collective action, but not by individual states. This would require a technically fully integrated, highly sophisticated system with an even more challenging and inventive system for verification. The technical hurdles – notably for installing the necessary degree of security against tampering – would be challenging, but do not appear out of reach in a 30- to 40-year perspective.

By reducing the utility of small nuclear arsenals resulting from breakout while diminishing the risks of retaliation for states engaging in enforcement action at the same time, such multilateral ballistic missile defence systems might add to the dissuasive effects of the enforcement system.

BMDs, as well as limits to the number of ballistic missiles, would not only reduce the incentive to break out, but also serve as a hedge against any threat by a perpetrator to retaliate against military efforts aimed at preventing that actor from completing nuclear weapons development or, if nuclear weapons are already available, at removing these nuclear assets (Perkovich and Acton 2008, 87). It goes without saying, though, that the problem of unconventional delivery in such a situation cannot be addressed by missile defences. In any case, for the time being, strict limits on national interceptor deployments should be agreed in a kind of multilateral ABM treaty in order to eliminate incentives for building up, rather than down, nuclear arsenals, and to make possible the reduction of strategic nuclear forces (Krepon 2003, Chapter 8).

You might call this combined cooperative system of offensive and defensive enforcement capabilities *deterrence erga omnes*. There is no doubt that there is an inherent element of dissuasion in its structure and in its strategic meaning. But it is so different from today's deterrence thinking, rooted in unilateral, national, self-help capabilities, that using the same term for both systems would be intellectually confusing and politically counterproductive.

The possibilities discussed above will need a lot of fleshing out in terms of strategic, operational, technical, and institutional considerations. They are meant to stimulate relevant thinking. In the context of this chapter, their function is to demonstrate in what direction(s) we will have to think 'out of the box' in order to do justice to the requirements, but also the opportunities inherent in an NWFW. However, these opportunities will arise only if we take care to frame new ways of thinking about security. It is to that challenge which the next sub-chapter turns.

Laying the foundations of a security culture without nuclear weapons

Mainstream thinking about politics and sometimes even about political culture has been dominated by rationalist-utilitarian modes of thinking. Humans are depicted as cool calculators of their supposed interest in maximizing utility. This (oversimplified) anthropology is then reified for collectivities and transferred from individuals to states. It is a view very popular in the social sciences – but it is unfortunately wrong, because it is incomplete. Humans do calculate rationally, but these calculations are inevitably intermingled with emotions; in seeking to maximize utility, humans are guided by motives like pride, fear, revenge, justice, love, friendship and loyalty, compassion, empathy – to mention only a few. How these motives are framed and brought together is very much a matter of culture, frequently expressed in written and unwritten norms that enable and constrain the activities of humans, whether the common people or elite policy-makers (Lebow 2008; Mercer 2010; Singer 2007). This makes it necessary not only to affect the utility calculus so as to deflect motivations away from nuclear weapons and the deterrence system that they constitute, but even more so to influence the culturally embedded norms that tell people what to do and what not to do.

From this vantage point, by far the most important aspect for stabilizing the NWFW will involve creating a very strong normative system that outlaws nuclear weapons without conditions and exceptions; moreover, a system which elites, the military, experts and common people have all internalized. For this reason, the nuclear weapons complexes and their virtual deterrence must disappear, because their very existence is contradictory to such a strong norm and thus stands as an ever-present danger that the norm might be destroyed.

Several scholars have noted a 'nuclear taboo' which, depending on the source, is defined as the norm not to use nuclear weapons or not to have them (Tannenwald 2007; Daase 2003). Taboos are the strongest form of prohibitive norms, approaching absolute character in substance and effectiveness (on prohibitive norms, see Nadelman 1990; on taboos, see Steiner 1956). Taboos form part of the life-world: they are fully integrated into the mind and emotional set-up of those belonging to the related community and are thereby completely habitualized. They have unquestionable status and are thereby removed from the realm of contestation so characteristic of most other established norms (Wiener 2008). This removal is reflected in the aversion to even articulate, or speculate about, any breach of the taboo or to debate variances of its meaning. Breaches of the taboo are subject to heavy and automatic sanctions, including massive blaming and shaming of the perpetrator. Measured by this standard, it is obvious that no such taboo currently exists in the nuclear sector.

Some argue for the existence of a taboo by pointing to the fact that in the South Pacific societies where the term originates, chieftains were authorized to touch tabooed items; this privileged permission counted as part of the taboo norm. In the case of nuclear weapons, they maintain, this corresponds to the authority of the nuclear-weapon states under the NPT to possess nuclear weapons (Daase 2003). However, this argument overlooks the fact that Article VI of the NPT prescribes that NWS must work towards eliminating their nuclear arsenals –in stark contrast to the position of tribal leaders and classical taboos (Becker-Jacob et al. 2013).

The main argument against there being a true taboo is the existence of entire techno-bureaucratic machineries whose sole *raison d'être* is to prepare for breaches of the political taboo if and when their political masters deem this necessary. The breach of the taboo is the contested subject of expert and occasionally public debate, rather than being completely silenced. For this reason, the current use of the term 'taboo' in this connection is metaphorical. 'Nuclear taboo' simply refers to a particularly strong norm against using nuclear weapons. And that is how Nina Tannenwald (2007) uses the term in her seminal work. It lacks the absolute character of taboos in the classic, anthropological sense.

That said, the concept of a taboo is useful for understanding the direction in which security cultures must change in order for an NWFW to come into being and then become and remain stable. The outlawing of nuclear weapons, promoted through the campaign on their inhumane character, must approach and pass over the threshold of a classic taboo in order to establish a sufficiently strong global norm with the required stability. A multi-pronged strategy is needed to achieve this objective. In the following paragraphs, some ideas for parts and parcels of such a strategy are proposed.

A first and particularly important element is the further pursuit of the campaign to expose the inhumane character of these weapons, and their total incompatibility with the rules of international humanitarian law because of their indiscriminate and cruel effects and their capacity to cause unnecessary suffering over an extremely long period. The sophistic reply is that there are modes of employment which could avoid these consequences, so that nuclear weapons use could be compatible with humanitarian law. But that misses the point. What is essential here is not the constructed outlier mode of use (such as use in a desert against an isolated bunker), but expectations concerning the average consequences of nuclear use in the range of the probable. In this perspective, mass murder is the rule and not the exception. Today's doctrines and nuclear strategies, as far as they are known, do not tell otherwise. As the strategy of outlawing nuclear weapons as inhumane becomes increasingly successful, the stronger the concept of human security will become, relative to the conventional and far more abstract concerns about national security.

It is essential to include religious actors in such a campaign. All religions see in humans on the one hand, and nature on the other hand, the creation of god(s) (on religion and nuclear weapons, see Hashmi and Lee 2004). The mass killing of the former and the utter destruction of the latter are horrifying sins. There is a tradition whereby religious leaders of various faiths have condemned nuclear weapons and their use. In the East–West nuclear arms race, Catholic bishops and Protestant churches have made important critical contributions to the ongoing debate. As the disarmament process progresses, leaders of all religions should be called upon to condemn nuclear weapons publicly, more and more. Since religion remains one of the most basic normative references for billions of people, this aspect is of great importance.

And finally, when a world total without nuclear weapons has been achieved, it should become obligatory for all states to amend their constitutions to include a general prohibition against nuclear weapons, with a corresponding change of national criminal law making all acts contrary to this proscription severely punishable. These legal changes should be registered, reviewed and screened for publishable 'best practices' at UN level. Each year, the UNGA should devote at least one full session day to this issue.

Furthermore, educational curricula should be used to confirm and strengthen the taboo in young people. Even in primary school, the story of how wise leaders rid the world of the most dramatic threat to human survival could help to inculcate the taboo in a particularly effective and positive way. In higher education, the nuclear danger should be vividly demonstrated and the evolution of the taboo thoroughly documented. It should be done likewise in basic military curricula, notably regarding the sections on humanitarian law that are taught at almost every military academy. The scenarios for nuclear war that were elaborated on during the Cold War might be addressed in some detail, in order to condition the military mind in a completely 'conventionalized' frame. And, like the military, nuclear physicists, engineers and chemists will also need to be trained to understand the effects of nuclear weapons and the ethics of their renunciation. Every student of these faculties should take a solemn pledge never to commit to research and development of these evil devices. That measure can enhance the probability that there will be whistle-blowers around when we need them.

At the level of the United Nations Office for Disarmament Affairs, there should be a register to which states would report all constitutional, legal and training measures taken to develop an anti-nuclear-weapons culture. The office/department should have the authority to review these reports and to visit the countries in order to witness teaching and instruction units, and peer-review their quality and effectiveness. Best practices would be identified and circulated and discussed in special conferences of member states.

There are certainly more possibilities for amending the strategy in order to make it more effective. The examples given above are meant to be illustrative, not all-encompassing or exclusive. In the practices of the nuclear abolition movement and its many non-governmental organizations, ranging from centrist security experts to convinced absolute pacifists, we can find many more examples worth studying and spreading.

Conclusions

The stability of a world without nuclear weapons cannot rest on virtual nuclear deterrence longer than for a brief transition period, as this mode of providing security is still *inside* the nuclear weapons world and contains an intrinsic pressure towards re-climbing the ladder towards physical nuclear arsenals. National deterrence, even in purely conventional form, although better than virtual arsenals, re-produces security dilemmas and enemy images that are not conducive to stabilizing a world without nuclear weapons. The concept of deterrence must be redefined as a collective endeavour, and security relations between the great powers be based on concertation, with clear priority to common interests in global security over investing in geostrategic competition. The combination of collective security and 'concertation' (see above) should allow a sophisticated enforcement system for the NWFW that will minimize the incentives for nuclear hedging, while maximizing confidence in the reliability of one's partners and the credibility of the commonly erected security system.

The process which can produce this change consists of a parallel, mutually enforcing feedback circle between arms control/disarmament steps and political steps to defuse disputes among the major powers as well as regional disputes. The sterile debate on whether disarmament can move forward only after all political conditions have been met, or whether conflict management can become possible only when antagonists have been thoroughly disarmed needs to give way to a dynamic and dialectic understanding of the interrelationship between the two issue areas. The final phase of the Cold War gives ample proof of the vast possibilities. Denying them on the basis of this evidence is yet another indication that motivational bias prevails.

This process should be used to establish a new culture of security in and between states. In the end, the stability of a world free of nuclear weapons will not hinge on technical precautions, which will never be perfect or absolutely foolproof. Human behaviour, collective as much as individual, is rooted in cultures and in the norms they entail. Today's nuclear security culture is a mixed bag. Abhorrence of nuclear weapons and fear of their use live side by side with deep convictions as to their necessity, with neglect and disinterest, and with the resigned feeling that nothing can be done. In order to stabilize an NWFW, these feelings of abhorrence must be strengthened and convictions of the necessity of nuclear weapons must be worn down. The campaign to draw attention to the humanitarian costs of nuclear war and the inhumane attributes of nuclear weapons, eventually aimed at the erection of a true nuclear taboo, has set us on the right path. It must be broadened to draw in multiple types of actors who have influence on the normative structure of present societies, and to address all those social and professional spaces which impact on national security cultures. This is a Herculean task – but then, ridding the world of nuclear weapons is truly no small thing: it goes far beyond the routine business of everyday security policy, on the one hand, and, on the other hand, single-issue protest movements against certain deployments or particular weapons.

Change in the normative setting of a society results from the contestation of established norm systems. For nuclear weapons, such a contestation began long ago and received a mighty push forwards by the 'Gang of Four' and President Obama's Prague speech. Because of the powerful counterweighing forces, this momentum can never be taken for granted. We must keep it going, through a tenacious strategy of transformation, underpinned by carriers with sufficient stamina for the long haul.

Notes

1 A more recent example is Levi and O'Hanlon (2005), which reflects a largely technopolitical rationalization of the Bush administration's arms control policy.
2 In summer 1991 I spent an unforgettable hour on the beach of Almeria, Spain, together with a high-ranking Soviet diplomat who had become a friend over the years. He told me that NATO's plan in spring 1989 to replace the Lance short-range nuclear missile by a more potent system had stimulated activities in Moscow towards a *coup d'état*, as it indicated that the United States had stolen a march on the Soviets in the INF Treaty. Whether NATO would adopt a deployment decision (as supported by the USA and the UK) or not (as requested by Germany) was seen as a litmus test for Gorbachev's policy towards the West. When the massive German opposition succeeded in producing a postponement *sine die* of the decision, the danger of a coup faded (for more than one year). Had Gorbachev been removed from power in spring 1989, history would probably have taken a radically different course.

Bibliography

Adler, E. and Barnett, M. (eds) (1998) *Security Communities*. Cambridge: Cambridge University Press.
Becker-Jacob, U., Müller, H. and Seidler-Diekmann, T. (2013) Regime Conflicts and Norm Dynamics: Nuclear, Biological, and Chemical Weapons. In Müller, H. and Wunderlich, C. (eds) *Norm Dynamics in Multilateral Arms Control Interests, Conflicts, and Justice* (pp. 51–81). Athens, GA: University of Georgia Press.
Berry, K., Lewis, P., Pélopidas, B., Sokov, N. and Wilson, W. (2010) *Delegitimizing Nuclear Weapons: Examining the Validity of Nuclear Deterrence*. Monterey, CA: James Martin Center for Nonproliferation Studies, Monterey Institute of International Studies.
Booth, K. and Wheeler, N. (2007) *The Security Dilemma: Fear, Cooperation and Trust in World Politics*. Basingstoke: Palgrave Macmillan.
Daase, C. (2003) Der Anfang vom Ende des nuklearen Tabus. Zur Legitimitätskrise der Weltnuklearordnung. *Zeitschrift für Internationale Beziehungen*, 10(1): 7–41.
Drell, S. and Goodby, J. (2009) *A World Without Nuclear Weapons: End State Issues*. Stanford: Hoover Institution.
Evangelista, M. (1999) *Unarmed Forces: The Transnational Movement to End the Cold War*. Ithaca, NY: Cornell University Press.
Evangelista, M. (2004) Turning Points in Arms Control. In Herrmann, R.K. and Lebow, R.N. (eds) *Ending the Cold War: Interpretations, Causation, and the Study of International Relations* (pp. 83–106). Basingstoke: Palgrave Macmillan.
Feiveson, H, Blair, B.G., Dean, J., Fetter, S., Goodby, J., Lewis, G., Nolan, J.E., Postol, T. and von Hippel, F. (1999) *The Nuclear Turning Point: A Blueprint for Deep Cuts and De-alerting of Nuclear Weapons*. Washington, DC: Brookings Institution Press.
Hagerty, D.T. (2012) The Nuclear Holdouts: India, Israel and Pakistan. In Ogilvie-White, T. and Santoro, D. (eds) *Slaying the Nuclear Dragon: Disarmament Dynamics in the Twenty-First Century* (pp. 219–248). Athens, GA: University of Georgia Press.
Hashmi, S.H. and Lee, S.P. (eds) (2004) *Ethics and Weapons of Mass Destruction: Religious and Secular Perspectives*. Cambridge: Cambridge University Press.
Holbrad, C. (1970) *The Concert of Europe: A Study in German and British International Theory, 1815–1914*. London: Longmans.
Homolar, A. (2015) *US Security Policy: Origins, Politics and Contemporary Challenges*. London: Taylor & Francis.
Krepon, M. (2003) *Cooperative Threat Reduction, Missile Defence and the Nuclear Future*. Basingstoke: Palgrave Macmillan.
Lebow, R.N. (2008) *A Cultural Theory of International Relations*. Cambridge: Cambridge University Press.
Lebow, R.N. and Stein, J.G. (1994) *We All Lost the Cold War*. Princeton, NJ: Princeton University Press.
Levi, M.A. and O'Hanlon, M.E. (2005) *The Future of Arms Control*. Washington, DC: Brookings Institution Press.
Mazarr, M. (1997) *Nuclear Weapons in a Transformed World. The Challenge of Virtual Nuclear Arsenals*. Basingstoke, New York et al.: Palgrave Macmillan.
Mercer, J. (2010) Emotional Beliefs. *International Organization*, 64(Winter): 1–31.
Milne, T. and Wilson, H. (1998) Aldermaston and Nuclear Disarmament. *Bulletin of the Atomic Scientists*, 54(6): 24–25.
Müller, H. (2010) Enforcement of the Rules in a Nuclear Weapon-Free World. In Hinderstein, C. (ed.) *Cultivating Confidence: Verification, Monitoring, and Enforcement for a*

World Free of Nuclear Weapons (pp. 33–66). Washington, DC: Nuclear Threat Initiative.

Müller, H. and Schörnig, N. (2006) *Rüstungsdynamik und Rüstungskontrolle. Eine exemplarische Einführung in die Internationalen Beziehungen*. Baden-Baden: Nomos.

Nadelman, E.A. (1990) Global Prohibition Regimes: The Evolution of Norms in International Society. *International Organization*, 44(4) (Autumn, 1990): 479–526. Available from: www.jstor.org/stable/2706851.

Nitze, P. (1997) Is It Time to Junk Our Nukes? *Washington Quarterly*, 20(3): 97–101.

Nolan, J.E. (1999) *An Elusive Consensus: Nuclear Weapons and American Security after the Cold War*. Washington, DC: Brookings Institution Press.

Ogilvie-White, T. and Santoro, D. (eds) (2012) *Slaying the Nuclear Dragon: Disarmament Dynamics in the Twenty-First Century*. Athens, GA: University of Georgia Press.

Perkovich, G. and Acton, J.M. (2008) *Abolishing Nuclear Weapons*, Adelphi Paper 396. Abingdon: Routledge.

Price, R.M. (1997) *The Chemical Weapons Taboo*. Ithaca, NY: Cornell University Press.

Sauer, T. (2011) *Eliminating Nuclear Weapons: The Role of Missile Defence*. London: Hurst.

Schell, J. (1998) The Gift of Time. The Case for Abolishing Nuclear Weapons, *The Nation*, February (Special Issue).

Shelling, T.C. (2009) A World Without Nuclear Weapons? *Daedalus*, Fall 2009: 124–129.

Schulz, M. (2009) *Normen und Praxis: das Europäische Konzert der Großmächte als Sicherheitsrat, 1815–1860*. Munich: Oldenbourg Verlag.

Singer, T. (2007) The Neuronal Basis of Fairness. *Novartis Symposium*, 278: 20–30.

Steiner, F. (1956) *Taboo*. London: Cohen & West.

Stützle, W. (1988) 1987 – The Turning Point? In *SIPRI Yearbook 1988. World Armaments and Disarmament*. Oxford: Oxford University Press.

Tannenwald, N. (2007) *The Nuclear Taboo: The United States and the Non-use of Nuclear Weapons since 1945*. Cambridge: Cambridge University Press.

White, P.C., Pendley, R.E. and Garrity, P.J. (1992) Thinking about No Nuclear Forces: Technical and Strategic Constraints on Transitions and End-points. In Karp, R.C. (ed.) *Security Without Nuclear Weapons? Different Perspectives on Non-Nuclear Security* (pp. 103–112). Oxford, Oxford University Press.

Wiener, A.A. (2008) *The Invisible Constitution of Politics: Contested Norms and International Encounters*. Cambridge: Cambridge University Press.

6 Verification requirements

Andreas Persbo

Introduction

For many, achieving 'global zero' has become the Holy Grail of nuclear arms control. How to get there, however, remains hazy and elusive, and the goal is hidden away in a distant future difficult to discern or grasp. Several conditions must be fulfilled before nuclear abolition can become reality, the principal one being the elimination of any degree of utility, whether military or political, of nuclear weapons. Weapons cannot disappear until they have no value to the possessor or their value has reduced to such a degree that other alternatives become possible. Until then, abolition will remain very difficult, perhaps impossible, to achieve. There is much to be said of the value of nuclear weapons. They can serve as a currency of immense power – and, despite the arguments of some, they do have perceived military utility as well.

Nuclear weapons have been an important part of international relations theory for decades. Deterrence adherents argue that international peace and stability during the past six decades has been – ultimately – a nuclear peace. The logic seems appealing. The threat of mutual assured destruction means that no rational actor will consider starting a major conflict because that would mean the end not only of the enemy, but also of himself. All-out nuclear war is suicidal by nature, as was recognized early on. As Bernard Brodie wrote in 1946, 'Thus far the chief purpose of our military establishment has been to win wars. From now on its chief purpose must be to avert them. It can have almost no other useful purpose.'[1] It is precisely the terrifying nature of these weapons that makes them useful as a deterrent. Highlighting their awesome character therefore plays into the hands of deterrence adherents, who, confronted with the humanitarian effects of weapons use, might perhaps respond, 'Yes, I know that they are doomsday weapons which cannot be used, and that is their ultimate reason of being.'

Deterrence theory has been brought into popular culture through films such as Stanley Kubrick's *Dr Strangelove* (1964) and John Badham's *WarGames* (1983). In the former, while discussing the concept of a doomsday device, the doctor argues, 'deterrence is the art of placing in the mind of the enemy the *fear* to attack ... the Doomsday Machine is terrifying, simple to understand, and completely credible and convincing'. This popular statement neatly encapsulates the thinking of the time, but also the thinking of today. And *WarGames*, while far less sophisticated than Kubrick's masterpiece, features a final scene where a rogue supercomputer, on the brink of unleashing devastating conflict, eventually concludes that thermonuclear war is 'a strange game. The only winning move is not to play' (*WarGames* 2015).

Nuclear weapons remain prevalent in defence planning even now, some two decades after the collapse of the Soviet Union and the end of the Cold War. However, deterrence relationships have become more complex. In South Asia, for instance, Pakistani nuclear weapons are pointed at the long-standing Indian adversary, whereas weapons on the other side of the border are pointed at both Pakistan and China. In the Far East, the desperately impoverished Democratic People's Republic of Korea has started to develop its own peculiar brand of nuclear deterrence against its southern neighbour and the USA (see, e.g. Lewis 2013). And, in the former, public support for the development of a nuclear arsenal of its own reportedly remains high (Keir and Persbo 2013).

In fact, despite the coherent logic of deterrence, nuclear weapons have recently been portrayed by former deterrence strategists as a destabilizing factor, something fundamentally dangerous. This reformulation of thinking, however, does not go as far as saying that the theoreticians of the past were wrong, or that the Cold War balance of terror was fundamentally unstable. No, it is the emergence of these new complicated deterrence relationships that troubles the minds of former Cold Warriors. The thinking of statesmen such as Henry Kissinger, William Perry, George Shultz and Sam Nunn goes like this: 'the risk of accidents, misjudgments or unauthorized launches [is] growing more acute in a world of rivalries between relatively new nuclear states that lacked the security safeguards developed over many years between the two superpowers' (see, e.g. *The Economist* 2011). The underlying assumption, thus, is that there are responsible weapons-holders, and irresponsible ones. For some, nuclear weapons enhance security; for others, that they constitute a detrimental force. The overriding conclusion appears to be that deterrence does not work in all circumstances and at all times.

Several authors have in the past outlined means and ways in which the perceived utility of nuclear weapons can be reduced, or perhaps eliminated. That discussion is also brought to the fore in Harald Müller's chapter in this volume. It is less straightforward to discuss nuclear abolition in terms of establishing norms against their use or retention than it is to discuss ways in which acquiring nuclear weapons can be made more difficult and costly. That does not mean that those arguments are without value. Having a commonly accepted norm that it is unlawful to use nuclear weapons, for instance, clearly diminishes their utility for the military planner, and by extension reduces overall demand for these weapons. Making it time-consuming and costly to acquire them is a supply-side measure which, while not reducing demand per se, keeps the numbers of weapons at lower levels than if such measures were not in place.

However appealing it is to engage further in a discussion about the concepts and values underlying deterrence and disarmament, this chapter leaves it here, as an important backdrop for the ensuing pages. The following sections will assume that the deterrence knot has been solved, and that nuclear weaponry has lost political and military utility – however unattainable that may seem at present.

Therefore, this chapter focuses on *the role of verification* in a world which has attained nuclear-weapons-free status. The reader will hence be brought into an imagined place, not yet in existence, to face questions that have not yet materialized. For some, this might devalue the discussion in the chapter, but it really should not. The simple fact that nuclear weapons still hold utility – in some shape or form – does not mean that practical questions concerning verification should not be asked, or that they are without meaning.

After all, present policies will need to be shaped by the vision of the end-state. There remains a vast amount of political, technical and theoretical work ahead of anyone seeking to abolish nuclear weapons. Even though the end-state may be decades away, there is no point in delaying preparations for departure: even the longest of journeys must start somewhere, and more often than not with a simple step.

A world without nuclear weapons

Thinking about verification requirements for nuclear disarmament will require a large amount of speculation. Verification requirements will vary significantly, depending on the type and form of assumptions made. The utility of the item under inspection is one important variable, but there are others too, such as the international climate at the time. Fundamentally, there is today no consensus on what is meant with the term 'a world free of nuclear weapons' – and thus no established view on how the general climate will look.

Is this future world simply a place where there are no nuclear explosives in existence? If one subscribes to this view, and some do, the means for re-manufacturing weapons will remain untouched. Nuclear reactors will still produce plutonium, and uranium enrichment plants will still produce fuel. At the extreme end of this vision, the former nuclear-weapon states (NWS) may still be allowed to maintain and run their former nuclear-weapons laboratories and associated facilities, as a kind of 'virtual deterrent'. Many disarmament proponents would find the latter scenario deeply unappetizing.

True abolitionists view 'a world free of nuclear weapons' as a space without weapons – where the demand for them has been eliminated, but also where the capacity of states to re-establish their arsenals is curbed. This approach is not without its pitfalls: what constitutes a capacity to re-establish a nuclear arsenal? Is it enough to dismantle the infrastructure required for the manufacturing and testing of weapons, or would further steps be needed?

Could it be that the phrase 'a world free of nuclear weapons' fundamentally means a place where there are in function no reactors capable of producing plutonium and no enrichment plants in operation? If so, can we truly achieve nuclear zero without destroying the nuclear industry as a whole? The true abolitionist would argue 'no'. Taking this position therefore unsettles all those who hold that the peaceful use of nuclear power is an undeniable good, and that such use should be increasing, not decreasing. Whether or not nuclear energy is on the rise or whether it is in decline is a matter of debate. According to the World Nuclear Association, an industry group, 'nuclear power provides about 13.5% of the world's electricity, almost 24% of electricity in OECD countries, and 34% in the EU'; moreover, 'its use is increasing' (World Nuclear Association 2012). On the other hand, recent nuclear safety failures have considerably strengthened the hand of those who foresee a future based on alternative energy sources. On balance, however, it would appear today that the future is likely to be more nuclearized, not less.

It should also be kept in mind that even if all uses of the atom vanish from the Earth, a disarmed stated could rearm, given the political will and resources to do so. A country that controls the raw materials and the necessary industrial infrastructure and technical and scientific knowledge will always be able to hedge against the loss of nuclear weapons. The marginal costs of acquiring nuclear weapons appear to be decreasing, not increasing, as nuclear knowledge becomes more widespread.

The DPRK, with an annual GDP per capita well below US$1,000, has proven that manufacturing nuclear weapons is not beyond the reach of even a desperately impoverished country.[2] This should not be surprising to anyone. Nuclear weaponry is based on technologies developed some 70 years ago, in turn drawing on science insights of almost a century ago. In all likelihood, our knowledge of the atom, and how to harness its might, cannot ultimately be contained – despite the best efforts of those advocating nuclear non-proliferation.

It may be more appropriate to speak of 'unarmed states' rather than 'disarmed states',[3] recognizing that any state with the capacity to enrich or reprocess nuclear material is practically speaking on the threshold of weapons acquisition. That means there are today nine armed states, but also perhaps 30 more unarmed. Some of these may have the capability to weaponize their material within months, some within years – they are not armed, but they have immediate capability to arm themselves. The remainder of the international community, some 150 states, are disarmed – they are not armed, and they lack the immediate capability to arm themselves. For many of these 150 states, however, armament is not an impossibility, should they decide to invest in nuclear industry and science[4] and gain access to the necessary raw materials.

Irreversibility becomes an economic argument, a matter of will and desire. The key questions are how difficult, and above all how costly, it will be for a country to reverse a state of disarmament. Or, to put it another way, how difficult and costly it is for any state to arm itself. The more facilities a state decides to get rid of, and the more fuel cycle options it foregoes, the more irreversible its disarmament will be.

If a country has no nuclear facilities, and no stocks of fissile materials, it cannot produce weapons without (re-)establishing a major industrial infrastructure. Not having armed in the first place, such countries remain in a fully disarmed state. This line of argument implies that the question of irreversible nuclear disarmament is closely associated with the question of the future of nuclear energy. Nuclear energy infrastructure will enable a country to produce weapons: that is the viewpoint of the true abolitionist. The only way to ensure a world free of nuclear weapons is to remove *all* capability to supply them.

However, if we instead assume that states, and the citizens they often represent, do not want to forego the nuclear energy option totally, we quickly find ourselves focusing on questions relating to *acceptable risk*. What kind of nuclear processes constitutes an acceptable risk? Is it an acceptable risk to allow for enrichment by any government? Is it an acceptable risk to allow for reprocessing? And, if so, how should these highly sensitive processes be regulated?

VERTIC has examined these questions in some detail in its report *Irreversibility in Nuclear Disarmament: Practical steps against nuclear rearmament* (Cliff *et al.* 2011). The aim of this study was to examine and develop the concept of irreversibility as it relates to nuclear disarmament. It found that, while the term 'irreversibility' is increasingly used in discussions of nuclear disarmament, its meaning in this context remains largely undefined and understudied. In particular, little consideration has been given to the specific steps that would have to be taken to achieve a level of disarmament irreversibility. Further, the report found that it is not useful to treat nuclear disarmament in a binary sense – without, however, coming down on one side or the other on how to ensure that weapons do *not* re-emerge in a world where the use of the atom remains prevalent.

In light of the discussion above, can it credibly be said that a state is 'disarmed' simply because its weapons are gone or because it never acquired them in the first place? Would it not instead be that armament, disarmament and rearmament are different sides of the same coin, different aspects of the same problem? If so, this leads to an important conclusion: that the resources and time needed for rearmament is a topic urgently in need of study. The nuclear weapon itself is just the tip of a large iceberg, a massive investment in industrial infrastructure, resource extraction and scientific training, yet one within reach of most states, be they rich or impoverished. Is it not reasonable to conclude that, for a country like the USA, with vast natural and human resources at its disposal, rearmament will be easier than for countries such as Pakistan or North Korea? Few studies in the public domain have critically examined the constitution or reconstitution times for nations at differing stages of economic development.

In terms of verification, the regime will need to be able to handle several top-level tasks. During the transition to zero, it must be able to verify that nuclear explosives are being destroyed. When the transition is complete, it needs to verify that explosives do not re-emerge in the former NWS. It must be able to verify that the disarmed remain disarmed; and at all times during the transition it needs to verify that nuclear weapons do not emerge elsewhere.

Whereas the traditional nuclear abolitionist movement has not concerned itself much with non-proliferation (focusing more on the injustice of non-nuclear-weapon states (NNWS) having to shoulder the safeguards burden without much in return), upholding and defending strict rules on non-proliferation, as well as protecting international safeguards, may be one of the greatest contributions to nuclear disarmament today. This is discussed later in this chapter.

Preparing for future verification challenges requires considerable investment in thinking about details and particulars. So far, not nearly enough energy and thought have been devoted to trying to solve the problems. This has left the arms control and disarmament community as a whole, whether based inside or outside government, in nuclear- or non-nuclear-weapon states, in a state of perpetual unpreparedness and, perhaps, resignation. Verification solutions have traditionally been discarded when the next big arms control challenge comes along, often leaving little time for preparation.

Where should we start if we were to start work now? Should we start our examination by looking at the warheads, how they can be verifiably dismantled? Should we rather focus on weapons components, such as the fissile material that they contain? With so many possible end-states representing a world with no nuclear weapons, it becomes difficult to address the question of verification properly. As noted above, however, there are three processes that require consideration:

- *Verifying arms reductions.* How can we verify that states are reducing their armaments levels to stated degrees? This will include addressing questions such as whether it is required to verify each individual warhead as it is being dismantled, or if it is simply a matter of verifying that a certain amount of nuclear material is being withdrawn from military use. Views differ on the need for intrusiveness and accuracy at various stages of this process.
- *Verification that disarmed states remain disarmed.* This is arguably one of the more difficult questions. How can we ensure that no nuclear weapons are possessed clandestinely by a state that professes to have rid itself of them? How do you verify that production processes in the former NWS are converted to peaceful use, and that they remain in such use?
- *Verification that currently unarmed states do not arm.* Here, there is already a developed system in place, run by the International Atomic Energy Agency. However, safeguards in the NNWS community would need to be maintained, and perhaps even strengthened, as the playing field becomes more equal. In a world where no nation has immediate access to the most destructive weapon devised by man, any nation may gain an instant military advantage should it decide to weaponize.

The following sections of this chapter address all three aspects in turn.

Verifying arms reductions

The focus of this chapter is on how to lock in an end-state of nuclear disarmament once it has been achieved, not on the process of getting to zero. However, before that discussion, it may be useful to recapitulate some of the ways in which nuclear disarmament as a process may occur.

To date, most disarmament-related treaties or arrangements have focused on counting delivery vehicles. Fewer arrangements have been put in place for examining the verification of the final disposition of weapons-usable nuclear material, or their transfer to civilian use.

Unlike the verification of delivery vehicles, the verification of warhead dismantlement using national technical means is insufficient to achieve the necessary levels of confidence in the actual process of dismantlement. Because inspectors must be allowed access to nuclear dismantlement sites, NWS would need to accept some level of inspection intrusiveness. This will require a trade-off between inspector access and national security (however defined). If no trade-off in this area can be foreseen, the verification enterprise will have to focus exclusively on fissile material disposition and control. Even here, however, sensitive design features will remain, notably the quantity and composition of the material disposed of. Material properties and quantities are often among the most heavily guarded secrets of an NWS – sometimes more so than the internal configuration of the weapon itself.

What if inspectors were to be given access to the dismantlement process? In such cases, it is broadly agreed that the inspection team could only have some confidence that the warhead had been dismantled and the associated material disposed. It is not enough just to watch the process: observations must be backed up by something else, like supplementary site or item documentation. While these documents (for instance, maintenance records) could give peripheral information about the device, they would not, by themselves, prove or disprove that the item under disassembly is a bona fide nuclear weapon. The activity clearly supports the verification effort, but does not provide clarity by itself. This leads to the distinction between transparency and verification. The former provides confidence that a declared activity is taking place, whereas the latter *confirms* such activity. Generally speaking, a good verification regime should incorporate both elements.

To confirm that a specific warhead has been dismantled has proven to be one of the most technically challenging aspects of dismantlement verification. The basic problem is to confirm the presence of a device that one is, in fact, not allowed to know much about. The inner workings of the bomb are a closely guarded secret in all NWS. Especially sensitive is the amount of fissile material, as well as its composition and location within the device. That does not mean, however, that such information cannot be included in a verification regime. To some degree, the transfer of information from this classified domain to a domain where uncleared inspectors may work can be done through the deployment of specialized equipment, such as an 'information barrier'.[5] Such technology, if properly developed, may allow inspectors access to the device itself, while safeguarding against the release of classified information.

However, any information barrier is a technical piece of equipment, and can be altered. Indeed, modifying equipment to give a fake reading is an old evasion technique. How, then, can inspectors be sure that the equipment they are using has not been tampered with beforehand? One solution is to design the equipment in ways that make modification exceptionally difficult – like sealing the device into a tamper-proof enclosure. Another solution is to construct the device in ways that minimize vulnerable areas where modifications could be made or false signals introduced, such as circuitry or wiring. Yet another solution is for the inspected party to produce the equipment in multiple copies. The inspector can then take a sample away for review, while the remaining systems are placed under seal. This is the most workable solution, since it allows the inspected party to ensure that the equipment is not rigged to collect and divert classified data, while the inspector, if the sample size is large enough, can be confident that the equipment will not show false readings. However, much equipment will be wasted in the selection process, making it important to build equipment cost-effectively – and that can be a difficult task indeed.

Maintaining a credible chain of custody of the treaty-limited item will be essential. A solid chain of custody will allow inspectors to be reasonably certain that any item they have already inspected remains unaltered throughout the inspection process. It is advisable to start the chain as early as possible, perhaps as early as deployment or storage sites.

As implied above, all inspection exercises have one thing in common: they all aim to find a balance between the inspectors' need for access and the inspected party's need to maintain confidentiality. An important aspect of research into the verification of warhead dismantlement is the management of the potential proliferation risks associated with these activities. This obviously has to be addressed, given the non-proliferation obligations contained in the NPT. The inspected party hence has a legal obligation not to give unfettered access to all and sundry.

However, the proliferation risks associated with verified warhead dismantlement are probably exaggerated when compared to other classification aspects. Most restrictions on access are likely to be prompted by national security concerns: for instance, the thickness of walls, security patterns and response times and the size and composition of the workforce. Other classifications will relate to the intended use and power of the weapon, such as design information relating to delivery, detonation altitudes, yield and safety features, as well as deployment and maintenance information. Naturally, NWS will always seek to err on the side of caution.

Clearly, for their part, inspector confidence will increase with the level of access granted. High levels of access will correspond to high levels of confidence – but also, potentially, an elevated risk that sensitive design information may be released. Sensitive information can be ensured complete protection only if no access at all is granted. At the other extreme, full access – such as X-raying weapons and components – is likely to give nearly foolproof affirmation that a device is authentic, but it will also reveal highly sensitive information. A trade-off is likely to be possible somewhere between the no-access and full-access scenarios, but this trade-off would invariably mean the risk of some information being released.

This points to the urgent need for the NWS to review their classification policies and decide which information can, at the end of the day, be released without consequences for proliferation.

While the inspectors and the inspected will have seemingly irreconcilable interests in terms of access, both will presumably want the verification regime to succeed. No study to date, however, has thoroughly explored where the inspectors' demand for information optimally intersects with what the inspected party is willing to supply. As noted above, if all aspects of nuclear weapons are kept secret and cannot be divulged, Pareto improvements – where additional inspection access does not leave the inspected party worse off – cannot occur. Fortunately, this is not the case: if it were, decommissioned nuclear weapons would not be on display in museums and other public spaces. This means that at least visual inspection is likely to be granted. And, so, we may assume that a Pareto optimal intersection can be found somewhere. It is not at all clear, however, where that intersection can be found, or to what degree the results would vary depending on the inspected state party.

It is concerning that issue that no research thus far has managed to strike a reasonable balance between inspector access and host restrictions. Giving complete and unfettered access is obviously not desirable. Indeed, the dangers can be acute in areas where fissionable material is being processed. For instance, great care must be taken in cleaning areas where sensitive material has been stored or used, so that minute samples of material, which may reveal classified material, cannot be collected. Such samples can be collected fairly easily, for instance by brushing a piece of clothing against a surface or using the soles of the inspectors' shoes. That sampling is involved may not be immediately clear to any escort accompanying the inspectors.

Studies attempting to identify Pareto efficiency in disarmament verification might take their starting point in complete access, and then work backwards. The question becomes whether each additional restriction emplaced on inspector access will act to inhibit the verification process. If not, it cannot be assumed that the inspection will be marginally worse off by the restriction, and further restrictions can be explored. Once a layer of restriction on the margin inhibits the inspection process, further Pareto improvements cannot be made. Studies on the access problem must be broad and must avoid focusing too much on technical factors or solutions. The human factor in dismantlement verification should be considered, not least through psychologically oriented studies.

If warhead eliminations are to be verified, the construction of a dedicated dismantlement facility is an idea worth serious consideration. Carrying out dismantlement in a dedicated facility would, in many ways, be preferable to current arrangements, where dismantlement activities take place in existing nuclear-weapons facilities. Managing the verification exercise to ensure that inspectors are kept away from day-to-day operations – if for no other reason than to ensure their own safety – often presents a major problem for site operators. Issues such as these would be eliminated with a facility built exclusively for the purpose of warhead dismantlement.

In addition, such facilities can be designed and built in ways that incorporate and facilitate verification activities. In a dedicated facility built to a commonly agreed design, inspectors would be able check the plant against the floor plan before inspection activities commenced, to make sure that no hidden trapdoors, concealed spaces, extra piping or other undeclared constructions had been secretly incorporated. This would help in ensuring that no items could be swapped or spoofed during dismantlement operations conducted out of the inspector's view. The benefits of a dedicated, verification-oriented facility are obvious – but, that said, construction costs might easily spiral, and such a facility would in any case require separate environmental, safety and health assessments, a separate security evaluation, and an operational readiness review. Not an easy task, or a quick one. Despite the cost, this would, however, make the task of providing inspectors access to the facility much easier. It would also, quite naturally, make the verification task much simpler.

Verifying that the disarmed remain disarmed

The scale of an abolition undertaking cannot be underestimated. There are reportedly still about 20,000 nuclear weapons in existence worldwide, several thousand of which are awaiting dismantlement in Russia and the USA (International Panel on Fissile Materials 2011, 4). Precise figures are not in the public domain.

Exactly how long it would take to dismantle one weapon is not a matter discussed in the public domain, but could take anything between three and 36 working days (Munger 2012). In addition, how many weapons are currently being dismantled per year is not known. Data from the International Panel on Fissile Materials (IPFM) indicate that the USA is dismantling on average 580 weapons per year, and the Russian Federation some 200 to 300. At the peak of the dismantlement campaign in the 1990s, the USA managed to dismantle some 1,300 weapons per year (International Panel on Fissile Materials 2011, 5).

It is unknown whether such a campaign can be sustained today. Anecdotal evidence indicates that US dismantlement sites are running close to capacity and that storage space for dismantled components is becoming scarce. Assuming that no expansions to existing dismantlement sites were necessary – probably an unrealistic assumption – it would, at present dismantlement rates, take some 15 years to fully dismantle the US arsenal and about four decades to remove the Russian arsenal. Considering that some weapons will take longer than others to dismantle, an implementation timeline of at least two decades does not sound unlikely.

To speed up the process, existing disposal facilities may need to be expanded, modified to enable inspections, or new facilities will need to be built. While no precise projections are available, complete nuclear disarmament is likely to be a lengthy process, which also will require significant funding.

The disarmament process will not end simply because there are no more weapons in existence. Weapons-usable material will also need to be dealt with. According to the International Panel on Fissile Materials (IPFM), there are in the world approximately 1,390 metric tonnes of uranium enriched to over 90 per cent in the isotope U-235. In addition, world stockpiles of non-civilian plutonium are about 230 metric tonnes. How much of this material resides in weapons is not known at present. In addition, these figures are subject to significant uncertainties.

From this material, more than 80,000 nuclear weapons could theoretically be produced (or about 60,000 additional weapons). Global stockpiles are currently shrinking as the USA and Russia move to eliminate excess material (ibid., 8, 16). However, while some countries are getting rid of their stocks, or holding them in reserve, others may still add to the balance.

Much as with dismantling warheads, reducing material stocks is not a cheap endeavour. An indication of how costly this can be is gleaned by quickly examining efforts to date. Under the 2000 Plutonium Management and Disposition Agreement (PMDA), the United States and Russia have each pledged to dispose of 34 metric tonnes of surplus weapons-grade plutonium. The price tag on the Russian side alone is estimated to be approximately US$3.5 billion, so the average cost of disposing of one single kilogram of plutonium in Russia stands at US$102,900. Simple extrapolation puts the present cost of disposing of the world's stockpile of weapons-grade plutonium to approximately US$24 billion (DTIRP n.d.). Once the plutonium stockpile has been dealt with, the significantly larger uranium stockpile will remain. Merely transferring this material to international safeguards would increase the workload on the IAEA Department of Safeguards by some 30 per cent.[6] The costs associated with disposing of this material are not known at present.

It can be assumed that costs will come down as new facilities are built to handle the flow – hence achieving good economies of scale. All the same, the expense is likely to run into the billions of dollars, and only some of the costs will be recovered as former military metal is converted for civilian use.

Handling a single kilogram of material as sensitive as weapons-grade uranium or plutonium is a serious undertaking. This will be a challenge never faced before: to handle, down-blend and dispose of literally millions of kilograms of material, all suitable for weapons use. If warhead dismantlement is expected to take more than a decade, the massive verification task that will follow – verifying that all material has been declared and is in use for peaceful purposes – can be expected to take even longer.

Work has already started on laying the foundations of a potential verification regime. The United States and Russia have, for instance, finally invited the IAEA to verify activities under the PMDA. This agreement was initially signed in 2000 by US President Bill Clinton and Russian President Vladimir Putin. At the time, the USA intended to use 25.5 tonnes of its amount as fuel in nuclear reactors and planned to immobilize the remaining 8.5 tonnes through vitrification. For its part, Russia wanted to use all 34 tonnes of its amount in mixed oxide fuel elements.

Both sides intended to construct industrial-scale disposition facilities by 2007. Construction of these facilities is still under way. They also undertook to stop reprocessing plutonium until the 34 tonnes were disposed of and to conduct any future reprocessing under effective, mutually agreed monitoring. At the time, it was thought that these verification measures would become part of the Trilateral

Initiative negotiated with the IAEA, Russia and the USA (Trust and Verify 2000).

The Trilateral Initiative (which ran between 1996 and 2002) clearly holds special relevance for the PMDA. However, to date, little is known about the Trilateral Initiative, and its comprehensive final report remains 'in confidence' to this day. A major aspect of the Trilateral Initiative was the development of 'information barrier' technology (see above), designed to allow inspectors to take measurements of nuclear-weapon components without gaining access to sensitive design information. The technology developed under the project was never put to the final test of real-life implementation. Significantly, however, all parties concluded that the same technology was robust enough to be used by the IAEA in nuclear facilities, with no danger of proliferative material being revealed in the process.

The USA and Russia should agree to make public the work already covered, and open it up for international peer review. Remaining disagreements should not be beyond a solution (Persbo 2010).

- The first issue concerns equipment authentication: how can inspectors be sure that the equipment they are using has not been tampered with? Several possible options were proposed by the Working Group. The preferred option was for the nuclear-weapon states to produce many copies and for the IAEA to authenticate a sample, while the rest would remain under seal. This, as noted above, is an elegant solution to the authentication problem.
- The second question relates more to compliance. What happens if an anomaly is detected? What would the status of the remaining items be, and how could the anomaly be resolved?
- Finally, there is the question of material shapes. The United States wanted Russia to submit roughly the same amount of plutonium in roughly the same forms as those used by the USA itself. But, while the USA decided to put the entire pit under verification, the Russian side wanted to melt its pits into two-kilogram balls and pack two balls each into specialized containers (the so-called AT-400R). The USA, however, had no intention of converting its pits.

Another important element for ensuring that the disarmed state remains disarmed will be the Fissile Material Treaty (also referred to as the Fissile Material Cut-Off Treaty, FMCT). All five nuclear-weapon states have ended production within a non-binding moratorium. However, fissile material production is continuing in South Asia. India and Pakistan are trying to define how much material they think they would need to preserve their own deterrence. Many in that region argue that excessive transparency as to material holdings could expose military weaknesses. They also say that an imbalance in stocks could tilt the brittle military balance on the subcontinent. It is likely that India and Pakistan would choose to produce a comfortable cushion of material before signing any control regime.

A ban on production would not reduce already worked-up stocks of material. It would simply preserve the status quo, where it exists, in fissile material inventories. The ban would have limited relevance for general nuclear disarmament – but that is not to say that a ban would be pointless. After all, parties cannot produce new material. Stockpiles can legitimately only go down. This has relevance also in a world where weapons have been disposed of. Weapons-grade fissile material would have few uses – supplying fuel for nuclear submarines, surface ships and deep-space satellites and rovers would be the notable exceptions – so production of new material should be allowed only under controlled circumstances.

Some would argue that, ultimately, the ban on fissile material should dispose of already-existing stocks. From the perspective of irreversibility, this argument makes undeniable sense. A full-scope FMCT would put all means of production of material in the nuclear-weapon states under safeguards. As noted above, this is likely to be costly, but is ultimately desirable.

Verifying that nuclear weapons do not emerge elsewhere

To achieve full compliance with Article VI of the Nuclear Non-Proliferation Treaty, the recognized NWS are likely to be required to reduce their nuclear arsenals in a way that is both irreversible and verifiable. However, ridding the world of nuclear weapons is one thing: preventing their re-emergence is quite another altogether.

In a nuclear-weapons-free world, the military playing field returns to a conventional state. Given the technological and numerical superiority of most of today's NWS, conventional equality is unlikely to occur. However, the balance of power will shift radically if any one actor decides to bolster its conventional forces with the nuclear option. Given the continued reliance on nuclear power for energy supplies, many governments will be in a position to break out relatively quickly, should they so desire. Nuclear abolition may spell the end for unconventional weapons – but it will not end the nuclear age.

The final settlement on nuclear weapons is very likely to be similar to that embodied in the 1996 Chemical Weapons Convention.[7] Here the parties declared that they were 'determined for the sake of all mankind, to exclude completely the possibility of the use of chemical weapons.' They further considered 'that achievements in the field of chemistry should be used exclusively for the benefit of mankind' (see the preamble of the treaty).

Although the Chemical Weapons Convention has often been heralded as a disarmament treaty, its first provision is essentially a non-proliferation clause. This strongly suggests, at least as far as chemical weapons are concerned, that there is a firm link between capabilities for acquiring a weapons system and the stability of the disarmed condition. It is not enough simply to get rid of weapons in the state's possession (this language appears further down in the treaty's principal article); the treaty must also assure that no state reacquires them.

Under Article I.1 the parties cannot 'develop, produce, otherwise acquire, stockpile or retain chemical weapons, or transfer, directly or indirectly, chemical weapons to anyone'.[8] The Organisation for the Prohibition of Chemical Weapons does not refer to this as non-proliferation, but rather as 'preventing the re-emergence of chemical weapons'. Further,

> This is a notion that is much wider than mere non-proliferation. In the context of the CWC, it covers industry verification, data monitoring; nationally and by the Organisation; transfer controls; effective national implementation and dissemination of the ethical norms of the Convention through outreach, education and public diplomacy.
>
> (Uzumcu 2013)

In the nuclear field, however, some challenge that there is a similar interconnection between non-proliferation and disarmament. Those scholars and diplomats argue, often forcefully, that the armament choices of states are disconnected from the weapons holdings of the NWS. That might be correct in certain circumstances. Armament of any kind rarely happens in a vacuum, and is more likely to be prompted by the behaviour of neighbours and prevalent strategic threats, not by the behaviour of some tangential nuclear-weapon state (the DPRK's behaviour, for example, is unlikely to be inspired by the weapons holdings of the United Kingdom). Considerations of national security (perhaps even prestige) will weigh heavily on any government's choice to weaponize its uranium resources. A country suffering from a severe inferiority in conventional forces compared to its strategic rivals may opt to develop unconventional weaponry as an ultimate guarantee.

Undeniably, however, any state that feels under nuclear threat will want to equalize the situation. Any honest application of the theory of deterrence will point to one conclusion: to safeguard against a nuclear attack, ensure that you have capability to respond in kind. From that perspective, a statement such as that 'as long as some states possess nuclear weapons, others will seek them, too' (Lodgaard 2010, 87) is logically unassailable. If, in addition, one also believes that nuclear weapons are a stabilizing good, then nuclear weapons possession for all nation-states would, presumably, be a good thing.

It is becoming easier to acquire nuclear weapons. In 1997, IAEA historian David Fischer wrote:

> Once the main scientific and technical breakthrough to a nuclear device had been made and had become public property, replicating such a device would be largely a matter of engineering. Hence, technical fixes to prevent proliferation would not work in the long term. Today, the technical ability to make a simple nuclear device is within the reach of 40 to 50 nations and the number of technically capable nations is bound to grow.
>
> (1997, 21)

Fortunately, possessing capability does not mean that states generally rush to acquire nuclear weapons whenever their security situation deteriorates. On the contrary, over the past four decades only a handful of new nuclear actors have emerged, and most of them had been considering their weapons options already at the time of the entry into force of the NPT.

At present, the NNWS parties to the NPT are under a similar prohibition as parties to the CWC with respect to the acquisition of nuclear weapons. In a sense, it could be said that these countries have chosen to remain disarmed. Their compliance with this obligation is indirectly verified through bilateral safeguards agreements concluded with the IAEA. The exclusive purpose of these safeguards is to verify the 'fulfilment of [the state's] obligations assumed under this Treaty with a view to preventing diversion of nuclear energy from peaceful uses to nuclear weapons or other nuclear explosive devices' (NPT, Article III.1).

The safeguards agreement itself, however, uses a slightly different formulation. The purpose of safeguards is the

> timely detection of diversion of significant quantities of nuclear material from peaceful nuclear activities to the manufacture of nuclear weapons or of other nuclear explosive devices or for purposes unknown, and deterrence of such diversion by the risk of early detection.
>
> (INFCIRC/153, part II, paragraph 28)

This discrepancy allows for a state to be in non-compliance with its safeguards agreement, but not necessarily at the same time with the NPT. Although unlikely, a deliberate diversion of nuclear material does not necessarily need to be for weapons. However, the ultimate goal is the same: to prevent, or at least complicate, the misuse of materials which could legitimately be used only for peaceful purposes.

The commitment by NNWS parties to subject their materials, their facilities and the territory of their nations to international inspection constitutes their single most influential contribution to nuclear disarmament. It is unfortunate, from that perspective, that safeguards obligations are formulated as *obligations*, or burdens. In most cases, countries do not appear to undertake safeguards to assure their neighbours that they are not developing nuclear weapons, or because they are suspected of developing weapons. Instead, they shoulder this undertaking to show transparency, commitment and international responsibility.

The safeguards regime can be seen as the foundation on which all disarmament measures ought to be built. If the ultimate goal is to equalize all parties to the NPT, to bring them all under equitable material safeguards, then how can one argue for less-intrusive safeguards in the non-nuclear world? Would that not be akin to letting the foundation rot? What would happen when the nuclear-armed world reduces its weapons and material holdings, and ultimately brings all its materials under safeguards? If the foundation is rotten, would not the structure collapse?

Some might be uncomfortable with an argument of this kind. Why, they might argue, should the NNWS be scrutinized by their powerful weaponized neighbours, while receiving nothing in return?

The NPT is indeed an unequal treaty in this respect, as in many others. Its Article IX.3 creates two classes of states: those who had nuclear weapons before 1 January 1967 and those who did not. Any newcomer to the nuclear weapons business will, for the purposes of the treaty, be treated as a non-nuclear-weapon state.

In India, for instance, leaders have 'decried the NPT as an unequal treaty that created an unfair caste system of nuclear haves and have-nots', whereas others had 'objected to the "pace" with which the NWS had moved to eliminate their own weapons and specifically demanded a "date certain" for the abolition of all nuclear weapons' (Pubantz and Moore 2008, 314). It is undeniable that the NPT contains few trade-offs for the non-nuclear-weapon states, whereas it safeguards, protects and to some degree legitimizes the status quo as regards the nuclear balance of power.

There are no easy counter-arguments to present to those that argue that the basic deal contained in the NPT is unbalanced, perhaps even fatally flawed. With hindsight, it would have been good to have stronger provisions on technological exchange. Moreover, the disarmament commitment could perhaps have been formulated in language less open for wide-ranging interpretation. However, the Non-Proliferation Treaty is a product of its time, a period where two competing ideological blocs, amply stocked with all kinds of weapons of mass destruction, were wrestling for control over their perceived dominions.

In the end, to quote Chancellor Otto von Bismarck, 'Politics is the art of the possible' (*die Politik ist die Lehre vom Möglichen*). The NPT is the best agreement that was possible then, and it has largely stood the test of time. It contains the basic building blocks for a world free of nuclear weapons – that much is clear.

Nuclear abolition may be many decades away. Meanwhile, the leadership and commitment shown by the NNWS community should remain unwavering. This means continuing to commit fully and without reservation to the work of the IAEA. This means keeping the safeguards system fully funded, and supporting its further development, no matter how bitter that might feel. Leadership is always a hard and ungrateful task, and it becomes especially hard when so little appears to be given in return, but that is simply the nature of good governance.

Towards multilateralism in disarmament

Safeguards, as administered by the International Atomic Energy Agency, will become increasingly important in a world free of nuclear weapons. Fissile material will need to be accounted for, and the absence of undeclared stockpiles of these materials would need to be confirmed.

It is likely that verification in a nuclear-weapons-free world will look very similar to safeguards in NNWS, but on a much greater scale. The fuel cycles of the two major NWS, the United States and Russia, are fundamentally different, and much larger, than cycles found elsewhere. It will be challenging to take them on, and to bring them under full-scope safeguards. There are considerable uncertainties in stockpile numbers, and it may take many decades before anything resembling a complete determination on the NWS' initial declaration can be drawn.

However, empowering the IAEA Secretariat to be able to address some of the technical tasks is a step that can be taken today. The IAEA already has a reasonably completed technical protocol for material disposition, but it will need to start preparing for future verification challenges as well.

For member states to engage with the IAEA on issues relating to warhead dismantlement verification, it includes thinking about how the Agency needs to change to be able to take on the task. However, sceptics may ask: why investigate the potential of having the IAEA involved in disarmament verification? Would it not be better to create an alternative body, perhaps subsidiary to the UN Security Council, for this task (see, e.g. Ekéus 2012)?

Of the various reasons for giving the task to the IAEA, three primary ones should to be mentioned here:

- First, all the nuclear-armed states, with the exception of the DPRK, are members of the IAEA. It therefore constitutes an already-existing, natural meeting place for the states with the highest stake in nuclear disarmament.
- Second, the Agency has been doing nuclear verification, in one way or the other, ever since it was founded, and has a vast amount of technical knowledge and experience at its disposal. Ultimately, the disarmament task will revolve around nuclear material. It makes more sense to lodge weapons specialists in Vienna, where there is a peer group available, than in, say, New York, where there is none.
- Third, since the Agency is already conducting verification activities in most of the nuclear-armed states, it has experience in dealing with the states in question. All NPT outliers (the DPRK, India, Israel and Pakistan) have one or several safeguards agreements in force with the IAEA.[9]

Despite these advantages in respect to an IAEA role in disarmament verification, opinion nevertheless appears split as to whether it should be put in charge of verifying nuclear disarmament. Some here argue that the Agency is not an obvious choice for disarmament verification, pointing to the practice to date of monitoring disarmament action through bilateral verification processes that are bespoke and owned by the parties.

Second, and perhaps more prevalently, it has been argued that the existing structure and purpose of the IAEA safeguards system mainly concerns the safeguards obligations of NNWS. Sometimes, the view is also expressed that IAEA inspectors would somehow be placed in a situation where they would learn military secrets, which would compromise their suitability as a credible inspectorate.

All of these points can be addressed.

- First, it is widely recognized that disarmament processes would need to become multilateral at some point in the future (see, e.g. Browne 2008). That, by itself, weakens the argument that verification processes by definition ought to be bilateral.

- Second, while it is largely correct to state that the present structure of the IAEA is mostly geared towards verifying NNWS obligations under the NPT, it is a gross exaggeration to claim that this is the only function that the Agency was envisioned to fulfil. The Agency's mandate is relatively clear on the matter, and it has been covered extensively in the literature (see Cliff and Keir 2012, 4; Ebahtimy and Persbo n.d.; Kofstadmoen and Reistad 2010). The question is not if, but how, the Agency could be reformed to handle such a future verification challenge.
- Third, any inspectors, from any type of inspection regime, would be placed in a situation where they could learn military secrets. This is nothing that applies solely to the IAEA. Moreover, the Agency already has long experience in dealing with industrially sensitive or commercially secret information. Despite some public debate on the matter, such confidential information very rarely meets the public eye. Granted, the Agency would need to apply extremely stringent levels of security on the most sensitive information, and this would require some preparatory work by the organization.

It would be counter-intuitive not to make best use of the knowledge and expertise that exists in the IAEA concerning verification. The agency knows how to protect commercially, politically and militarily sensitive information. The agency could organize teams with weapons inspectors, supplemented by a cadre of administrative and logistical support – as it has done in the past. The IAEA has a major head start in terms of skills and experience; carrying out capacity-building and limited reorganization within the IAEA is a realistic prospect.

There is also a strong legal case for involving the IAEA in future multilateral disarmament verification efforts. The IAEA Statute provides for the Agency's right to apply safeguards, at the request of parties, to 'any bilateral or multilateral arrangement, or at the request of a state, to any of that state's activities in the field of atomic energy'. Disarmament verification is therefore implicitly included in the IAEA mandate.

However, it is not enough simply to simply identify and promote the IAEA as the body that should be called upon to verify nuclear arms reductions. It must be capable of delivering on the assigned task as well.

While the IAEA has done some amount of disarmament verification in the past, current capacity for dealing with this type of work is clearly lacking within the organization. This need not be written in stone. It is up to the member states of the IAEA to shape its role and to equip it to handle whatever role the membership finds suitable. Building up capacity for dealing with future verification challenges should be a priority. Capacity-building would necessarily be organized along two lines:

- building institutional knowledge within the IAEA, and safeguarding against the loss of knowledge through proper documentation in manuals, equipment specifications, operational procedures and work instructions; and

- investing in member-state capacity to furnish the IAEA with substantive and financial support for maintaining readiness for a role in disarmament verification, and ensuring that verification missions can be deployed in a timely and cost-effective fashion.

Capacity-building within appropriate individual member states of the IAEA is an essential adjunct to building capacity within the IAEA itself. After all, the Agency does not exist in isolation. It draws funding and guidance from its member states, and its manpower is drawn from the nationalities of its members. If the community of members (which includes all nuclear-armed states save one) can become incrementally more subject-area aware and more sophisticated in its views in relation to the whole issue of verification, the IAEA would progressively find itself in a better position to leverage its resources onto future verification challenges. This should be done through a programme of capacity-building, gap analysis and 'tool-box' development and training within the IAEA itself.

Conclusions

A world free of nuclear weapons is – beyond doubt – still many decades away. Even if the order were given today it would take several decades before the world would be ultimately rid of nuclear weapons. There are many critical decisions that need to be taken between now and then. It remains unrealistic, perhaps even naive, to expect the major powers to come together overnight and agree on something as ambitious as a nuclear weapons convention. Today there is no convergence of views on what a nuclear-weapons-free world would look like – or if it is even desirable.

The end-state described in this chapter may not be so very different from what the end-state may look like. The way to get there is unlikely to be straightforward or quick. Given the value that nuclear weapons hold for some, a step-by-step approach is highly advisable. This would devalue weapons over time, and allow for deterrence alternatives to be sought.

Achieving and maintaining the end-state portrayed here will require an international body capable of monitoring and verifying compliance throughout the transition, and in the nuclear-weapons-free world itself. At present, many of these capabilities are today handled by the International Atomic Energy Agency. This organization will undeniably have an important role to play in the future – perhaps not the IAEA as we know it today, but a stronger, more powerful version. In the meantime, the IAEA needs to be able to show that it can handle future verification challenges. Only then can it be viewed as a credible actor in the disarmed future, with a credible role in that future.

Hence, it is in Vienna that we must begin on the path to strengthening our abilities for dealing with future tasks. It is in Vienna that nuclear- and non-nuclear-weapon states alike can – and should – come together to start the process. After all, the IAEA already verifies that unarmed states remain so, through its safeguards system. It would be logical to add a disarmament component to this.

Article VI of the Nuclear Non-Proliferation Treaty calls on 'all states' to take measures towards nuclear disarmament. This means that taking practical steps towards nuclear disarmament is the shared responsibility of all, not only the nuclear-weapon states.

Legal obligations notwithstanding, there is also the practical imperative. Here we should recall the words of Des Browne in 2008, in his then capacity as UK Secretary of State for Defence, it is:

> of paramount importance that verification techniques are developed which enable us all – nuclear-weapon states and non-nuclear-weapon states – to have confidence that when a state says it has fully and irrevocably dismantled a nuclear warhead, we all can be assured it is telling the truth.

Notes

1 For an overview of deterrence theory, see Cowley and Parker (1996), 130.
2 Estimating North Korea's GDP is difficult. See the estimates of the South Korean Central Bank (2012) for more information.
3 In English, being unarmed is to be 'not equipped with or carrying weapons' whereas to disarm is 'take a weapon or weapons away from (a person, force, or country)'. One state is readily reversible, the other less so.
4 Of course, there are limitations to the capabilities of states. It does appear unfeasible for countries such as the Maldives or Tuvalu (just to give two examples) to acquire weapons. They lack the infrastructure and, more critically, the natural resources to drive a weapons effort.
5 An information barrier works like a coffee filter, allowing unclassified information (the water) to flow through, while capturing and retaining the sensitive information (the ground coffee).
6 According to the safeguards statement for 2012, the Department is currently safeguarding some 177,473 significant quantities of nuclear material. The present stockpile of weapons-grade material represents an additional 55,600 significant quantities.
7 Convention on the Prohibition of the Development, Production, Stockpiling, and Use of Chemical Weapons and on their Destruction, adopted on 3 September 1992.
8 See Article I.1(a) of the Convention, available at www.opcw.org/chemical-weapons-convention/articles/article-i-general-obligations/ (accessed 3 April 2013).
9 The IAEA's mandate in respect to the DPRK is currently in limbo. North Korea has a facility-specific safeguards agreement in place for a Soviet-supplied research reactor (INFCIRC/252, 14 November 1977). That was suspended when North Korea, for a period of time, adhered to so-called comprehensive safeguards. Technically, this agreement will be reactivated once the Agency gets confirmation that the DPRK is no longer a member of the NPT. The NPT membership has so far not furnished such confirmation. See International Atomic Energy Agency (2011). Application in all other states is routinely implemented, with few problems.

Bibliography

Browne, D. (2008) Laying the Foundations for Multilateral Disarmament. [Online] available from: www.labour.org.uk/des_browne_conference_on_nuclear_disarmament [accessed 18 March 2013].

Cliff, D. and Keir, D. (2012) *Multilateral Verification: Exploring new ideas*. VERTIC brief 17(January).

Cliff, D., Elbahtimy, H. and Persbo, A. (2010) *Verification of Warhead Dismantlement: Challenges, solutions and prospects*. IAEA-CN-184/204

Cliff, D., Elbahtimy, H. and Persbo, A. (2011) *Irreversibility in Nuclear Disarmament: Practical steps against nuclear rearmament*. VERTIC, September 2011. [Online] available from: www.vertic.org/media/assets/Publications/Irreversibility_Report_Sept_2011.pdf [accessed 2 April 2013].

Cowley, R. and Parker, N.G. (eds.) (1996) *The Reader's Companion to Military History*. [Online] available from: www.houghtonmifflinbooks.com/epub/militaryhis.shtml [accessed 5 February 2016].

DTIRP [Defence Treaty Inspection Readiness Programme] (n.d.) Plutonium Management and Disposition Agreement (PMDA). [Online] available from: http://web.archive.org/web/20140723061149/http:/dtirp.dtra.mil/tic/synopses/pmda.aspx [accessed 16 April 2013].

The Economist (2011) The growing appeal of zero: Banning the bomb will be hard, but not impossible. 16 June 2011. [Online] available at: www.economist.com/node/18836134 [accessed 2 April 2013].

Ekéus, R. (2012) The Iraq Action Team: A model for monitoring and verification of WMD non-proliferation, SIPRI essay. [Online] Available from: www.sipri.org/media/newsletter/essay/Ekeus_Sep [accessed 4 April 2013].

Fischer, D. (1997) History of the IAEA. [Online] available from: www-pub.iaea.org/mtcd/publications/pdf/pub1032_web.pdf [accessed 4 April 2013].

International Atomic Energy Agency (2011) Application of Safeguards in the Democratic People's Republic of Korea. [Online] available from: www.iaea.org/About/Policy/GC/GC55/GC55Documents/English/gc55-24_en.pdf

International Panel on Fissile Materials (2011) *Global Fissile Material Report 2011, Creative Commons*. [Online] available from: www.fissilematerials.org/library/gfmr11.pdf [accessed 5 February 2016].

INFCIRC/153, part II, paragraph 28. (Information Circular from the International Atomic Energy Agency).

Keir, D. and Persbo, A. (2013) Monitoring the Nuclear Weapons Situation on the Korean Peninsula. [Online] available from: www.vertic.org/pages/posts/monitoring-the-nuclear-weapons-situation-on-the-korean-peninsula-473.php [accessed 2 April 2013].

Kofstadmoen, H. and Reistad, O. (2010) *The Role of IAEA in Multilateral Disarmament Verification*, IAEA-CN-184/280. [Online] available from: www.iaea.org/Public/root/SG_SYMPOSIUM/Documents/PPT

Lewis, J. (2013) Writing on the Wall. [Online] available from: http://lewis.armscontrolwonk.com/archive/6505/writing-on-the-wall [accessed 2 April 2013].

Lodgaard, S. (2010) The relationship between nuclear disarmament and nuclear proliferation. In Krieger, D. (ed.) *The Challenge of Abolishing Nuclear Weapons*. New Brunswick and London: Transaction.

Munger, F. (2012) How long does it take to dismantle bomb parts? *Knox News*, 31 August 2012. [Online] available from: http://blogs.knoxnews.com/munger/2012/08/how-long-does-it-take-to-disma-1.html [accessed 14 March 2013].

NNSA [National Nuclear Security Administration] *Dismantlement Fact Sheet*. [Online] available from: http://nnsa.energy.gov/mediaroom/factsheets/dismantlement-0 [accessed 14 March 2013].

Persbo, A. (2010) *Technology and science for nuclear disarmament*. Wilton Park, United Kingdom. [Online] available from: www.vertic.org/media/assets/Events/WPJune2010/100624_WiltonPark.pdf

Pubantz, J. and Moore, J.A.J. (2008) *Encyclopedia of the United Nations*. New York: Infobase.

South Korean Central Bank (2012) Gross Domestic Product Estimates for North Korea for 2011. [Online] available from: www.nkeconwatch.com/nk-uploads/DPRK-GDP-2011-BOK.pdf [accessed 15 March 2013].

Trust and Verify (2000), 92(July 2000). [Online] available from: www.vertic.org/media/assets/TV/TV92.pdf [accessed 18 April 2013].

Uzumcu, A. (2013) *The Chemical Weapons Convention: Making disarmament happen*. Presentation to the Vienna Centre for Disarmament and Non-Proliferation, 19 March 2013. [Online] available from: www.opcw.org/index.php?eID=dam_frontend_push&docID=16213 [accessed 3 April 2013].

WarGames (2015) *WarGames*. [Online] available from: http://en.wikiquote.org/wiki/WarGames [accessed 2 April 2013].

World Nuclear Association (2012) *World Energy Needs and Nuclear Power* (updated July 2012). [Online] Available from: www.world-nuclear.org/info/Current-and-Future-Generation/World-Energy-Needs-and-Nuclear-Power/#.UVq-AVt4ZQo [accessed 2 April 2013].

7 Missile defence as an alternative to nuclear deterrence?

Tom Sauer

More and more experts, both in and outside governments, are now arguing that, with the further spread of nuclear weapons to unstable countries like Pakistan and North Korea, as well as to possible non-state actors, the goal of nuclear elimination should be taken seriously. That is what Harald Müller points out in his illuminating chapter. At the same time, the US missile defence programme, which has been legitimized as an instrument to counter nuclear proliferation, seems to getting more effective, at least at first sight. While missile defence had been a rather marginal phenomenon in the past, President George W. Bush made it one of his major foreign and defence policy objectives. The Anti-Ballistic Missile Treaty (ABM Treaty) has now been abolished, and missile interceptors have been installed in Alaska and California. Obama's European Phased Adaptive Approach consists of three phases. The first part, declared operational in 2012, involves Aegis destroyers with SM-3 missiles in the Mediterranean, a radar in Turkey and a command and control centre in Ramstein (Germany). Under Phase 2, completed in 2015, four ships are to be located in Spain, and Romania would host SM-3 interceptors and a radar on land. The third phase would field interceptors in Poland in 2018. The fourth phase was cancelled in 2013 (Rose 2013).

In much of the literature, nuclear elimination and missile defence are not automatically – let alone systematically – linked. Most proponents of missile defence avoid the debate about nuclear elimination, and many nuclear pacifists have little to say about missile defence.

The goal of this chapter is to relate these two phenomena. Does the renewed interest in nuclear elimination since 2007 diminish or support the demand for missile defence? Will states completely dismantle their offensive strategic capabilities only if they possess reliable defensive capacities? Or will US missile defence hamper further reductions in Russia and China, thereby halting the move towards elimination at some time? Will the need to eliminate nuclear weapons require or facilitate the elimination of ballistic missiles, which in turn would make missile defence redundant?

On the rare occasions when the concepts of nuclear elimination and missile defence have been connected (Glaser 1990; Glaser and Fetter 2001), this was always a theoretical exercise, because the prospects of effective missile defence and nuclear elimination were not very realistic. This seems to be changing now.

While President George W. Bush was probably the harshest opponent of arms control of all US presidents since the beginning of the atomic age, President Obama has publicly spoken out in favour of global zero during his 2008 presidential campaign and since (Obama 2009). The picture is similar but less clear cut with respect to missile defence. While President George W. Bush supported missile defence as much as President Reagan did, President Obama downgraded missile defence on his list of priorities, as he first wanted to be convinced that it is technically feasible and economically sensible. On the other hand, Obama has continued to spend nearly twice as much on missile defence as President Clinton.

Nuclear elimination with or without (large-scale) missile defence?

If nuclear deterrence 'works', as its proponents claim, by definition missile defence is unnecessary. That is the reason why the USA and the former Soviet Union agreed to negotiate and adhere to the ABM Treaty. That is also why France is not a great fan of NATO missile defence (NTI 1 April 2009). But, nowadays, it seems that nuclear deterrence must be complemented with missile defence. That means implicitly admitting, at least in part, that nuclear deterrence is not up to the job any more. That undermines the remaining relevance and utility of nuclear weapons, and is an additional argument for nuclear elimination.

The biggest criticism that can be made vis-à-vis extra-atmospheric missile defence systems – including the US ground-based mid-course system and the Aegis SM-3 missiles – is that their technological performance depends on the capabilities of the enemy, in particular the ability to build countermeasures (decoys etc.). And any nation capable of producing an ICBM and fitting it with a nuclear warhead is also capable of building countermeasures (Sessler 2000; US Defense Science Board 2011; Coyle 2013). On the other hand, it is not unreasonable that enemies should expect installed missile defence systems to work.

Assuming further nuclear reductions, should the build-down of the global nuclear arsenals be accompanied by a build-up of missile defence systems? A scenario-type approach will be used in this chapter. In the event that missile defence is somehow retained in the future, two important variables show up in our analysis: the degree of cooperation on missile defence, and the timeframe.

With respect to the degree of cooperation, two scenarios can be distinguished: the first option is 'unilateral' missile defence, which corresponds to a missile defence system that covers one major country (e.g. the USA) and possibly its allies (e.g. NATO allies). The second option is 'global' missile defence, which is a missile shield that protects all (major) states of the globe against launches from 'rogue' states and against accidental launches.

Regarding the timeframe, we distinguish the medium term, in which the world is heading towards elimination; and the long term, which would correspond, according to our assumptions here, to a nuclear-weapons-free world.

Table 7.1 Future missile defence scenarios

	Medium term (nuclear deterrence)	Long term (nuclear elimination)
Unilateral missile defence	1	Highly unrealistic
Global missile defence	2	3
No missile defence	Highly unrealistic	4

A last possibility is to abandon (large-scale) missile defence systems, either in the medium or the long term. Thus, six possible future missile defence scenarios can in theory be distinguished (see Table 7.1).

Two of these scenarios are highly unrealistic, and are not further analysed. The first is the one in which missile defence will be totally prohibited in the short or medium term. Given the massive sums (US$10 billion per year) invested, and the long history of the bureaucratic survival of missile defence programmes, it is highly unlikely that missile defence will be totally eliminated in the short or medium term.

A second unrealistic scenario is that regional powers like Russia and China will agree to give up their nuclear weapons in the long term while the USA unilaterally retains an extensive missile defence capability (Perkovich and Acton 2008, 27). As universality is a necessary condition for a nuclear-weapons-free world, the corollary is that unilateral missile defence should not be allowed. Another important condition for nuclear elimination is the abandonment of preventive strike doctrines as well as the means of executing such attacks (for example, prompt global strike capabilities). The combination of conventional superiority and missile defence on the part of the USA makes Russia, China and 'rogue' states feel existentially threatened. The latter will never give up their nuclear weapons unless the current collective security regime is substantially strengthened.

Consequently, for each timeframe, two realistic scenarios remain: for the medium term, unilateral missile defence and global missile defence; for the long term, global missile defence and no missile defence. For each scenario, the scenario, its advantages and disadvantages and its likelihood will be described. We will then be able to draw some preliminary conclusions, including conclusions that may be helpful for the choices confronting us in the short term.

Unilateral missile defence in the medium term (scenario 1)

This first scenario imagines a world which is not much different from today. The USA and its allies possess nationwide, strategic missile defence, while this is not the case (or is less so) for Russia, China and the rest of the world.

The major disadvantage of this scenario is that, with the downsizing of nuclear weapons arsenals in the medium term, two geostrategic factors will become more important: the quality of the offensive nuclear force and (to a lesser extent) the perceived effectiveness of missile defence. Unfortunately from the perspective of global stability, there is a fundamental imbalance with regard to these two factors in favour of the USA (Lieber and Press 2006a; 2006b; Lantis *et al.* 2006/7). As a result, Russia has consistently argued against US missile defence, especially on its borders in Europe. On various occasions, Moscow has also threatened retaliatory measures like installing short-range Iskander missiles in Kaliningrad (NTI 17 December 2013). In 2015, Russia also threatened to aim its nuclear missiles at Danish ships because of their role in the NATO shield (Jensen 2015). This also means that the odds are that Russia and China will halt their nuclear weapons reductions at a certain point, and that the nuclear disarmament process will come to a halt (Butt and Postol 2011). The Russian articles of ratification to New START allow Moscow to withdraw in the event of extensive US missile defence, and, according to the US Bipartisan Strategic Posture Commission, 'China may already be increasing the size of its ICBM force in response to its assessment of the U.S. missile defense program' (Perry and Schlesinger 2009, 32; see also Zhang 2011; Peck 2015). This interruption of the nuclear disarmament process is not in the interests of the USA and its allies, as proliferation will continue and missile defence will not be effective in neutralizing this threat.

It could also be pointed out that the nuclear deal reached with Iran in July 2015 makes a US missile defence shield less necessary (Thielmann 2015). However, the limited threat of North Korea remains, for the time being.

This first scenario is above all highly unstable, and therefore not very likely to endure for long. As a result, in the medium term the USA and its allies will basically have to choose: either limit their missile defence capabilities to such an extent that they are not perceived by Russia and China as destabilizing, which corresponds to a status quo of the current situation; or else cooperate with Russia and China on a global missile defence system (see scenario 2). With respect to the former, the question then becomes how limited these defensive capabilities would have to be. With shrinking numbers of offensive nuclear weapons, the odds are that any nationwide strategic missile defence capability will be perceived as too large. Only theatre missile defence capabilities, like those that protect a small part of the country, will not be regarded as destabilizing. Theatre missile defence capabilities that can easily be plugged into or extended to a strategic capability (like THAAD or Aegis) will have to be strictly limited as well. This option may also require the reintroduction of a kind of ABM treaty. This scenario appears the most likely in the medium term.

Global missile defence in the medium term (scenario 2)

The major stable alternative to a limited unilateral missile shield in the medium term is a 'global' missile defence system against 'rogue' states and incidental launches. Because all major stakeholders (including Russia and China) by definition participate in such a project, it can be extensive and can include strategic missile defence. On the other hand, the system does not need to be very extensive, because it would supposedly act against accidental launches and in defiance of rogue states, which, in all likelihood, will possess only a one-digit number of nuclear warheads that can be transported by long-range ballistic missiles.

As long as there are nuclear weapons, the threat of their use, even accidental, will persist. A global missile defence shield – assuming that the technology is effective – may help to limit the damage in case of such an attack.

Another advantage is that such a system will build trust among the major states in the world. This is an asset that the nuclear-weapon states will need when they reduce their nuclear arsenals to very low numbers. There may thus be a positive feedback loop from global missile defence to the more encompassing project of nuclear elimination.

But how realistic is this scenario in the medium term? Difficult hurdles will have to be overcome. There are also conceptual clarifications to be made. Are we talking about all states in the world except the 'rogue' states? If not, which ones are included and which are excluded? On the basis of what criteria shall the international community decide? Which countries can be categorized as 'rogue' states, and who is going to determine that? For example, President Clinton once stated that the USA would share the missile defence technology with friendly, 'civilized' states:

> I don't think that we could ever advance the notion that we have this technology designed to protect us against a new threat; a threat which is also a threat to other *civilized nations* who might or might not have nuclear powers ... and not make it available to them ... I think it would be unethical not to do so'.
>
> (Quoted in Graham 2003, 280)

His statement seemed a reaction to presidential candidate George W. Bush, who supported a missile shield that would also protect the NATO allies, something the Clinton administration had neglected. But did President Clinton also mean to include Russia and China, let alone Iran and North Korea, in the category of 'civilized nations'?

The George W. Bush administration invited Russia to participate, but was silent on China (Dyvad 2005). President Obama has followed a similar policy line, although his administration states that it wants to talk with China about strategic issues, including missile defence (Zhang 2011, 565). But this offer apparently does not include active participation in missile defence. Nevertheless, a global shield will require the inclusion of China as well, as former UK Foreign Secretary David Miliband has argued (Miliband 2009, 38).

Further, there are more practical day-to-day command and control problems. In which states are the defensive interceptors going to be installed? Who is going to decide about their use (NTI 12 March 2010)? As these interceptors will have to be launched quickly in case of emergency, there will be no time to bring all world leaders together and decide what to do. Or will there be an international organization responsible for global missile defence? If so, how should this organization function? How will it make decisions? And what about cost-sharing?

However, the main hurdle in building global missile defence is the presence of distrust among the major actors in the world (NTI 26 August 2009; Fitzpatrick 2009/10, 10; Weitz 2010). Not only will the USA be uncertain whether the initial level of cooperation with Russia and China, if existent, will remain: there is the additional problem that Russia and China may cheat by exporting shared missile defence technology to rogue states. Both problems are inherent to international cooperation in general, as the realist school in international relations would point out.

That is why many believe that the USA will *not* be eager to share this sophisticated technology with states like Russia and China (Stone 2000). As Harald Müller put it,

> It would require the US to share and transfer cutting-edge technology with countries its military elite still regards as rivals and potential enemies ... Over the last years, the US inclination to transfer sensitive technologies has diminished rather than grown, even within the Western Alliance.
> (Müller 2001, 17)

This reasoning applies even more after the Ukraine crisis. The system components regarded as top secret are the sensing and homing techniques. This kind of technology is not even shared among NATO allies. The request by some European allies for technology sharing and technology transfer from THAAD to MEADS, for instance, has been rejected by the Pentagon (Pullinger *et al.* 2007, 26). Just before entering the Bush administration, Condoleezza Rice was also highly sceptical about US–Russian missile defence cooperation:

> Moscow should understand that any possibilities for sharing technology or information in these areas would depend heavily on its record – problematic to date – on the proliferation of ballistic missile and other technologies related to weapons of mass destruction. It would be foolish in the extreme to share defences with Moscow if it either leaks or deliberately transfers weapon technologies to the very states against which America is defending.
> (Rice 2000)

Similarly, many observers see US missile defence as part of an overall doctrine of defence superiority and overall primacy (Cronberg 2005; Heurlin 2005). This too will make it highly unlikely that the USA will share its missile defence technology (Müller 2008; Heurlin, 2005). Dmitry Rogozin, then Special Envoy of the Russian President, in an interview to *Yaderni Kontrol* in September 2003, agreed:

> I am not sure that this idea [of missile defense cooperation] has a future.... What is the point for [the Americans] in sharing with us? I wouldn't if I were in their shoes. Until these projects of cooperation with Russia acquire concrete outlines and real investments are in the pipeline, I will remain a

skeptic. Let us face it; the US does not have much of a reputation on this issue.

(Arms Control and Security Letters 2003)

Further, Russian Foreign Minister Sergei Lavrov does not believe in far-reaching cooperation in this regard: 'The US, as everyone knows, has never given control to anyone, will not now and obviously will never give up control of their strategic systems' (NTI 16 April 2009). Stephen Sestanovich, a US expert at the Council on Foreign Relations, concurs: 'For that kind of cooperation [the Americans] would have to have more trust than people really do now toward the Russian military' (NTI 8 June 2007).

On the other hand, the USA and Russia have already agreed to cooperate on missile defence to a certain extent (Kassianova 2005). But, up until now, the outcome of the talks has been rather meagre, apart from some joint table-top exercises. It is restricted to the field of theatre missile defence, and also this low level of cooperation was not making progress, even before the Ukraine crisis.

Russia and the USA have also shown some interest in cooperating on strategic missile defence, but each time that Russia has been interested the USA seemed unenthusiastic, and vice versa. When push came to shove, they could not agree on concrete proposals. For instance, President Gorbachev, while initially highly sceptical of missile defence (for example during the Reykjavik summit in 1986), proposed in October 1991 that both superpowers 'study the possibility of creating joint systems to avert nuclear missile attacks with ground- and space-based systems' (Graham 2003, 21). In January 1992, President Yeltsin went even further. Speaking at the UN, Yeltsin proposed deploying and jointly operating 'a global system of protection of the world community based on a revised American SDI and advanced technologies developed by the Russian military-industrial complex' (Graham 2003, 22). Six months later, President George H.W. Bush and Yeltsin agreed to develop a Global Protection System. A high-level group chaired by Denis Ross and Georgi Mamedov was set up to explore the establishment of an early-warning centre.

But the Clinton administration lost interest. President Putin raised the subject of missile defence cooperation, especially boost-phase, in an interview on NBC in June 2000 (Graham 2003, 279–281). The Clinton–Putin summit a few days later did call for setting up a Moscow-based information exchange centre for missile launches, for example to prevent the authorized use of nuclear weapons after false alarms and to exchange data about launches conducted by third countries. The latter, however, was not realized.

In turn, the George W. Bush administration reintroduced the idea of US–Russian missile defence cooperation in the context of its proposals to withdraw from the ABM Treaty. In a speech at the National Defense University on 1 May 2001, President Bush stated:

> This new cooperative relationship should look to the future, not to the past.... It should be premised on openness, mutual confidence, and real

opportunities for cooperation, including the area of missile defence. It should allow us to share information so that each nation can improve its early-warning capability and its capability to defend its people and territory. And perhaps one day we can even cooperate in a joint defense.

(Graham 2003, 359)

This time, however, President Putin apparently lost interest. Nevertheless, the US–Russian Joint Declaration on the occasion of the signing of the SORT Treaty on 24 May 2002 called again for joint research and development of missile defence technologies. In July 2002, the Ad Hoc Working Group on Theater Missile Defense, established in the framework of the NATO–Russia Council, met for the first time. But Russia did not reply to the US invitation to observe the IFT-10 flight test in December 2002, an exhibition of Patriot PAC-3 or a visit to the missile defence base in Fort Greeley in Alaska (Webster 2003, 24).

To sweeten the US offer for a third site in Europe, the Bush administration repeated the idea of cooperating with Russia on missile defence. Initially, Russia again did not show much interest, except for including the former Soviet radar in Azerbaijan in a joint system as an alternative for the Czech radar. The latter was proposed by President Putin at the G-8 Summit in Heiligendam on 7 June 2007 (Ward 2007). According to Ted Postol of MIT, the Russian proposal was technologically sound (Postol 2007). The Bush administration was interested in the Azeri radar, but only as a complement – not an alternative – to the Czech radar. Russia disagreed. Putin said that he was less concerned with US interceptors in Iraq, Turkey or on Aegis ships. At their last summit in Sochi in 2008, Bush and Putin seemed to come closer to a deal (Buckley and Dombey 2008). But, again, the US proposal that included Russian inspectors at the Polish site did not go far enough for the Russians, who wanted Russian inspectors to be stationed in Poland on a permanent basis. Both superpowers once again agreed to disagree. These proposals have not yielded any concrete results and, as Walter Slocombe writes, 'have [not] gone much beyond the communiqué stage. All have foundered on issues of joint control, access to information, and generally uneasy relations' (Slocombe 2008, 22).

In their first meeting, Obama and Medvedev agreed to work together on a study of a joint assessment of the missile threat in the world and to establish a Joint Data Exchange Centre on missile launches (Cooper 2009). Immediately after the Obama administration had cancelled the Bush plan for a third site in Poland and the Czech Republic, NATO Secretary General Rasmussen in his first public speech invited Russia to cooperate with NATO on missile defence (Rasmussen 2009). Earlier, US Secretary of State Hillary Clinton had stated, 'Just as we had to build a mutual defense with Europe in the 20th century, we have to build it in the 21st century. It is my hope that we will persuade Russia to be part of that defense' (NTI 5 March 2009). Russia reacted by blowing warm and cold at the same time. Dmitry Rogozin, Russia's Ambassador to NATO, was not completely negative: 'If we are convinced that the European missile defense initiative is not part of a U.S. theater missile defense system, such [cooperative] efforts are possible' (NTI 30 September 2009). Taking into account that the European and US missile defence system are meant to be highly integrated, one may wonder how deep Russia's interest in this proposal for cooperation is.

Russia also asked for more technical details as a condition for cooperation. A NATO–Russian working group on missile defence was established in December 2009. But the saga continued to unfold. One month later, Russian Foreign Minister Lavrov presented a new condition: 'we have told the U.S. and NATO that it is necessary to start everything from scratch – to jointly analyze the origin and types of missile proliferation risks and threats'. That is apparently not the US approach. Lavrov continues: 'But [the US has] simply told us: these are the systems we plan to develop, and you will have to contribute your radars. This is not the kind of approach we are ready to support' (NTI 26 January 2010; NTI 30 April 2010). To what extent Lavrov's remarks are diplomatic language for a plea for cooperation on an equal basis, or whether they are another way of saying 'no', is unclear. Even if it is the former, agreeing on such delicate issues on an equal basis will be extremely difficult.

For starters, the USA and Russia disagree on a common threat assessment (for example, Iran). Even Secretary of State Hillary Clinton doubted whether such cooperation is politically feasible: 'I can imagine [US–Russian cooperation] but I am not sure the Russians can imagine it' (NTI 23 February 2010). Russian President Medvedev created an opening right after having signed New START in April 2010 (NTI 9 April 2010). When Obama and Medvedev met in June 2010, they pledged again to continue work on establishing a Joint Data Exchange Centre. However, when it ratified New START in 2011, the US Senate stated in the ratification resolution that the US government had no right to disclose any sensitive missile defence information to Russia (NTI 29 March 2012). Nevertheless, in a personal letter to President Putin, President Obama went ahead and shared anti-missile data (NTI 16 May 2013). The issue was discussed at the Russia–NATO Council in October 2013 without making any progress. Thereafter, the Ukraine crisis put an end to this ritualistic missile defence cooperation debate (NTI 27 March 2014).

Given all of these practical but especially political difficulties with just one other regional power – Russia – the odds are that a global missile defence project is not realistic in the medium term.

Global missile defence in the long term (scenario 3)

For different reasons, the construction of a global missile defence system – corresponding to a nuclear-weapons-free world (according to our assumptions) – may be easier to realize in the long term than in the medium term. First, the problem of which states have to be covered should in principle be resolved, as all states will be nuclear-weapons-free, so all of them will be entitled to be covered by the missile shield. Second, in a nuclear-weapons-free world, Russia and China should have more reasons to go along with a cooperative missile defence system, as the chances of destabilizing consequences are much lower.

Third, missile defence will have matured further. As a 'thick' defence against a large-scale nuclear attack is not needed, and as the only danger will be the breakout of one state with one or a couple of nuclear weapons, the technological requirements become less stringent and therefore more feasible. Fourth, due partly to the process of getting rid of nuclear weapons, relations among the great powers may have improved to such an extent that cooperation on missile defence becomes politically less sensitive, and therefore politically more feasible. Fifth, a global missile defence may help the last sceptics of elimination to overcome their doubts (Kampelman and Seitz 2001). In short, as Oliver Thränert argues, 'if successful, NATO–Russian missile defence cooperation could become the nucleus for a wider missile defence that could provide some reassurance against nuclear breakout if a world free of nuclear weapons is ever achieved' (Thränert 2009/10, 74).

On the other hand, there are also good reasons why global missile defence may become less likely over time. In a nuclear-weapons-free world there is in principle much less need for a missile defence system. As there will be no nuclear weapons around, there is no need to protect oneself against nuclear weapons any more, except in case of breakout. Breakout scenarios are unlikely to include ballistic missiles, especially if a nuclear-weapons-free world goes together with a ban on ballistic missiles (see scenario 4). Even without such an additional ban, fitting a nuclear explosive on a ballistic missile is much more difficult for cheaters than delivering nuclear weapons by lorry, ship or aeroplane.

No missile defence in the long term (scenario 4)

For several reasons, the option of a prohibition on missile defence is preferable in a nuclear-weapons-free world. Given the technological complexities of missile defence, the political difficulties of a global missile shield, as well as the problem of squaring the idea of global missile defence with the vision of elimination in the interim period, the most desirable scenario in the long term is a ban on missile defence.

Verifying a ban on ballistic missiles is easier than verifying a ban on nuclear weapons, as endogenous ballistic missiles have to be tested (even more so than nuclear weapons), and that can be easily observed by satellites. As Graham and Mistry argue, 'A verification system may not detect the development of every single missile component in secret production sites, but missile components must ultimately be integrated and new missiles must be flight tested, and flight testing can be detected' (Graham and Mistry 2006).

A ban on defensive ballistic missiles opens up enormous opportunities to expand the ban to include offensive ballistic missiles as well, which in turn will increase the prospects for a nuclear-weapons-free world (see Schelling 1987; Adelman 1991; Glaser and Fetter 2001; Frye 1992, 1996; Lumpe 1993, 1995; Lichterman *et al.* 2002, 33; Andreasen 2004; Graham and Mistry 2006). In principle, nuclear deterrence strategies do not require the existence of missiles. Bombers can temporarily do the job as well, as was the case at the beginning of the nuclear age.

In addition, a nuclear-weapons-free world will require substantial changes to the current collective security system. Not only will doctrines of preventive attacks (like the Bush doctrine) have to be drastically restricted, but the capabilities necessary for such doctrines should also be limited. In particular, space-based weapons and global strike conventional weapons should be outlawed. This would in fact imply that all long-range missiles, for offensive as well as defensive purposes, must be prohibited before the last nuclear weapons are destroyed.

A ban on ballistic missiles also removes the danger of a massive and swift unauthorized (nuclear) attack, or an authorized attack after a false alarm. Bombers can be recalled. As Randall Forsberg argued,

> in about 15 minutes the two or three top officers on a US Trident submarine can launch 24 missiles carrying 192 nuclear warheads.... In a world without ballistic missiles, launching hundreds of nuclear weapons at distant cities would take many hours and involve scores or even hundreds of people.
> (Forsberg 1987, 190)

Also, President Reagan, influenced by his Undersecretary of Defence Fred Iklé (Iklé 1973) and START negotiator Max Kampelman, toyed with the idea of banning (offensive) ballistic missiles. President Reagan proposed this in a letter to President Gorbachev in July 1986.

Crucially, a ban on ballistic missiles is much easier to implement and much more effective than trying to construct a reliable missile defence system. Alton Frye agrees: 'in terms of technical feasibility and reliability, a prohibition on testing, production, and deployment of ballistic missiles is incomparably simpler than an active defense against them' (Frye 1996, 107–108).

The proposal to ban ballistic missiles has met with new interest from another angle as well (Cooper 2013). The 1987 bilateral INF Treaty prohibited medium-range and intermediate-range nuclear weapons – the first treaty that banned a particular category of missiles, albeit only for two states. Today, an increasing number of states (such as India, Saudi Arabia, Pakistan, North Korea, Iran) are in the process of acquiring such missiles as well. They endanger global security, including the security of Russia (and of US allies). Canada proposed a multilateral extension of the INF Treaty for the period 1993–95 in the framework of the Missile Technology Control Regime (MTCR). Also, Russia came up with the idea of multilateralizing the INF Treaty or even abolishing the bilateral INF Treaty, as a reaction to the missile defence plans of the George W. Bush administration. According to a bilateral US–Russian statement delivered at the UN General Assembly in October 2007:

> The Russian Federation and the United States call on all interested countries to discuss the possibility of imparting a global character to this important regime through the renunciation of ground-launched ballistic and cruise missiles with ranges between 500 and 5,500 kilometers, leading to the destruction of any such missiles and the cessation of associated programs.
> (NTI 26 October 2007)

In his first presidential campaign, Barack Obama proposed the idea (Ryan 2007), and William Perry and George Schulz later supported it in an op-ed (*New York Times* 11 April 2010). Also, UN Secretary-General Ban Ki-Moon has called for 'new weapons bans, including of missile and space weapons' (Ki-Moon 2008).

Of course, a ban on ballistic missiles has its own drawbacks. For one thing, critics may ask: what are the repercussions of such a ban for launching satellites into space? One answer is that the proposal to ban ballistic missiles would still allow missiles for satellite launches. Missiles for satellite launches do not need heat-shielding materials because they are not meant to survive re-entry into the atmosphere. That is a major difference with ballistic missiles for offensive or defensive purposes. Frye argues: 'with careful, transparent management of the design, testing, production, and operations of space-launch vehicles, containing the danger of clandestine missile deployments would pose no insuperable difficulties' (Frye 1996, 108). An alternative solution would be the creation of an international space consortium.

Most proposals for a ban on ballistic missiles would allow short-term ballistic missiles with a maximum range of, for instance, 100 km (Andreasen 2004, 121). Also, cruise missiles would be allowed. However, Leon Sloss, writing at the end of the Cold War, saw a problem in this regard:

> If both the Soviet Union and the United States were, for example, to rely heavily on bombers, but both also deployed long-range, stealthy submarine-launched cruise missiles that could attack the relatively small number of bomber bases, we might find this a very unstable situation with very strong incentives for a first strike by both sides.
>
> (Sloss 1987, 188)

The recent controversy about the possible INF Treaty violation by Russia touches upon similar sensitivities. This may be an argument for forbidding cruise missiles as well.

Politically, it will not be easy to convince Russia to agree to a ban on ballistic missiles. As former Clinton NSC official Steven Andreasen has stated, 'Russia may view a global [Zero Ballistic Missile Treaty] regime as unequal, and seek concessions in other areas (for example, the elimination of long-range heavy bombers and nuclear cruise missiles, or limitations on precision-guided conventional munitions)' (Andreasen 2004, 124). However, he goes on to say 'every ICBM and SLBM not under Russian command today – whether American, British, French or Chinese – is a threat to Russia. A global [Zero Ballistic Missile Treaty] regime would at least simplify, if not improve, Russia's strategic position' (ibid., 124–125).

Therefore, although more thinking is needed for carefully weighing the costs and benefits, a ban on offensive and defensive ballistic missiles seems the best alternative to missile defence – which is an extremely expensive technological solution that, technically speaking, does not work. With a ban in place, the threat of ballistic missiles (with or without nuclear weapons) can simply not arise in the first place – or, at least, it would have greater difficulty in arising.

Conclusions

Assuming that nuclear elimination becomes a priority in the fight against nuclear proliferation and nuclear terrorism, and assuming that missile defence will not become reliable under real circumstances, then the best option seems to be zero offensive and zero defensive ballistic missiles. Nuclear elimination does not need missile defence; on the contrary, missile defence that is limited to one or even two regional powers (like the USA) but excludes others (like Russia and China) will substantially hinder the road to global zero.

Second-best would be to limit the existing missile defence capabilities to theatre missile defence, excluding those theatre missile defence systems (like advanced SM-3 missiles on Aegis ships) that can easily be plugged together to form a strategic missile defence capability. As the US Bipartisan Strategic Posture Commission stated, 'The United States should ensure that its actions do not lead Russia or China to take actions that increase the threat to the United States and its allies and friends' (Perry and Schlesinger 2009, xvii). This means the restoration of a kind of ABM treaty.

Third-best, but unlikely, in the event that large-scale strategic missile defence systems are allowed they should be shared with all major powers. Otherwise new arms races with both defensive and offensive weapons could develop, in turn preventing the realization of the only solution to the threat of nuclear proliferation: *a world without nuclear weapons.*

To conclude, then, missile defence must be recognized as more a liability than an asset if we are to climb down the nuclear arms ladder and achieve a world free of nuclear weapons.

Bibliography

Adelman, K. (1991) How to limit everybody's missiles. *New York Times*, 7 April.
Andreasen, S. (2004) Reagan was right: let's ban ballistic missiles. *Survival*, 46: 117–130.
Arms Control and Security Letters (2003), 7, 141, September.
Buckley, N. and Dombey, D. (2008) Optimism on missile shield deal. *Financial Times*, 8 April.
Butt, Y. and Postol, T. (2011) Upsetting the reset. *Federation of American Scientists Special Report*, 1(September).
Cooper, D. (2013) Globalizing Reagan's INF Treaty. *The Nonproliferation Review*, 20: 145–163.
Cooper, H. (2009) Promises of 'fresh start' for US–Russia relations. *New York Times*, 2 April.
Coyle, P. (2013) Back to the drawing board: the need for sound science in U.S. missile defense. *Arms Control Today*, January/February. [Online] available from: www.armscontrol.org/act/2013_01-02/Back-to-the-Drawing-Board-The-Need-for-Sound-Science-in-US-Missile-Defense.

Cronberg, T. (2005) US missile defence: technological primacy in action. In Heurlin, B. and Rynning, S. (eds) *Missile Defence* (Chapter 2). London: Routledge.

Dyvad, P. (2005) China's response to the US Missile Defence Programme. In Heurlin, B. and Rynning, S. (eds) *Missile Defence* (Chapter 6). London: Routledge.

Fitzpatrick, M. (2009/10) A prudent decision on missile defense. *Survival*, 51: 5–12.

Forsberg, R. (1987) Abolishing ballistic missiles. *International Security*, 12: 190–196.

Frye, A. (1992) Zero ballistic missiles. *Foreign Policy*, 88: 12–17.

Frye, A. (1996) Banning ballistic missiles. *Foreign Affairs*, 75: 99–112.

Glaser, C. (1990) *Analyzing Strategic Nuclear Policy*. Princeton, NJ: Princeton University Press.

Glaser, C. and Fetter, S. (2001) National missile defense and the future of US nuclear weapons policy. *International Security*, 26: 86–88.

Graham, B. (2003) *Hit To Kill*. New York, NY: Public Affairs.

Graham, T. and Mistry, D. (2006) Two treaties to contain missile proliferation. *Disarmament Diplomacy*, 82. [Online] available from: www.acronym.org.uk/dd/dd82/82tgdm.htm.

Heurlin, B. (2005) Missile defense in the US. In Heurlin, B. and Rynning, S. (eds) *Missile Defence* (Chapter 3). London: Routledge.

Iklé, F. (1973) Can nuclear deterrence last out the century? *Foreign Affairs*, 51: 267–285.

Jensen, T. (2015) Russia threatens to aim nuclear missiles at Denmark ships if it joins NATO Shield. *Reuters*, 22 March.

Kampelman, M. and Seitz, F. (2001) Missile defense: a global approach. *Washington Post*, 8 April.

Kassianova, A. (2005) Roads not (yet) taken: Russian approaches to cooperation in missile defence. In Heurlin, B. and Rynning, S. (eds) *Missile Defence* (Chapter 4). London: Routledge.

Ki-Moon, B. (2008) Five steps to a nuclear-free world. *Guardian*, 23 November.

Lantis, J., Sauer, T., Wirtz, J., Lieber, K. and Press, D. (2006/7) The short shadow of US primacy? *International Security*, 31: 174–193.

Lichterman, A., Mian, Z., Ramana, M.V. and Scheffran, J. (2002) Beyond missile defense. *INESAP Joint Working Paper* (January).

Lieber, K. and Press, D. (2006a) The rise of nuclear primacy. *Foreign Affairs*, 85: 42–54.

Lieber, K. and Press, D. (2006b) The end of MAD? The nuclear dimension of US primacy. *International Security*, 30: 7–44.

Lumpe, L. (1993) Zero ballistic missiles and the Third World. *Arms Control Today*, 23: 218–223.

Lumpe, L. (1995) Arms control options for delivery vehicles. *Physics and Society*, 24: 2–5.

Miliband, D. (2009) *Lifting the Nuclear Shadow: Creating the Conditions for Abolishing Nuclear Weapons*. London: Foreign and Commonwealth Office.

Müller, H. (2001) Nearly mortal dilemma: the Europeans and the US plans for NMD. *Nuclear Control (Yaderni Kontrol)*, 6: 15–22.

Müller, H. (2008) *Old wine in old bottles: missile defenses in today's strategic environment*. Paper presented at the International Peace Research Association (IPRA) Conference, Leuven, 15–19 July.

New York Times (2010) How to build on the START Treaty. 11 April.

NTI (8 June 2007) Putin raises questions with missile defense offer. *NTI Global Security Newswire*.

NTI (26 October 2007) Washington backs wider global missile ban. *NTI Global Security Newswire*.

NTI (5 March 2009) Clinton plans 'serious' talks on missile defense with Russia. *NTI Global Security Newswire.*
NTI (1 April 2009) France poses questions on NATO missile shield. *NTI Global Security Newswire.*
NTI (16 April 2009) Russia waiting for concrete US missile defense proposal. *NTI Global Security Newswire.*
NTI (26 August 2009) U.S., Russia unlikely to cooperate on missile defense, experts say. *NTI Global Security Newswire.*
NTI (30 September 2009) U.S., Russia should cooperate on missile defense, Obama says. *NTI Global Security Newswire.*
NTI (26 January 2010) Russia resists partnering with U.S. on missile defense. *NTI Global Security Newswire.*
NTI (23 February 2010) Clinton calls on Russia to participate in missile defense. *NTI Global Security Newswire.*
NTI (12 March 2010) NATO Commander supports partnering with Russia on missile shield. *NTI Global Security Newswire.*
NTI (9 April 2010) Medvedev offers to work with U.S. on missile defense. *NTI Global Security Newswire.*
NTI (30 April 2010) NATO weighs reviving conventional forces pact with Russia. *NTI Global Security Newswire.*
NTI (29 March 2012) House Speaker questions Obama antimissile negotiations comments. *NTI Global Security Newswire.*
NTI (16 May 2013) Obama reportedly offers Putin deal on sharing of antimissile data. *NTI Global Security Newswire.*
NTI (17 December 2013) Russia is fielding nuclear-capable missiles in territory bordering NATO. *NTI Global Security Newswire.*
NTI (27 March 2014) Washington suspending missile defense cooperation talks with Moscow. *NTI Global Security Newswire.*
Obama, B. (2009) Presidential speech in Prague, 5 April. [Online] available from: www.whitehouse.gov/the-press-office/remarks-president-barack-obama-prague-delivered.
Peck, M. (2015) Get ready, America: here comes China's ballistic missile defences. *The National Interest*, 28 October.
Perkovich, G. and Acton, J. (2008) Abolishing nuclear weapons, Adelphi Paper 396.
Perry, W. and Schlesinger J. (chairpersons) (2009) *America's Strategic Posture.* Washington, DC: US Institute of Peace.
Postol, T. (2007) A ring around Iran. *New York Times*, 11 July.
Pullinger, S., Gasparini, G., Neuneck, G. and Pasco, X. (2007) *Missile defence and European security.* Brussels: European Parliament, EP Subcommittee on Security and Defence.
Rasmussen, A. (2009) *NATO and Russia – A New Beginning.* Brussels: Carnegie.
Rice, C. (2000) Exercising power without arrogance. *The Chicago Tribune*, 31 December.
Rose, F. (2013) Implementation of the European Phased Adaptive Approach. Remarks by the US Deputy Assistant Secretary of State at the Polish National Defense University, 18 April.
Ryan, K. (2007) Expand or scrap missile ban. *Los Angeles Times*, 16 October.
Sessler, A. (ed.) (2000) *Countermeasures: A Technical Evaluation of the Operational Effectiveness of the Planned US National Missile Defense System.* Union of Concerned Scientists/MIT Security Studies Program.

Schelling, T. (1987) Abolition of ballistic missiles. *International Security*, 12: 179–183.
Slocombe, W. (2008) Europe, Russia and American missile defence. *Survival*, 50: 19–24.
Sloss, L. (1987) A world without ballistic missiles. *International Security*, 12: 184–189.
Stone, A. (2000) Idea: share shield technology with Russia; senators say don't rule it out if it enables missile defense, but Pentagon unenthusiastic. *USA Today*, 7 February.
Thielmann, G. (2015) It's official: there will be no Iranian ICBM in 2015. *The National Interest*, 24 November.
Thränert, O. (2009/10) NATO, missile defense and extended deterrence. *Survival*, 51: 63–76.
US Defense Science Board (2011) *Task Force Report on Science and Technology Issues of Early Intercept BMD Feasibility*. Washington DC.
Ward, A. (2007) Putin in surprise offer to US on missile defence. *Financial Times*, 8 June.
Webster, P. (2003) Just like in old times. *The Bulletin of the Atomic Scientists*, 59: 30–35.
Weitz, R. (2010) Illusive visions and practical realities: Russia, NATO and missile defense. *Survival*, 52: 99–120.
Zhang, B. (2011) US missile defence and China's nuclear posture: changing dynamics of an offence–defence arms race. *International Affairs*, 87: 55–69.

8 Nuclear disarmament
A Chinese view

Jingdong Yuan

In January 2007, four senior US statesmen – George Shultz, William Perry, Henry Kissinger and Sam Nunn – wrote a seminal opinion piece in the *Wall Street Journal*, in which they called for a drastic reduction of the existing nuclear arsenals of the United States and Russia to reduce the chance of nuclear war and to prevent terrorist groups from gaining access to nuclear weapons (Shultz *et al.* 2007). A newly elected President Obama announced in April 2009 in Prague that great efforts would have to be made to make the world free of nuclear weapons. New START, a treaty between the United States and Russia, was subsequently signed, committing both countries to reduce their operational nuclear weapons to 1,550 each. In June 2013, in Berlin, President Obama renewed the call for further reducing US/Russian nuclear arsenals by a third, to around 1,000 weapons each (Cortright and Väyrynen 2010).

However, the momentum for abolishing nuclear weapons seems to have stalled since then. Indeed, while nuclear-weapon states pledge nuclear disarmament, none of them has genuinely demonstrated a serious willingness to give up these arsenals. Nuclear weapons continue to feature prominently in their defence doctrines and military planning. In the United States, billions are being spent and are budgeted on extending the life-span of the existing arsenals and producing new nuclear warheads. Russia has recently announced it will introduce some 40 new ICBMs into its nuclear arsenal. Also, other nuclear-weapon states are engaged in increasingly expensive nuclear modernization programmes, with no signs of slowing down (Mecklin 2015; BBC 2015; Kristensen and Norris 2014). Meanwhile, the crisis in Ukraine and the Russia–West confrontation, heightened territorial disputes in East Asia and continuing tensions in South Asia further exacerbate the security dilemmas between rivalling states, many of them nuclear-armed. These developments cast a shadow over the prospects of nuclear disarmament and intensify interstate rivalry, while elevating the importance of extended deterrence and raising questions about it. All of these foreshadowed the 2015 NPT Review Conference, which ended with a failure to agree on a final document.

What went wrong? And what must be done to renew and carry through the important task of achieving a world free of nuclear weapons, and to make sure nuclear disarmament will be irreversible, legal and permanent? Professors

Harald Müller and Andreas Persbo's contributions to this volume seek to address these questions. For Professor Müller, a major obstacle to a nuclear-weapons-free world (NWFW) is 'the hegemony of existing mentalities', in particular the fixation on deterrence to the extent that all other alternatives are not even considered in discussions of nuclear policy. For Müller, the very concept of nuclear deterrence (and hence the argument for its preservation, often by the organizations that benefit from it) constitutes a serious obstacle to nuclear zero.

Müller rightly points to the illogic of the 'virtual arsenals' as part of deterrence. Essentially, any such arsenals are a guarantee that nuclear weapons will be retained, because any sensible governments would rather prefer the ready availability of nuclear arsenals, however shrunk they may be, to the ability and speed with which nuclear arsenals can be reconstituted, i.e. 'the devil they don't know'. Calling for the liberation of a cultural and psychological fixation on nuclear weapons, Müller believes the arms control and disarmament process itself can be transformative in reversing the military-industrial complex's pursuit of armament and profits, which has been facilitated at times by transformative figures such as Reagan and Gorbachev – who had arrived at the same conclusion about nuclear weapons and nuclear war ('A nuclear war cannot be won and must never be fought,' said Reagan in his 1984 State of the Union address) and almost struck an agreement on abolition at the 1986 Reykjavik summit.

But how would a world without nuclear weapons rid itself of the perennial curse of security dilemmas? Müller's remedy is the formation of a concert of powers, very much like the nineteenth-century Concert of Europe, which secured a century of peace. Such a concert would fundamentally change the nature of relationships between great powers in an NWFW and should be built on the principles of equality, mutual respect for core interests, and an agreed governance structure. This concert of powers would not only provide the precondition for achieving a world free of nuclear weapons, but also serve as the enforcer of global and regional peace and stability through collective action.

Müller is correct in pointing out that, while an NWFW could benefit from the existence of conventional deterrence, unilateral and asymmetrical distribution of long-range power projection (precision strike) capabilities could actually undermine strategic stability among the major powers. One way to address this is to limit the number of long-range precision strike missiles while at the same time developing and sharing ballistic missile defences. But, perhaps most importantly, Müller notes that for an NWFW to reach fruition and be maintained a fundamental step must be taken: a change in mentality, with the development and embracing of a new norm, a culture of minimizing and eliminating a role for nuclear weapons in national security, and a real taboo against the very existence of nuclear weapons, let alone their use in any conceivable way. This reference to the inhumane nature of nuclear weapons and the call for engaging religious groups to join the campaign to rid the world of nuclear weapons resonate with the recent international efforts to 'identify and pursue effective measures to fill the legal gap for the prohibition and elimination of nuclear weapons' (Reaching Critical Will 2015).

Nuclear disarmament: a Chinese view 113

Whereas Müller's chapter focuses on how to get to a nuclear-weapons-free world, Andreas Persbo's contribution focuses on verification measures to ensure that an NWFW can be maintained, cheating detected and deterred and future nuclearizing prevented. He is less concerned with the political process of getting to zero, and more on what verification can and should do to sustain a stable zero. Persbo indicates that, in order to deal with various situations, several types of verification mechanisms and focuses will have to be put in place. He lists three: verifying arms reduction, verifying whether disarmed states remain disarmed and verifying that currently unarmed states do not arm. The first two relate to disarmament; the last one refers to non-proliferation.

Persbo raises important questions regarding verification. Should the focus of verification be on counting delivery vehicles or nuclear warheads? He indicates that, barring intrusive on-site inspections, relying solely on national technical means could hardly ensure confidence. He also reminds us that verification may encounter difficulties, as nuclear-weapon states tend to guard information regarding weapons design in terms of the quantity and composition of the material disposed of dismantled warheads. The sensitivity and secrecy surrounding the inner workings of nuclear bombs make it challenging even to confirm whether a nuclear warhead has indeed been dismantled.

Persbo's analysis also draws attention to the cost factor in nuclear disarmament and verification. It is not cheap to dismantle nuclear warheads: the work must be conducted with meticulous care and the highest level of professionalism in handling, transporting, storing and safeguarding such material. Costs can involve making disposal facilities available, training and providing competent personnel, and sufficient funds for down-blending weapons-grade fissile materials to reactor-usable fuel. Billions of dollars are needed to sustain the nuclear disarmament undertaking. The pace has already slowed down significantly in recent years, partly because existing facilities have been reaching full capacity and partly because of political reasons.

A final challenge to verification is how to ensure that the pursuit of the peaceful use of nuclear energy does not serve to promote nuclear proliferation. Given the dual-use nature of nuclear technology, there is growing concern that the 'nuclear renaissance' of recent years could lead to more countries gaining access to nuclear fuel cycle technologies, including uranium enrichment and spent-fuel reprocessing, thereby increasing the chances of nuclear proliferation – and making it imperative for the international community to maintain and strengthen safeguards measures (Ford 2010). The Iranian and North Korean nuclear issues are clear examples of such challenges. As a result, the IAEA would be required to carry out more inspections, which in turn will require more funding and additional staff. But this is not just an issue of resources and technical matters: the IAEA has typically been tasked with detecting and reporting proliferation activities – can it now be empowered to verify nuclear disarmament as well?

Challenges of the Second Nuclear Age

While the Müller and Persbo chapters provide compelling and convincing arguments on the need to go beyond traditional thinking about security and the role of nuclear weapons in order to move the nuclear zero agenda forwards, and the necessary verification measures to ensure the irreversibility of nuclear disarmament, the road to an NWFW remains littered with obstacles. One fundamental issue is the interplay between nuclear disarmament and strategic stability. Intuitively, it would seem that the two should be complementary, but in reality that is not always the case. The reduction or removal of nuclear weapons hardly make the security dilemma and great-power rivalry disappear; and, paradoxically, some military developments that ensue as a result or in anticipation of lower nuclear numbers can serve to destabilize rather than stabilize strategic balances between major powers. Thus, the idea of a concert of powers remains a state to be desired and to be pursued when and if possible – not a reality to be celebrated.

This leads to the more important question of the interrelationship between nuclear disarmament and world order. If the Cold War world order was characterized by US–Soviet rivalry, East–West confrontation and the shadow of nuclear winter if the two superpowers should come to blows, then the post-Cold War order has until recently been one dominated by US unipolarity. The rise of the rest – rapidly developing markets such as India, Brazil and Indonesia, among others, in the aftermath of the 2007–8 global financial crisis, the growing schism between Russia and the West over Ukraine, and the emerging Sino-US competition in the Indo-Pacific provide the backdrops against which nuclear disarmament and the world order must be assessed. To the extent that Washington seeks to retain its primacy, with a world order reflecting US dominance in global politics, further nuclear disarmament will become difficult, as it reinforces and prolongs the unipolar moment, especially as regards widening the gap in conventional capabilities between the USA and the rest of the world.

The issue here is how an NWFW will affect the international, regional and national security of those key players that must be involved to make it possible. Chinese perspectives on world order, for instance, advocate non-zero-sum, relative, and common security as the basis of major-power relations, and oppose any state's unilateral pursuit of absolute security at the expense of others. Indeed, Beijing considers the role of nuclear weapons in national security strategy as a more important benchmark than the numerical status of nuclear arsenals as regards the path to nuclear zero. It has persistently advocated that all nuclear-weapon states adopt a no-first-use (NFU) policy as a first step towards diminishing and eventually eliminating the role of nuclear weapons (Lewis 2014). For over five decades, China has maintained a relatively small nuclear arsenal and insisted that its engagement in multilateral nuclear disarmament is predicated on further and deeper reductions of the nuclear arsenals of Russia and the USA. While acknowledging President Obama's nuclear-free world endeavour and noting the change in the 2010 Nuclear Posture Review, Chinese analysts have also pointed to US nuclear modernization programmes and efforts in enhancing overall conventional capabilities, which in turn could undermine China's limited nuclear deterrence, rendering it less secure (Twomey 2013; Lu 2015). This concern makes the realization of a 'concert of powers' concept difficult, given the lack of mutual trust, perceived asymmetry and hence insecurity. If anything, Beijing has been actively pursuing a modernization programme precisely because it feels the need to secure a reliable nuclear deterrence that can survive a first strike by others and still retain the ability to retaliate. And that means that China is unlikely to participate in multilateral nuclear disarmament in the near term (Kulacki 2015).

Even if Beijing's security concerns could be addressed, it would remain to be seen if and when China would be willing to participate in multilateral nuclear disarmament – and, more importantly, would be ready to accept intrusive and comprehensive verification, as can be anticipated with the lower numbers of nuclear weapons. For years, Washington has sought to initiate a dialogue with Beijing on nuclear-weapons issues, but with little progress thus far. Part of the reason concerns the equivocal US attitude towards accepting mutual vulnerability in bilateral nuclear relations and its refusal to adopt NFU; for its part, China, as the weaker party and influenced by a strategic culture that emphasizes secrecy and surprise, and which is suspicious of transparency demands, would resist intrusive verification. In fact, China has never declared or confirmed the exact number of nuclear weapons it possesses and deploys, or its stockpile of weapons-grade fissile materials (Lewis 2014; Mahnken 2011).

This raises a critical issue about verification, as Persbo acknowledges – the level of intrusiveness and the reluctance or even resistance to accepting it, due to national security concerns. In addition, one precondition for verification would presumably be to determine a baseline account of a state's total inventory of nuclear warheads and weapons-grade materials, which is difficult to establish in the first place. As one recent report states, 'Such records will take time to develop, and there are currently no agreed-on mechanisms for recording, sharing, or verifying this information' (NTI 2014, 18). While Persbo's discussion of the three processes addresses many of the technical issues of verification in detailed and convincing analysis, the more challenging question remains political and is driven by security considerations: how far the nuclear-weapon states are willing to go down the path to zero; the extent to which comprehensive and intrusive verification is accepted; some degree of trust that no defection is likely to take place among disarmed parties; and the ability of the international verifying body to monitor and enforce agreed rules, backed by consensus among major powers.

Furthermore, many of the points articulated in the Müller/Persbo chapters make excellent sense in the context of the traditional superpower nuclear arms races, arms control and disarmament during the Cold War and immediately afterwards, and relate primarily to US–Russian experiences and practices. However, in the Second Nuclear Age – where more nuclear-weapon states have emerged, with varying nuclear doctrines and sizes of nuclear arsenals, each involved in various types of conflicts, ranging from territorial disputes to intense rivalry for regional dominance, and facing different and more complex deterrence relationships – the same logic may not resonate (Bracken 2012; Koblentz 2014). That said, it is also clear that nuclear proliferation often can find a convenient excuse in the slow pace of nuclear disarmament, a commitment NWS should honour as stipulated in Article 6 of the NPT (Knopf 2012/13). The 2015 NPT Review Conference has again highlighted this issue, and the chapters by Professors Müller and Persbo are a timely reminder of the linkage and its importance for the future of nuclear non-proliferation regime. As two past chairmen of the NPT Review Conferences note, the failure of the 2015 conference reflected, above all, the deep feeling of impotence on the part of most of the treaty's non-nuclear-weapon states over the failure to extract from the five recognized possessors of nuclear weapons a clear commitment to an effective, legally binding process towards nuclear disarmament in a sure, predictable and time-bound manner (Dhanapala and Duarte 2015, 8).

The first and foremost obstacle to nuclear disarmament and an NWFW remains the nuclear-weapon states themselves. Signs of slowdown, if not setback, can be observed in US–Russian implementation of strategic nuclear arms reductions. New START, signed between the USA and the Russian Federation in 2010, sets an overall limit of 1,550 strategic nuclear warheads for each country – a further 74 per cent reduction of nuclear weapons set by the 1991 START. Both Russia (January 2011) and the USA (December 2010) have ratified this new treaty. Enforcement and verification measures have been in effect, notwithstanding the recent deterioration of relations in connection with the Ukraine crisis. However, moving below 1,550 to a lower number is likely to involve major obstacles, for Russia and for the USA. Without any further reduction between the two nuclear superpowers, it is unlikely that second-tier nuclear powers like the UK, France and China will be willing to participate in multilateral nuclear disarmament negotiations (Horner and Kimball 2014).

Any further reductions of nuclear weapons in the USA and Russia will have to overcome political, security and technical hurdles. Politically, the crisis in Ukraine and US–Russia tensions have significantly narrowed the opportunities for further negotiation. For instance, in 2013 the US proposed to Russia that the two countries cut a further one-third of the numbers of strategic nuclear arsenals set by New START. This has yet to be taken up by Moscow and, given the current circumstances, it seems unlikely any time soon. At the same time, Russia has reportedly violated the 1987 US–Soviet Intermediate-Range Nuclear Forces (INF) Treaty by testing a new medium-range, ground-launched cruise missile. Moscow has raised concern over the US plan to field the Mark-41 (MK-41) missile launcher in Romania and Poland as part of its missile defence system in Europe (Collina 2014). The INF Treaty, signed in 1987 by US President Ronald Reagan and Soviet leader Mikhail Gorbachev, eliminated an entire category of weapons from the respective nuclear arsenals – in this case the 2,700 ground-based missiles with ranges between 500 and 5,500 km. The Treaty obliges the two countries to not 'possess, produce, flight-test' such missiles. Only a few years ago, the two countries had entertained the idea of multilateralizing the INF Treaty to include missiles of similar ranges in other states, including China.

The security hurdles to future nuclear disarmament can prove significant, especially given the real, perceived and evolving imbalances in the military capabilities of Russia and the USA, as well as between the USA and the other key players that need to be engaged in multilateral nuclear disarmament processes (Goodby 2010). Further deep reductions in the US and Russian nuclear arsenals might tempt some second-tier nuclear powers to seek parity. In a broader context, it has become widely accepted that nuclear disarmament, or nuclear arms control for that matter, has not and cannot become an end in itself: it must serve the objectives of achieving overall strategic stability and security for all concerned (Freedman 2009). In other words, as long as imbalances – perceived or actual – exist and are being created, further disarmament will not be possible. The US development and deployment of conventional global prompt strike (CGPS), space and missile defence capabilities introduce elements of uncertainty, cause controversies and ultimately could slow down or even derail the global nuclear disarmament process. These systems could impact the threat assessments of relevant powers, inducing similar efforts, countermeasures or both – leading to arms races in new areas. Such actions/reactions undermine strategic stability, erode trust and at times poison relations between major powers; moreover, they have yet to demonstrate their intended objectives of deterring certain groups or states from undertaking WMD-related activities, or defeating and destroying them as necessary.

Missile defences continue to be a major point of contention between the United States on the one hand and China and, to some extent, Russia, on the other, because of their negative impacts on strategic stability among these major powers. No credible solution has been found for maintaining or enhancing these systems without causing serious concerns for those other powers not ostensibly the targets of such systems. On the one hand, missile defence developments make it hard for smaller nuclear-weapon states to participate in multilateral nuclear disarmament, a critical step towards nuclear zero; on the other hand, with smaller nuclear arsenals and lower numbers, missile defences become critical in responding to any breakout and dissuading unilateral attempts to gain advantage. However, unless such systems are collectively owned – cooperative missile defences, as Müller suggests and hopes for – they would only make matters worse for nuclear disarmament. Given their utility in both offensive and defensive posture, a bold proposal would be to ban ballistic missiles altogether – along with, if not prior to, complete nuclear disarmament. But tell that to policy-makers and defence strategists (Wilkening 2010/11)! The weaponization of space, and certainly the speed and scope with which developments are taking place, pose serious problems, not only in military terms but also as regards commercial activities. An arms race into outer space would be highly deplorable, because the likely participants to engage in these ventures are also the most active users of space for economic and commercial purposes. In a world so interconnected and interdependent on critical, continuous and instantaneous communication to function, anti-satellite weapons and their use would wreak havoc with our global village.

Finally, CGPS, while itself growing out of the post-Cold War reduction of nuclear arsenals and a US defence posture less dependent on nuclear weapons, could actually reinforce and elevate the importance of nuclear weapons, especially for powers with inferior conventional capabilities that may feel threatened by the United States. While CGPS capabilities can serve to prevent nuclear proliferation, maintain deterrence and reduce the role of nuclear weapons, they also allow the USA to retain critical industrial capacities, know-how and skills for a safe, secure and reliable nuclear arsenal. However, one potential CGPS use could be linked to the Air-Sea Battle Concept in response to what has been described as growing Chinese anti-access and area-denial A2/AD capabilities, with serious consequences (Acton 2013). Indeed, US pursuit of strategic primacy (nuclear and conventional modernization, missile defences and long-range precision strike capabilities) would challenge China's long-standing nuclear strategy of assured retaliation with a relatively small nuclear arsenal. A shift in Chinese nuclear strategy oriented towards a more offensive posture would not only require building a larger inventory but also lead to uncertainties in US–China strategic stability and East Asian security (Cunningham and Fravel 2015).

The Second Nuclear Age presents serious challenges to an NWFW. This is especially the case with the Indo-Pacific, a region of divided nations, territorial disputes, emerging rivalry and great-power competition, and one without fully developed security institutions. The risks that incidents might escalate into military conflict are clear and present. This further highlights the challenges facing the region and key powers: the role of nuclear weapons, extended deterrence, WMD proliferation and crisis management in the absence and in need of confidence-building measures. Extended deterrence is indeed alive and well in this region. Paradoxically, the reduction of US nuclear arsenals only makes Washington's commitment to providing nuclear umbrellas to its allies Japan and South Korea all the more critical. The prospect of lower nuclear numbers – a necessary step towards nuclear zero – could instead result in diminishing confidence in US extended deterrence, with the unpleasant scenarios of Tokyo and Seoul pursuing nuclear weapons of their own (Moltz 2013).

The nuclear future of the Indo-Pacific remains unsettled and evolving. Unlike the Cold War superpower nuclear face-off between the USA and Russia, the region's landscape is more complex, with dyad rivalry coexisting and even interacting with triangular balancing, hedging and aligning. The region has seen steady increases in defence spending and continuing nuclear modernization programmes. The strategically important Indo-Pacific has always been an integral part of great-power competition and rivalry. Interactions involving the region's key players and extra-regional actors continue to define and shape the nature of cooperation and conflict, now more than ever (Tellis *et al.* 2014).

Nuclear weapons still feature prominently in the national security policies of many Indo-Pacific countries – informed not only by direct competition in dyads where one contender is considerably weaker in conventional terms and is thus inclined to retain and strengthen nuclear deterrence, but also driven by the need to modernize existing nuclear arsenals and their delivery systems, especially where survivability, reliability, and therefore a secure second-strike capability are concerned (Alagappa 2008). India and Pakistan, for instance, have continued to develop new systems for delivering nuclear weapons and for expanding fissile material production capacities for military purposes. And, with the deployment of the Jin-class nuclear ballistic missile submarines, China is on the verge of deploying an operational sea-based second-strike capability.

These developments and project trends towards continuing nuclear modernization in the region warrant serious discussion on two critical questions. First, can assured nuclear second-strike capabilities, as the ongoing programmes in China, India and Pakistan presumably aim at achieving, prove conducive to crisis stability and arms-race stability – or, conversely, might they undermine strategic stability in the regional and subregional contexts? Second, would such developments enable and embolden those states to undertake risky actions, or pursue more-aggressive foreign policy adventures, with the (perhaps misplaced) confidence that they can get away with such actions as their assured second-strike capabilities provide some degree of security? In other words, what impact would these have on the stability–instability paradox and extended deterrence, regarding US allies in particular (Pifer *et al.* 2010)?

In South Asia, the India–Pakistan nuclear dynamics against the backdrop of continuing and at times escalating tensions between the two are not a good recipe for peace and stability. Given their geographic proximity and therefore near-zero warning time, both India and Pakistan face enormous pressure to use or lose their limited nuclear arsenals in a time of crisis. In any event, the introduction of nuclear weapons into the subcontinent cannot contribute to stability – instead creating opportunities for actions that are deeply destabilizing. Pakistan's asymmetric escalation nuclear posture enables it to engage in revisionist, small-scale adventures without fearing major conventional military counter-attacks from India, since New Delhi is concerned that this could trigger nuclear first-use on the part of Pakistan. The inherent risk is the intentional or inadvertent use of nuclear weapons, not least since misperceptions and miscalculations abound (Ganguly and Hagerty 2006).

But it is East Asia that has policy-makers and analysts on edge, given the growing tensions between China and Japan. Beijing's announcement in late 2013 of the establishment of an air identification zone triggered strong rebukes from Washington, Tokyo and Canberra, as well as other concerned capitals. Close and dangerous US–China aerial and maritime encounters in the Western Pacific and repeated face-offs between China and Japan in the vicinity of the disputed Diaoyu/Senkaku Islands all raise troubling prospects of incidents, escalation and military confrontation. In the context of an assertive and confident China and a USA equally eager to demonstrate to its allies the credibility of its commitment and obligation, there are growing concerns that, in the absence of crisis management and confidence-building measures, displays of resolve and low-intensity conflicts could get out of control and touch off major clashes (see Goldstein

2013). For Japan in particular, this raises the difficult question of how to respond to grey-area encounters, as there is no guarantee that US nuclear deterrence extends to them. The erosive effect of such developments would be a gradual loss of confidence in the credibility of the US nuclear security umbrella, and incentives for its allies to pursue independent nuclear capabilities – as indeed they have contemplated earlier (O'Neil 2013).

Keeping the dream of an NWFW alive

The year 2015 was a critical time for global and regional nuclear disarmament and non-proliferation, crisis management and conflict prevention, and the development of mechanisms for major-power relations. While differences and disputes are inevitable and indeed could even widen, it is not a foregone conclusion that the world will be left in a helpless and dangerous state of rising geopolitics and rivalry. There remain significant degrees of common interests among key players in pursing shared goals and, at the minimum, in preventing what analysts fear will be a tragic race to 1914.

With the 2015 NPT Review Conference failing to yield a consensus document, the gap widens between the NWS and NNWS regarding the NPT Article VI commitment to nuclear disarmament. Despite this setback, it is essential that the nuclear-weapon states, the USA and Russia in particular, continue their good-faith efforts in nuclear disarmament in order to meet the 13 'practical steps' of the 2000 Review Conference and the 64-point action plan set by the 2010 Review Conference. Progress or setback on the Iranian nuclear front could have critical impacts on the prospect of a Middle East free of weapons of mass destruction. That was a resolution first introduced at the 1995 NPT Review and Extension Conference, but little progress – 'including Israeli reluctance to make compromises and to participate in the process except on its own terms' – has been made since then. Related to the 2015 RevCon are also the extent and commitments of the five permanent Security Council members (P-5) towards disarmament – including the reduction and elimination of tactical nuclear weapons, diminishing the role of nuclear weapons in security policy, and the suspension of nuclear modernization programmes. New START has further reduced the US and Russian strategic arsenals to significantly lower levels, but the non-nuclear-weapon state parties to the NPT remain unsatisfied with the pace and scope of reduction.

The recent slowdown of nuclear disarmament needs to be reversed. Whereas the chapters by Müller and by Persbo serve to reignite the debate, discuss the possibilities and push the NWFW agenda forwards, the analysis above has shown that many obstacles remain. The national security apparatuses and doctrinal adherence to nuclear deterrence and virtual arsenals continue to be resilient, stubborn … and influential (Blackwell 2015). Top-down approaches working on changing the culture and psychology of worshipping and clinging to nuclear weapons require strong leadership and willingness to commit political capital to engineer transformational results. But equally important are bottom-up initiatives and greater emphasis on humanitarian concerns over the continued existence of nuclear weapons. The normative argument against such inhumane weaponry and the mobilization of masses to get their voices heard are important, and must be part of the movement to press for an NWFW. In contrast to the antinuclear movements from the 1950s to the 1980s, today's general public seems to have lost interest in the abolition of nuclear weapons (Wilson 2015). This must be changed.

Bibliography

Acton, J.M. (2013) *Silver Bullet? Asking the Right Questions About Conventional Prompt Global Strike*. Washington, DC: Carnegie Endowment for International Peace.
Alagappa, M. (ed.) (2008) *The Long Shadow: Nuclear Weapons and Security in 21st Century Asia*. Stanford, CA: Stanford University Press.
BBC (2015) *Putin: Russia to Boost Nuclear Arsenal by 40 Missiles*. [Online] 15 June. Available from: www.bbc.com/news/world-33151125.
Blackwell, J. (2015) The Bomb That Keeps on Ticking. And Keeps Us Safe. *Comparative Strategy*, December: 458–468.
Bracken, P. (2012) *The Second Nuclear Age: Strategy, Danger, and the New Power Politics*. New York: Times Books.
Collina, T.Z. (2014) U.S. Raises INF Concerns with Russia. *Arms Control Association*. [Online] 4 March. Available from: www.armscontrol.org/act/2013_03/US-Raises-INF-Concerns [accessed 5 February 2016].
Cortright, D. and Väyrynen, R. (2010) *Toward Nuclear Zero*. London: Routledge.
Cunningham, F. and Fravel, M.T. (2015) Assured Retaliation: China's Nuclear Posture and U.S.–China Strategic Stability. *International Security*, Fall: 7–50.
Dhanapala, J. and Duarte, S. (2015) Is There a Future for the NPT? *Arms Control Today*, July/August: 8–10.
Ford, C.A. (2010) Why Not Nuclear Disarmament? *The New Atlantis*, Spring: 3–20.
Freedman, L. (2009) A New Theory for Nuclear Disarmament. *Bulletin of the Atomic Scientists*, July/August: 14–30.
Ganguly, S. and Hagerty, D.T. (2006) *Fearful Symmetry: India–Pakistan Crises in the Shadow of Nuclear Weapons*. Seattle: University of Washington Press.
Goldstein, A. (2013) First Things First: The Pressing Danger of Crisis Instability in U.S.–China Relations. *International Security*, 37(4): 49–89.
Goodby, J.E. (2010) A World Without Nuclear Weapons: Fantasy or Necessity? In *SIPRI Yearbook 2010: Armaments, Disarmament and International Security* (pp. 17–34). Oxford: Oxford University Press for SIPRI.
Horner, D. and Kimball, D.G. (2014) Arms Control in the Near Term: An Interview with Undersecretary of State Rose Gottemoeller. *Arms Control Today*, 44(9): 8–15.
Knopf, J.W. (2012/13) Nuclear Disarmament and Nonproliferation: Examining the Linkage Argument. *International Security*, 37(3): 92–132.
Koblentz, G.D. (2014) *Strategic Stability in the Second Nuclear Age*. Council Special Report No. 71, New York and Washington, DC: Council on Foreign Relations.
Kristensen, H.M. and Norris, R.S. (2014) Slowing Nuclear Weapon Reductions and Endless Nuclear Weapon Modernizations: A Challenge to the NPT. *Bulletin of the Atomic Scientists*, 70(4): 97–107.
Kulacki, G. (2015) *The Chinese Military Updates China's Nuclear Strategy*. Boston, MA: Union of Concerned Scientists.

Lewis, J. (2014) *Paper Tigers: China's Nuclear Posture*, Adelphi Paper 446. London: International Institute for Strategic Studies.

Lu, Y. (2015) How to Approach Nuclear Modernization?: A Chinese Perspective. *Bulletin of the Atomic Scientists*, 71(3): 8–11.

Mahnken, T.G. (2011) *Secrecy and Stratagem: Understanding Chinese Strategic Culture*. Sydney: Lowy Institute for International Policy.

Mecklin, J. (2015) Disarm and Modernize. *Foreign Policy*, March/April: 54–59.

Moltz, J.C. 2013. Regional Perspectives on Low Nuclear Numbers: An Overview. *Nonproliferation Review*, 20(2): 195–204.

NTI (2014) *Innovating Verification: New Tools & New Actors to Reduce Nuclear Risks*. Washington, DC: Nuclear Threat Initiative.

O'Neil, A. (2013) *Asia, the US and Extended Nuclear Deterrence: Atomic Umbrellas in the Twenty-First Century*. London: Routledge.

Pifer, S., Bush, R.C. III, Felbab-Brown, V., Indyk, M.S., O'Hanlon, M.E. and Pollack, K.M. (2010) *U.S. Nuclear and Extended Deterrence: Considerations and Challenges*. Washington, DC: The Brookings Institution.

Reaching Critical Will. (2015) Article 36. Filling the Legal Gap: The Prohibition of Nuclear Weapons. [Online] available from: www.article36.org/wp-content/uploads/2015/05/A36-RCW-gaps-table-updated.pdf.

Shultz, G.P., Perry, W.J., Kissinger, H.A and Nunn, S. (2007) A World Free of Nuclear Weapons. *Wall Street Journal*, 4 January.

Tellis, A.J., Denmark, A.M. and Tanner, T. (eds) (2014) *Strategic Asia 2013–14: Asia in the Second Nuclear Age*. Seattle, WA, and Washington, DC: National Bureau of Asian Research.

Twomey, C.P. (2013) Nuclear Stability at Low Numbers: The Perspective from Beijing. *Nonproliferation Review*, 20(2): 289–303.

Wilkening, D.A. (2010/11) Nuclear Zero and Ballistic-Missile Defence. *Survival*, 52 (December 2010–January 2011): 107–126.

Wilson, W. (2015) Why Are There No Big Nuke Protests? *Bulletin of the Atomic Scientists*, 71(2): 50–59.

9 Stable at zero
Deterrence and verification

Patricia Lewis

The question about the future of nuclear weapons plagues a growing set of people who worry about the future of the world. And so it should. Nuclear weapons are qualitatively different in their effect to all other weapons that have been invented, deployed and used. And, although they have been reduced in numbers since the end of the Cold War, they still play a central role in the security postures of the possessor of nuclear weapons. Those in nuclear alliances with the United States (NATO allies, Japan, Australia and South Korea, for example) likewise place US nuclear forces in a central role in their defence planning. Unless we prise open the emotional attachment to nuclear weapons, rethink nuclear deterrence and understand the fears that nuclear disarmament would bring – and put in place measures to reduce the risks those fears portray – we are doomed to be in their thrall until they are used again.

The energy that is released in breaking and forming nuclear bonds are millions of times greater than the energy associated with molecular reactions in conventional explosives. The energy contained in a nuclear explosion has blast and heat effects orders of magnitude greater than conventional explosives, with the addition of a massive release of highly damaging prompt radiation and long-term deposits of radioactive isotopes that could spread far and wide (fallout). Depending on where and how many nuclear weapons explode, there is also a significant risk of long-term impact on global agriculture and food production due to soot particulates in the atmosphere blocking out sunlight. The numbers of people who would be killed, be maimed and suffer as a result of the use of nuclear weapons in populated areas far surpass those of conventional explosions in terms of numbers and degree of inhumane suffering. Indeed, one of the questions implicit in Andreas Persbo's paper is: will our era be known as the nuclear age, as our ancestors' are now described by the terms stone, bronze and iron?

One thing is certain; the effects of nuclear weapons are so devastating, so inhumane, that to use them again would be against the dictates of the public conscience. As Harald Müller strongly articulates, the framing of the nuclear weapons problem as a humanitarian issue makes complete sense. Chemical weapons and biological weapons have been banned on grounds of their inhumane, uncivilized effects; surely the case for banning nuclear weapons on the same basis is obvious. Many weapons systems and human behaviours have been banned as a result of their inhumane and devastating long-term impact on individuals and societies. Anti-personnel landmines and cluster munitions have been banned through treaties that have their roots in international humanitarian law (IHL). 2015 marked the centenary of the first massive use of chemical weapons on the battlefield of Ypres in World War I, which led to the 1925 Geneva Protocol that banned the use of chemical and biological weapons in conflict, which in turn led to the 1972 (biological) and 1993 (chemical) weapons conventions. Indeed, IHL is a barometer of the taboo effect.

A taboo, as discussed by Harald Müller, is (1) something forbidden because of what are believed to be dangerous supernatural powers; (2) banned on grounds of morality or distaste; and (3) banned as constituting a risk. There are a number of behaviours that can be considered taboo across cultures: incest, cannibalism, torture, murder and so on. But, however strongly held, taboos are broken. People commit heinous crimes even though such behaviours are strictly forbidden in their societies. So, although the use of nuclear weapons is often described as a taboo, such castigation may not be sufficient to prevent a future detonation and also may not hold in each nuclear weapon-possessing country.

Within IHL, the concept of taboo is expressed as the public conscience in the Martens clause in the preamble to the 1899 Convention (II) with Respect to the Laws and Customs of War on Land (ICRC 1899):

> Until a more complete code of the laws of war is issued, the High Contracting Parties think it right to declare that in cases not included in the Regulations adopted by them, populations and belligerents remain under the protection and empire of the principles of international law, as they result from the usages established between civilized nations, from the laws of humanity, and the requirements of the public conscience.

Also, in Protocol I, Additional to the Geneva Conventions of 12 August 1949 (ICRC 1977):

> Article 1.2: In cases not covered by this Protocol or by other international agreements, civilians and combatants remain under the protection and authority of the principles of international law derived from established custom, from the principles of humanity and from the dictates of public conscience.

The Martens clause enables the principles of international law, 'as they result from the usages established between civilized nations, from the laws of humanity, and the requirements of the public conscience', to be applied to cases and systems not covered by specific international agreements.

The 1977 Protocol I to the 1949 Geneva Conventions of 12 August 1949, relating to the Protection of Victims of International Armed Conflicts, specifically states that:

1   In any armed conflict, the right of the Parties to the conflict to choose methods or means of warfare is not unlimited.
2   It is prohibited to employ weapons, projectiles and material and methods of warfare of a nature to cause superfluous injury or unnecessary suffering.
3   It is prohibited to employ methods or means of warfare which are intended, or may be expected, to cause widespread, long-term and severe damage to the natural environment.

All of these restrictions apply to nuclear weapons. Nuclear weapons are inherently indiscriminate and will inflict unnecessary suffering that would violate any sense of decency or dictates and requirements of the public conscience. Indeed, if we look to the disgust and repugnance at the massive use of chemical weapons by Iraq in the 1980s and Syria since 2013 and how the 1925 Geneva Protocol and the 1993 Chemical Weapons Convention were applied, we can imagine how the world would be repulsed by the effect of a single use of a nuclear weapon in a densely populated area.

In 1996 in a landmark ruling, the International Court of Justice issued an Advisory Opinion on the Legality of the Threat or Use of Nuclear Weapons. The court examined current treaty law, customary law rules and state practice with regard to nuclear weapons and concluded unanimously that the principles and rules of international humanitarian law apply to the use of nuclear weapons. They added that: '... the threat or use of nuclear weapons would generally be contrary to the rules of international law applicable in armed conflict, and in particular the principles and rules of humanitarian law'.

The International Committee of the Red Cross (ICRC), the International Federation of the Red Cross (IFRC) and the Red Crescent Societies have taken up the issue with increased urgency and intensity in recent years. In 2011, the Council of Delegates passed a resolution[1] concerning the destructive power of nuclear weapons, the unspeakable human suffering they cause, the difficulty of controlling their effects in space and time, the threat they pose to the environment and to future generations and the risks of escalation they create, the continued retention of tens of thousands of nuclear warheads, the proliferation of such weapons and the constant risk that they could again be used. The delegates appealed to all states to ensure that nuclear weapons are never again used and to pursue in good faith and conclude with urgency and determination negotiations to prohibit the use of and completely eliminate nuclear weapons. Under the framework of humanitarian diplomacy, the Red Cross and Red Crescent Movement was called on to raise awareness of the catastrophic humanitarian consequences of any use of nuclear weapons, the international humanitarian law issues that arise from such use, and the need for concrete actions leading to the prohibition of use and elimination of such weapons and to engage in continuous dialogue with governments and other relevant actors on the humanitarian and international humanitarian law issues associated with nuclear weapons. Since then, the ICRC and the IFRC and the national societies have been active in studying possible responses to nuclear detonations, training delegates and attending international conferences.

The 2013 and 2014 Conferences on the Humanitarian Impact of Nuclear Weapons in Oslo, Nayarit and Vienna framed nuclear weapons from the perspective of humanitarian action and thus engaged a whole new set of participants and experts drawn from the humanitarian, health and development communities that includes a significant number of young people. The conferences have led to the 'humanitarian pledge' issued at the Vienna Conference in December 2014, in which states committed to 'follow the imperative of human security for all and to promote the protection of civilians against risks stemming from nuclear weapons' and to 'cooperate with all relevant stakeholders ... in efforts to stigmatise, prohibit and eliminate nuclear weapons in light of their unacceptable humanitarian consequences and associated risks' (Federal Ministry of the Republic of Austria 2014). By June 2016, 127 states had formally endorsed the pledge (ICAN 2015). A year after the conference, on 7 December 2015, the UN General Assembly adopted Resolution 70/48 (A/RES/70/48) on the humanitarian pledge for the prohibition and elimination of nuclear weapons, with 139 in favour, 29 against and 17 abstentions (UNGA 2015).

Reframing nuclear weapons issues from the perspective of humanitarian action is enabling a fresh injection of ideas quite separate from the stale discourse of deterrence and non-proliferation. Nuclear deterrence as a construct of belief relies on several premises that may or may not have held in the decades of the Cold War but are unlikely to hold for today's complexities or for the future.

There are huge fears about the spread of nuclear weapons to countries such as North Korea and to non-state actors. Sustained efforts were invested in talks with Iran to prevent another militarized nuclear programme in the Middle East. At the same time, the very countries that worked to dissuade Iran from developing nuclear weapons stress to their domestic audiences and allies that nuclear weapons are fundamental to their security and must be retained as a hedge against an uncertain future. Nuclear-weapons-possessors and their allies reassure others that the weapons are employed solely as a deterrent to would-be attackers and thus they server to prevent conflict. Nuclear weapons are said to have 'kept the peace' from 1945 and provide extended deterrence to nuclear alliances, thus also preventing regional war.

The problem with this belief system is that if nuclear weapons are such marvels that the threat of their use guarantees security and prevents conflict, why on earth would anyone want to give them up and – the obvious next question – why shouldn't everyone have them? Indeed, nuclear-weapons-possessors and their allies are fearful that nuclear disarmament would result in catastrophic conventional war. And, at the same time, they would have the rest of the world believe that they desire nuclear disarmament and are working seriously towards it. These two contradictory beliefs are fostering confusion and mistrust with the NPT and the international community. Nobody knows quite what or who to believe any more.

The continuing belief in nuclear deterrence is also contributing to nuclear proliferation. We learn from each other through imitation; it is how humans have developed as societies. It is how we have built cities and cultures. When we see somebody doing or making something useful, interesting and fun, we tend to copy and adapt it for our own needs. From the humble wheel to the smartphone, we innovate, imitate and adapt. What I see others having I want. When I have something desirable, it gives me status and others want what I have – even more so if they are denied it. We link possessions and services to ideas of social status and imbue them with senses of fairness or resentment. This seems to occur throughout human societies and in other animal groups too (de Waal 2011). And the higher the social status of the innovator or possessor, the more we are likely to aspire to possess the same things. For example, Bill Gates recently promoted an out of print book: 'Business Adventures remains the best business book I've ever read', Gates wrote. 'John Brooks is still my favorite business writer' (Tobar 2014). Almost immediately, demand for the book rocketed and there was a run on second-hand copies to the point of scarcity. The family of the now-deceased Brooks agreed to make *Business Adventures* available as an e-book and it has soared to new heights of popularity and has gone back into hard copy.

Even when the object or practice is against our health, safety and financial security, we will still imitate and adopt if it accords status: witness foot-binding, extreme plastic surgery and people purchasing expensive cars and houses that they cannot afford. The imitation of royalty has been a practice throughout recorded human history. In the 1860s, on marrying the Prince of Wales, Alexandra of Denmark sparked many a fashion in the British Isles, including imitating her pronounced limp through deliberately wearing shoes of different heights.

This is how the fashion industry works, as do the car and watch industries and so on. The powerful set trends. Film stars and popular singers sell everything from coffee to perfume because people imagine that, if they have the same things, they will somehow be conferred with connected status. Marketing departments and advertising agencies know this and know how to get us to want to buy stuff. Likewise, when all five of the permanent members of the UN Security Council say that they need to hang on to nuclear weapons, for their long-term security, we are likely to see over a period of time other insecure and vulnerable countries who will – wanting to be like them or to be seen to be like them – believe the theories of nuclear deterrence and put their faith in nuclear protection.

Nuclear weapons experts fall into one of three camps: (1) believers in nuclear deterrence as an effective way to stay the hand and prevent war through a fear of what might ensue; (2) sceptics of nuclear deterrence who question the validity of the nuclear deterrence framework in today's security environments (many of whom also challenge the validity of nuclear deterrence throughout the Cold War); and (3) those who remain unsure about whether nuclear weapons can provide an effective deterrence but determine that the risk of nuclear use is too high to support.

Harald Müller rightly identifies the persistence of the Cold War construct of nuclear deterrence as the key obstacle to nuclear disarmament. States that have developed and possess nuclear weapons often characterize them as tools to deter aggression in others. The requirement for extended nuclear weapons commitments within NATO and in Asia (Australia, Japan and South Korea) is an obstacle to nuclear disarmament. How is it possible for states that openly declare their reliance on nuclear weapons for their security to be taken seriously in calling for nuclear disarmament?

The construct of nuclear deterrence as an 'ultimate guarantee' is the very attribute that increases their attractiveness to weak and vulnerable states. The dominant narrative of nuclear deterrence can act as a driver for further proliferation, so that nuclear deterrence, instead of being a mechanism for the prevention of war, could be a contributory factor to the spread of the future use of nuclear weapons.

Nuclear deterrence may seem to be the 'sturdy child' of the nuclear era but it may be more aptly described as the sickly child, found wanting in physical and intellectual prowess, overprotected by parents who shield their offspring from exposure to the rough and tumble of the real world. Nuclear deterrence may be thought of as Anne, daughter of Lady Catherine de Bourgh in Jane Austen's *Pride and Prejudice*: the spindly child who is endowed with noble titles and vast amount of money goes through life in the cosseted halls of private schools, with indulgent professors who seek the patronage of the family title and whose inadequacies are overlooked, including by suitors who are prepared to marry solely for money and prestige.

So what to do?

Strategic and military planners are unlikely to ever agree (and, if they are truthful, be certain themselves) on the long-term deterrence effects of nuclear weapons. We can agree on the effects of their use and the horrors that would be unleashed if they were to be used again in conflict on populated areas. For this reason, their possession has been restricted. Only a very few of the of the 'true believers' in nuclear deterrence would go as far as Kenneth Waltz (2002) in saying that more countries should be allowed to possess nuclear weapons in order to stabilize regional insecurities. Most analysts and politicians do not think that the acquisition of nuclear weapons by North Korea has increased regional security or that Iran's acquisition would improve Middle East security. And the vehicle for ensuring that nuclear weapons do not proliferate is the Non-Proliferation Treaty, by which the 189 state parties have agreed to a set of provisions to prevent and verify non-proliferation and the eventual elimination of nuclear weapons. Only three states (India, Israel and Pakistan) have remained outside the treaty and have developed nuclear weapons capabilities.

So, whatever the beliefs and conceptual frameworks imbedded in the nuclear postures of the nuclear-weapon states and nuclear allies, they have committed themselves under international law to nuclear disarmament. So the question that begs to be answered is why few resources are invested in disarmament technologies, methodologies and negotiations compared with the resources invested in the armaments themselves? Nuclear-weapons-possessors produce regular plans for modernization, deployment and postures, but they don't produce the same set sorts of plans for nuclear disarmament. Where is the serious investment in verification technologies? The UK and the US have made some effort, along with Norway and VERTIC and the international treaty organizations IAEA, OPCW and CTBTO. However, as Andreas Persbo points out, so far the efforts devoted to solving the verification challenges have been inadequate, leaving the arms control and disarmament communities – inside and outside governments – in a state of perpetual unpreparedness.

The focus of Andreas Persbo's chapter is on the end-state of disarmament and how to lock it in so that it is irreversible – a significant confidence-building feature. He estimates that the dismantlement process is likely to take about 20 years – experience from the Chemical Weapons Convention suggests that it may take longer but – with the notable exception of Syria in 2013 – states with chemical weapons have not been incorporating them in their military planning since the CWC took effect. This is likely to be true in the event of a nuclear weapons treaty, whatever form it takes (a ban, a prohibition or a convention) – nuclear weapons will quickly become discounted as actual usable weapons in the arsenals of the possessing states once it is agreed to dispose of them under a legally binding treaty.

The foundations for verifying nuclear disarmament have already been laid, but nobody seems to be thinking about how to build the house, where the windows and doors will go and what sort of roof to have, let alone what would be kept in there and safeguarded.

The UK, the US and Norway have led the world in investing in nuclear disarmament and verification technologies. In 2007, the UK Foreign Secretary Margaret Beckett spoke at the Carnegie conference, where she called on the UK to become a 'disarmament laboratory' for the world. On 5 February 2008, the UK Defence Secretary Des Browne in a landmark speech at the Conference on Disarmament in Geneva outlined ideas for the UK to become 'a role model and testing ground' for key aspects of disarmament, including related technical research.

In 2008 at the Royal Society, British Pugwash, on the occasion of the centennial celebration of Sir Joseph Rotblat's birthday, took forwards the concept of a disarmament laboratory and the UK government responded by proposing a 'National Nuclear Centre of Excellence' with an initial funding of £20m, which incorporated disarmament and arms control objectives. With changes in political power, however, little has come of the idea, but British Pugwash is determined to develop the idea further and is proposing to help establish a British International Nuclear Disarmament Institute (BRINDI). It may be that future UK governments will embrace the idea again or perhaps the P-5 discussions that have so far yielded very little could be used to set up an international disarmament laboratory, based in Vienna, to harness the expertise at the IAEA and the CTBTO.

In the end, both Andreas Persbo and Harald Müller call for the sort of courageous leadership that we rarely see in today's political circles. In Prague in 2009, President Obama gave rise to hopes that we would see that sort of leadership blossoming in the United States but, because of domestic hamstrings and international events, he has little to show bar the Nuclear Security Summits and a visit to Hiroshima – all very important, of course, but hardly the visionary world free of nuclear weapons he promised, however long term. It is not too late to re-energize efforts towards a world without nuclear weapons. This won't be a world without war – we certainly do not have that with nuclear weapons – it will be a world without nuclear war. Not a bad idea at all.

Note

1 Working towards the elimination of nuclear weapons (ICRC 2011).

Bibliography

de Waal, F. (2011) Monkeys Join Wall Street Protest, *Huffington Post*, 10 November. [Online] available from: www.huffingtonpost.com/frans-de-waal/monkeys-join-wall-street-_b_1004370.html.

Federal Ministry of the Republic of Austria (2014) *The Humanitarian Pledge*. 9 December 2014, Vienna, Austria. [Online] available from: www.bmeia.gv.at/en/european-foreign-policy/disarmament/weapons-of-mass-destruction/nuclear-weapons-and-nuclear-terrorism/vienna-conference-on-the-humanitarian-impact-of-nuclear-weapons.

ICAN [International Campaign to Abolish Nuclear Weapons] (2015) Humanitarian Pledge. [Online] available from: www.icanw.org/pledge.

ICRC [International Committee of the Red Cross] (1899) Convention (II) with Respect to the Laws and Customs of War on Land and its annex: Regulations concerning the Laws and Customs of War on Land. The Hague, 29 July 1899. [Online] Available from: www.icrc.org/applic/ihl/ihl.nsf/Article.xsp?action=openDocument&documentId=9FE084CDAC63D10FC12563CD00515C4D.

ICRC [International Committee of the Red Cross] (1977) Protocol I, Additional to the Geneva Conventions of 12 August 1949, and relating to the Protection of Victims of International Armed Conflicts, 8 June 1977. [Online] available from: www.icrc.org/applic/ihl/ihl.nsf/Article.xsp?action=openDocument&documentId=6C86520D7EFAD527C12563CD0051D63C.

ICRC [International Committee of the Red Cross] (2011) Working towards the elimination of nuclear weapons, Council of Delegates of the International Red Cross and Red Crescent Movement, Geneva, Switzerland, 26 November 2011. [Online] available from: www.icrc.org/eng/resources/documents/resolution/council-delegates-resolution-1-2011.htm.

Tobar, H. (2014) Bill Gates resurrects 45-year-old book 'Business Adventures'. *Los Angeles Times*. [Online] available from: www.latimes.com/books/jacketcopy/la-et-jc-bill-gates-resurrects-business-adventures-20140715-story.html.

UNGA [United Nations General Assembly] (2015) A/RES/70/48. Humanitarian pledge for the prohibition and elimination of nuclear weapons. [Online] available from: www.un.org/en/ga/search/view_doc.asp?symbol=A/RES/70/48.

Waltz, K. (2002) Why Iran should get the bomb: nuclear balancing would mean stability. *Foreign Affairs*, July/August. [Online] available from: www.foreignaffairs.com/articles/137731/kenneth-n-waltz/why-iran-should-get-the-bomb.

Part III
Summary and conclusions

10 The vision and its implications for disarmament policy[1]

Sverre Lodgaard

> To discover new oceans, one must have the courage to lose sight of the shore
> (André Gide)

When Ronald Reagan and Mikhail Gorbachev discussed the elimination of nuclear weapons in Reykjavik, they seemed to take the consent of the other NWS for granted. Or they assumed that any objections would be overruled: others simply had to follow the lead of the two big ones. No reference is made to other NWS in the US and Soviet memoranda of conversation, or in the accounts of the discussions by Reagan, Shultz, Gorbachev and Dobrynin. This speaks to a fundamental feature of the Cold War: without a shred of doubt, the superpowers were dominant, certainly in their own eyes and most probably also in those of others. The other NWS were mere appendices to the bilateral dimension of the world order.

At the time, there were six NWS – the five veto powers of the UN Security Council plus Israel. Today, nine states possess nuclear weapons. A multicentric world has replaced the bipolar order, complicating the task of nuclear abolition. No longer can the others be subordinated to the two, and the strategic logic is not the same in all dyads. Non-governmental networks may also get hold of nuclear materials, and seizure of ready-made bombs cannot be excluded. When – 20 years after Reykjavik – the four US statesmen (Shultz, Nunn, Kissinger, Perry) revived the vision of a nuclear-weapon-free world (NWFW), they worried that the world of nuclear weapons had become too dangerous.

In Asia, furthermore, there is the view that nuclear weapons can be potent equalizers between a strong state and a much weaker one. With the Russian annexation of Crimea came similar claims: if Ukraine had kept the nuclear weapons that were on its soil when the Soviet Union broke down, Russia would have been deterred. As tensions between Russia and the West intensified, the Kremlin, too, accentuated that logic. Confronted with a conventionally superior NATO on its borders, Russia found nuclear weapons useful both domestically and internationally: domestically to mark strength in a nationalistic political setting; internationally to underline vital national interests. However ill-founded such arguments can be – the first use of nuclear weapons can bring terrible punishment at the hand of stronger opponents; Ukrainians never broke the Soviet codes – they can translate into realities, for security policies are based on perceptions and perceptions are fuelled by cultural codes, historical circumstances, national sentiments and personal preferences. There is much more to the matter than rational actor models can explain.

Today, the USA and Russia are modernizing their arsenals while the Asian NWS are expanding theirs. Since the conclusion of New START in 2010, there have been no disarmament negotiations. The international arms control regime, which has limited existing nuclear arsenals and the proliferation of nuclear arms, is under pressure. Thomas Schelling, one of the founders of arms control and a leading analyst of international security for more than half a century, nevertheless characterizes contemporary security affairs as a state of 'nuclear quiet'.[2] Compared with the frantic arms-racing of the Cold War, when East–West relations sometimes boiled down to little more than nuclear-weapon accountancy and related policy debates, this is understandable.

Equally understandable are Manpreet Sethi's concerns about the ongoing build-up and instabilities in Asia, where the trend is moving from worrisome to worse. The Asian NWS are geographically close, even bordering each other, whereas the USA and the Soviet Union were 5,000 km apart; China, India and Pakistan have territorial conflicts, while the USA and the Soviet Union had none (they fought wars in other parts of the world, but by proxy); in none of the Asian dyads has there been a consistent, long-term interest in arms control; North Korea and Pakistan are shifting back and forth between stability pursuits and brinkmanship; and there are lingering concerns about the security of Pakistani weapons because of the fragility of the regime and of terrorist activities in and around Pakistan. To Sethi, Asia is all but 'quiet'.

Nuclear weapons and major war

Except for the latest seven decades, mankind has lived without nuclear weapons, and wars have been fought over and over again. In the twentieth century, modern technologies made it possible to wage *world* wars – two of them in rapid succession. However, after the end of the Second World War there has been no major war between the leading powers. No Third World War.

One explanation, near at hand, assigns the absence of major war to the new factor in the equation – the nuclear weapon, which instils caution in the minds of leaders. This has been a matter of consolation, especially for those who experienced the horrors of the world wars. Obviously, the correlation may be spurious, and there is much to suggest that it is. On many occasions, the world has been on the edge of nuclear catastrophe by technical failure. Studies of these events, made possible as national archives have been declassified, have found significant elements of good luck in some of the fortunate outcomes. Yet the belief persists: nuclear weapons have kept war among the major powers at bay.

The sceptics of nuclear disarmament hold that things could have been worse. They argue that nuclear weapons have 'kept the peace'. By contrast, the proponents argue that the likelihood of nuclear war is unacceptably high and quite possibly growing, making it imperative to seek a world without these weapons. These are matters of belief, however: when they are framed in such terms, there is no rational choice [Sokov, Chapter 4].

For the sceptics, a functional equivalent must be found to the role of nuclear weapons in preventing a major new war. Thomas Schelling questions the wisdom of going to zero on that basis. What would happen in the event of another major war? Of course, one should hope that such wars would not happen in a world without nuclear arms, but they always did, and in a denuclearized world there would be a rush to rebuild and use nuclear weapons. In emphasizing the need to renounce war, the Russell–Einstein Manifesto on nuclear weapons, issued in 1955, argued along the same lines: '... Agreements ... reached in time of peace ... would no longer be considered binding in time of war, and both sides would set to work to manufacture H-bombs as soon as war broke out' (Wikipedia n.d.). In the starkest of terms, the Manifesto therefore presented two alternatives: find a way to abolish war, or the human race will come to an end.

However, while agreeing on the cardinal importance of avoiding major war, Schelling's understanding of the state of security affairs is very different from that of the Manifesto. He emphasizes the intellectual and practical efforts that have gone into the study and promotion of stability in a nuclear deterrence world, and recommends caution, so as not to throw the (arms control) baby out with the (nuclear weapons) bathwater. Similarly, he warns, thorough examination should be made of the dynamics of an NWFW, to clarify if it is feasible and realistic and superior to a world with (some) nuclear weapons. Would such a world be more secure than a nuclear deterrence world with security optimized by means of arms control? By contrast, the Pugwash Conferences on Science and World Affairs – the heir to the Manifesto and founded by some of its co-signatories – put the thrust on elimination: find a way to coexist without nuclear weapons, or perish.

History cannot tell us whether, in an NWFW, war will be more likely or less. Nor can assumptions about the transformative power of disarmament processes provide any definitive answers. For sure, doing away with nuclear weapons will require a great deal of cooperation between the major powers. Trust will be built on the way, so, most probably, the likelihood of major war will diminish. However, such a world is far away, and many unknowns – political and technological – may work in other directions, so the prudent position is the agnostic one.

The questions discussed in this book are therefore narrower. What does it take to make the world safe from *nuclear* war? What are the requirements of *stable* nuclear zero? How can the vision be a guide to action? If the major powers were to go to war again – and here there can be no guarantee – preventing nuclear apocalypse would be quite an achievement.

Stable nuclear zero

The vision

Schelling discusses a world where operational nuclear weapons have disappeared while the rest remains basically the same. In his conception of an NWFW, states maintain capabilities for the rapid reconstitution of nuclear weapons. Nuclear deterrence still applies, in virtual form, so the mentality that nuclear war might happen is still there. The assumption that another war would trigger a rush to rebuild and use nuclear weapons seems premised on US experience and behaviour in the run-up to and during the Second World War [Sethi, Chapter 2].

In response, Harald Müller emphasizes that elimination is a matter of large-scale political re-engineering, bound to progress in many small steps [Müller, Chapter 3]. To argue that, on the way to zero, everything else remains unchanged is fundamentally flawed. Throughout, it is essential to be mindful of the path-dependence of nuclear disarmament.

Some proponents of an NWFW also seem to accept the need for reconstitution capabilities. Others have chosen, for tactical reasons, to leave the question aside, so as not to overburden disarmament campaigns. Yet others favour versions where the capabilities are subject to *some* restrictions. Jim Goodby, for instance, has indicated that, to minimize the risk of breakout, the nations will have to agree on the answers to three important questions: what the necessary elements of an adequate reconstitution capability are; what activities, facilities or weapons-related items should be prohibited; and what can be done to assure early and reliable warning of a breakout attempt (Drell and Goodby 2009).

Going below zero is therefore a matter of more or less. The critical question is what it takes to get to *stable* zero. Analogous to the concept of a security community, originally introduced by Karl Deutsch (1962) in reference to the Nordic countries, stable zero is not a condition where the reintroduction of nuclear arms may be considered but is found inappropriate; it is a condition where resort to nuclear weapons has disappeared from the agenda. The ultimate objective can be defined in such terms.

The instabilities of a world of reconstitution capabilities and virtual deterrence, where nothing much has changed save for the elimination of operational nuclear weapons, are obvious. This would be a world of threshold states – and, assuming that the rights and obligations would be the same for all, their number might be higher than the current number of NWS. Müller, seconded by Jingdong Yuan, stresses the logical flaws of such versions: it is simply not plausible that governments that believe they need nuclear capabilities for the sake of deterrence would make the final move to elimination [Yuan, Chapter 8]. Rather than going for virtual capabilities, with which they are unfamiliar, they would stay with their remaining operational weapons, which they trust. As long as they feel that they need a deterrent, it is better to rely on the devil they know – operational weapons – than switch to the devil with which they have no experience – virtual capabilities.

In the following, we proceed from the assumption that, in order to make an NWFW stably non-nuclear, one must go in for more than merely eliminating the weapons as such. The aim must be to eliminate the fissile materials that have been dedicated to nuclear explosive uses; to institute strict international control of remaining materials; to dismantle the nuclear weapons infrastructure; and to redirect the workforce to other sectors. Nuclear materials that can be used to build weapons should be banned from civilian use as well. Highly enriched uranium (HEU) is not the big issue here – there is little HEU left in the civilian sector and what remains is being phased out – but plutonium continues to pose a problem. Technical fixes may or may not solve this: if not, a compromise must be struck to accommodate the civilian industry.

Not only do we assume that, in an NWFW, peaceful applications of nuclear energy would continue. Generally, such a world is likely to provide a more beneficial setting for nuclear industry, as suspicions that peaceful activities may be misused for military ends would have been much reduced. Despite the constraints that may be imposed on it, its representatives are therefore likely to welcome the elimination of nuclear weapons.

Others have emphasized that a world without nuclear weapons would be more sustainable as part of a double abolition: an end both to nuclear weapons and to nuclear energy. However, much like the compromise between the 'no' to nuclear weapons and the 'yes' to nuclear power built into the NPT, an NWFW is likely to entail the same dualism. If and when an NWFW comes into being, the energy situation may be much different from what it is today – but, if we want the vision to gain momentum, to demand an end to nuclear power is self-defeating. Restraints on peaceful applications by the haves were always seen as unacceptable discrimination by the great majority of have-nots, and that sentiment shows no sign of abating. Still, the links between peaceful and military applications are so substantial that some constraints must be agreed to make peaceful uses more proliferation-resistant; stringent safeguards have to be applied; and conventional enforcement capabilities must be erected to deter and stop potential rule-breakers.

However, had it only been for these and other material constraints, the world might not appear convincingly nuclear weapon-free. Not quite, for it would leave the impression that the constraints are necessary to stem reconstitution pressures. Therefore, to be convincingly stable, the security culture must be changed as well, in a way that makes nuclear options anathema. In a metaphorical sense the aim must be to make nuclear weapons *taboo* (see below).

International political order requirements

To get to an NWFW, there must be a qualitative shift in international security affairs. First of all, deterrence will have to yield in favour of cooperative security and common security thinking. Today, it is the other way around: nuclear deterrence is the name of the game, with cooperative security a mere add-on. Only by reversing the priorities can we build the 'mental springboard' from which states may dare to leap into a world without nuclear weapons [Müller, Chapter 5].

Disarmament is likely to be a protracted process passing through many stages. Actors have to create the political conditions for progress as they go. Big powers and smaller states will have to cooperate to make it happen. Successful steps will generate trust and encourage the participants to prepare for further steps. In other words, disarmament can assume the role of catalyst and amplifier of cooperative behaviour. Confidence and security-building measures (CSBMs) and arms control and disarmament have had that role before: starting with the Stockholm agreement on CSBMs in 1986, such measures helped to move the world out of the Cold War. Had it not been for these measures, we might have seen not the end of the Cold War, but an early end of Gorbachev [Müller, Chapter 5].

The further the process advances, the more difficult it becomes to envisage the nature of world affairs. Due respect must be paid to the unpredictability of it all. At the threshold of elimination, when the powers have to decide whether to make the leap into an NWFW, the world will be a different place. Quite possibly, it will be a more secure one, for at this point the major powers will have gone through a series of cooperative steps, building confidence between them. To which Harald Müller adds – in reference to John Mueller, Ned Lebow and Steven Pinker – that the value of war for the great powers is already in decline. For developed middle powers, it is in disrepute.

The first stages of a resumed disarmament process, commonly assumed to be US–Russian cuts leading to multilateral talks, will not presuppose any major change of world order. But the scope of the negotiations may have to be enlarged to include non-nuclear systems standing in the way of disarmament. At present, these are primarily ballistic missile defence and long-range, high-precision missiles carrying conventional arms. Space weapons and other nuclear-related technologies also present obstacles. Gradually, the current system may be transformed, substituting cooperation and mutual restraint for antagonistic behaviour. If disarmament is recognized as a high-priority global public good, it may become one of the organizing principles of international affairs, enhancing world security in many more respects than nuclear disarmament *per se* can do.

Contemplating the kinds of world-order changes that may be needed to sustain a disarmament process to zero, references have been made to the 'European concert' after the Napoleonic wars, when the European powers undertook to respect each other's vital interests and exercise restraint in a system characterized by a balance of power. Henry Kissinger, an authority on concert diplomacy, has described this as a system where:

> the great powers work together to enforce international norms.... Common action grows out of shared convictions.... Power emerges from a sense of community and is exercised by an allocation of responsibilities related to a country's resources. It is a kind of world order either without a dominating power or in which the potentially dominating power leads through self-restraint.
>
> (Kissinger, 2009)

A big-power concert may be based on equilibrium between the participating states, or it may be based on consensus about norms. Generally, the former has been considered less demanding than the latter, although there are few examples of sustained operation of *any* version of power concerts. Kissinger's 'without a dominating power [or one that] leads through self-restraint' squares reasonably well with the evolving multicentric world of the first decades of the twenty-first century. However, when power is shifting so rapidly – the multicentric world already has a dominant bipolar dimension (US–China) and China is about to surpass the US in economic strength – a lasting equilibrium may be dead on arrival. Better, then, to focus on norms – norms of mutual respect and self-restraint embedded in a growing body of international law, not least with a view to building a platform for effective enforcement action.

Conceptual requirements

Central to the field of security are the concepts of common security and cooperative security. Common security, introduced by the International Commission on Disarmament and Security Issues (better known as the Palme Commission after its chairman, former Swedish Prime Minister Olof Palme) in the early 1980s, says that, in the nuclear age, security is something one has to build together with one's adversary (ICSDI 1982). Unilateral measures will not do: the belief that the latest weapons acquisition will yield lasting gains was illusory then and is equally misguided now. Enhanced security at lower levels of arms must be pursued as a win–win proposition. Approached as a matter of unilateral gain or national sacrifice, it will lead nowhere.

In the 1980s, the concept of common security gained traction in Europe and the Soviet Union, but not in the United States. In Reykjavik, Gorbachev applied common security logic. Thirty years later, the European security system is back to the logic that marred East–West relations during the Cold War. Security policies are conducted on a unilateral action/reaction basis; no common institutions are strong enough to serve as a platform for joint deliberations on how to manage brewing crises; and international law has become an argument of convenience. The Russian annexation of Crimea violated all international law – and foremost among the critics were states that *usually* violate international law when resorting to force. Interestingly, however, China has begun to advocate non-zero-sum common security thinking, opposing unilateral pursuits of absolute security at the expense of others [Yuan, Chapter 8].

Whereas common security purports to be a holistic international security philosophy, cooperative security – based on acceptance and tolerance and anchored in international law – places greater emphasis on institutionalized cooperation. Using cooperative security as a guide, multilateral institutions must be strengthened to uphold international law. UN reform is important, for shaping a more representative Security Council and enhancing the organization's ability to develop and enforce international law.

Today, there is no consensual normative basis of global governance. The majority of states pretend to behave the way the UN Charter of 1945 said they should behave – with state sovereignty, territorial integrity and non-interference in internal affairs being the main pillars – while Western states have taken international law further, making state sovereignty conditional upon the way governments treat their own citizens. In the field of security, the Responsibility to Protect (R2P) doctrine strikes a balance between the institutionalized indifference of those who remain content with the norm of non-interference, and the unilateral interference of leading states projecting their arrogance of power (Thakur 2013). However, while the doctrine was unanimously endorsed by world leaders in 2005, it proved vulnerable to misuse the first time it was applied – in Libya in 2011.

Common security and cooperative security complement each other. In broad terms, they are helpful in organizing our thoughts and charting our way through unknown territory. At an advanced stage of nuclear disarmament, when the major powers have come to base their security on conventional forces and political accommodation, leaving only a residual role for nuclear weapons, collective security – the compass of the UN Charter – may also play an important role to stop other states that might take an interest in nuclear arms. Presumably, at that stage the major powers would have a common interest in meeting challenges to their own disarmament trajectories.

Anchoring the NWFW on principles

Sethi argues that, in order to make an NWFW stable and sustainable, it should be based on a set of widely acceptable principles: uniformity of commitments; verifiability; acceptance and tolerance; the rule of law and collateral measures. While these principles may seem too general and idealistic, Sokov argues that on closer examination they can be operationalized in ways that are not so demanding.

Uniformity of commitments

The sense of discrimination that has bedevilled the relationship between nuclear and non-nuclear-weapon states, especially in the framework of the NPT, leaves no doubt that in an NWFW the rights and obligations must be the same for all. The expectations that were created when the NPT was adopted – that the division of the world in two categories would disappear as the NWS met their obligation to disarm – point unambiguously in that direction.

Verifiability

The implication for verification is that, while the scope of verification activities would have to be more comprehensive for the former NWS than for the others, the intrusiveness and stringency should be the same for both categories. Ever since full-scope safeguards were introduced in the 1970s, the IAEA has monitored all declared activities of non-nuclear members of the NPT, building confidence in their peaceful nature. Since the mid-1990s, an Additional Protocol to the safeguards agreements has allowed the Agency to search for materials and activities that might not have been declared. These instruments would go a long way towards meeting the verification requirements of an NWFW as well. Presumably, additional requirements would be a matter of updating and strengthening the verification instruments in view of technological developments. The gaps that remain to be filled relate to the NWS and the verification of nuclear weapon dismantlement – hardly an insurmountable obstacle [Persbo, Chapter 6].

Acceptance and tolerance

Sethi's plea for acceptance and tolerance emanates from the insecurities caused by non-acceptance of particular political and economic systems and the accompanying threats of regime change. Her advocacy of human rights simultaneously with tolerance of systemic diversity is reminiscent of some of the principles of the 1975 Helsinki Final Act. In Helsinki, it was agreed that promotion of human rights was a legitimate activity, while interference in the economic and political systems of others was not.

Today, the principle of acceptance and tolerance must be qualified in reference to R2P. The triggering events of R2P action are war crimes, genocide, ethnic cleansing and crimes against humanity, thus aligning the doctrine with existing categories of international legal crimes (Thakur 2013). These are issues that will have to be visited and revisited in light of changes in the international political order.

The rule of law

The United Nations is the main institutional framework for the development of international law. However, it has kept pace neither with the power shifts of the international system nor with the speed with which modern warfare can be conducted, and it cries out for reform. Still, two fundamentally important international security functions remain anchored in the UN: the evolution of international law and the legitimation of the use of force. Under international law, military operations are justified either in self-defence or when mandated by the Security Council. There is no other legal justification.

Collateral measures

Collateral measures – Sethi's fifth principle – are needed to prevent the NWS from deploying more sophisticated non-nuclear weapons to compensate for the elimination of nuclear capabilities. Compensatory acquisitions are very much what current security thinking would suggest, reproducing the classical security dilemma. If it comes to the deployment of new weapons that are more thinkable and therefore more likely to be used – compared with nuclear weapons, they would almost certainly be – security concerns and fears could actually be aggravated. The history of arms control and disarmament agreements is full of compensatory measures that have limited or even annulled their benefits.

The concept of non-offensive defence (NOD) offers an attractive response to this problem. A NOD posture is a distinctly defensive posture that is strong enough for defence against an attack but unsuitable for the occupation of foreign territories (Møller 1994). The Conventional Forces in Europe (CFE) agreement, concluded at the end of the Cold War, had such a profile. It eliminated large numbers of weapons suitable for offensive operations.

In its pure form, NOD obviates the need for conventional deterrence of breakout from an NWFW agreement. For this purpose, long-range power projection capabilities are necessary. Such capabilities should, therefore, be balanced against the need to avoid dysfunctional compensatory acquisitions and made compatible with the desired defensive character of national military postures. This is a tall order. Can these diverging concerns be reconciled?

Harald Müller suggests that, for a transitional period, when the necessary anti-breakout capabilities rest in the hands of a few, military action against a rule-breaker may be qualified in two ways. First, it should require authorization by the UN Security Council; second, it should be made contingent on the international verification agency (currently the IAEA) finding that a country has embarked on a nuclear weapon programme. Unless or until the Security Council takes action, the NWFW agreement could define such a finding as permitting self-defence under Article 51 of the UN Charter.

At a later stage – when sufficient trust in collective action has evolved – national capabilities could be shaped so that no single state would be able to take effective action against a rule-breaker, only in combination with others. Alternatively, conventional capabilities might be regulated in such a way that they could promptly attack and destroy a limited number of targets, but not be sufficient to conquer and subdue a major enemy. Müller notes that these are critical questions that should be revisited repeatedly throughout the nuclear disarmament process, as the nature of world politics changes and new options arise [Müller, Chapter 5].

A security culture without nuclear weapons

Humans calculate rationally, but our choices are influenced by emotions and cultural codes as well. Therefore, to degrade the role of nuclear weapons and the deterrence logic that sustains their role in international security affairs, we must change not only the utility calculus of states but also the culturally determined norms that tell people what to do or not to do.

The nuclear age can be read and understood as a struggle between the utility and futility of nuclear weapons. The former has had the upper hand, but the usefulness of the weapons has been questioned by popular revulsion against their use. Their destructive effects – in particular the long-term harm that they inflict

– make them uniquely abominable. Sethi quotes US Secretary of State John Foster Dulles from 1953: 'since in the present state of world opinion we could not use an A-bomb, we should make every effort now to dissipate this feeling ...' (Kuznick 2011).

There is a certain truth to the observation that, the more time that passes without nuclear weapons being used, the stronger the norm of non-use becomes. Globalization and growing media coverage also raise the reputational costs of use. The nuclear powers have, however, done much to sustain the realism of nuclear-weapons use. During the Cold War, threat-based policies were employed: the threats were highlighted and exaggerated, and stronger nuclear forces were recommended in response. Shows of force in the vicinity of hot-spots around the world also helped to maintain the credibility of nuclear policies by raising the visibility of nuclear assets and alerting the conflicting parties to the stakes involved. Furthermore, new types of weapons were introduced that would arguably be more usable. A range of weapons tailored to particular needs was developed.

However, shows of force nearly disappeared with the presidential initiatives of 1991/2, which eliminated tactical nuclear weapons from surface ships and removed all nuclear deployments from foreign soil except airborne weapons in the low hundreds in Europe. Any introduction of new types of weapons was severely restricted by the national moratoria on testing and the signatures on the CTBT. By the turn of the century, the means to counter the creeping norm of non-use had therefore shrunk.

The response came in the doctrinal field. Washington expanded the scope to the point of allowing for the possible use of nuclear weapons in settings where the adversary possesses conventional weapons only. Further, according to the National Security Strategies of 2002 and 2006, the USA must deter and defend against the threat of weapons of mass destruction *before* they are unleashed – in other words, by preventive attack, in violation of international law (The White House 2002, 2006). The Russian and French doctrines assigned new roles to nuclear weapons as well, as did the British and Indian doctrines, only to a smaller extent.

The Obama administration turned the trend once again by issuing unconditional assurances not to use or threaten to use nuclear weapons against NPT members in good standing. The UK followed suit, and France and Russia made smaller modifications. The US Nuclear Posture Review of 2010 said, moreover, that the USA would work to establish the conditions for a transition to no-first-use (NFU). Five years later, however, US think tanks and scholars are calling – once again – for new nuclear weapons that are more usable, and for changes in the posture that would allow employment of tactical nuclear weapons in limited wars in a flexible manner.

The norm of non-use has been promoted with a view to making the use of nuclear weapons taboo. We are not there, however. Nuclear weapons are being modernized, preparations for use are going on all the time, and deterrence doctrines are being reaffirmed at appropriate intervals. But the notion of a taboo, in the sense of 'that which should not be touched', is the logical end-station. The humanitarian approach to nuclear disarmament is at the forefront in this respect, arguing that, on ethical and legal grounds, any use of nuclear weapons – not just first-use – should be banned [Lewis, Chapter 9]. Ethical arguments widen elitist approaches phrased in power and security terms and bring in new stakeholders. All the time, actors with religious convictions– who see in humans and in nature the creation of god – are important in such endeavours.

The main provisions of an NWFW agreement need to be codified in national law – in national constitutions and in national criminal law, prescribing severe punishment for weapons-oriented activities. Education curricula should be used to confirm and strengthen the prohibition in the minds of young people. The UN should inspire and monitor the efforts and invite joint discussion of best practices [Müller]. These and other measures are important for promoting and internalizing a taboo.

The vision as a guide to action

The four US statesmen who, on the twentieth anniversary of Reykjavik, revived the vision of an NWFW (Shultz, Perry, Kissinger and Nunn 2008) emphasized the relationship between vision and measures. To achieve a dynamic, interactive relationship between the two, we must be serious about both. We must be serious about the measures because without concrete steps towards disarmament the vision would appear illusory, void of realism. Being serious about the vision means that a convincing rationale for an NWFW must be spelt out, that the broadest possible agreement about it must be sought, and that the advantages of such a world should weigh in the assessment of specific steps to be taken. Otherwise, the pros and cons of each single step will be assessed in the framework of the existing international system at any time, with scant regard for the gains that an NWFW offers. That would deprive the steps of their full meaning and leave them hostage to the priorities of the day. The four leaders were therefore right in their emphasis on the vision: if the vision is not persistently invoked in the discussions of how best to promote disarmament and non-proliferation, efforts in this direction are unlikely to lead very far. The dynamism will be missing.

How can the vision be a guide to action? The following analysis starts from the vision and works itself back to the present, identifying likely implications for disarmament strategies in scenario fashion.

Beyond nuclear deterrence

The stated rationale for the acquisition of nuclear weapons has always been phrased in terms of national security. It centres on deterrence: deterrence by the threat of mutual assured destruction; deterrence of strong conventional forces; and extended deterrence. The USA maintains extended deterrence postures in cooperation with its allies in Europe and East Asia. Nuclear warfighting, the most insane of all doctrines, which contemplated nuclear exchanges between the

USA and the Soviet Union involving thousands of weapons back and forth, was abandoned together with the Cold War.

Deterrence is deeply ingrained in the mind-sets of the NWS and attracts potential proliferators by imitation. As long as this is the case, stable zero is out of reach – as explained above, stability is not compatible with virtual deterrence or a world of threshold states. If, then, belief in the utility of nuclear deterrence is the number one obstacle to an NWFW, how can we extricate ourselves from this mode of thinking? And what are the intermediate steps on the way?

The first question may be the hardest of all. It is easier to get rid of the weapons than the mind-sets that always justified them. However, moral and legal considerations do transcend deterrence, for the destructive effects of nuclear weapons are such that no sane leader should ever use them. Moral arguments resonate across borders, and legal instruments are essential to give them binding form. As explained by Patricia Lewis, international law already goes a long way towards de-legitimizing any use, especially because it is almost impossible to contemplate a use of these weapons that would be in conformity with international humanitarian law. Furthermore, moral and legal arguments are universally relevant and applicable to governments and to civil society. This is crucial: in order to succeed, disarmament must be seen as a global common good.

The humanitarian approach to nuclear disarmament puts the moral and legal arguments at the centre of the debate. Three international conferences – in Norway (March 2013), Mexico (February 2014) and Austria (December 2014) – engaged a whole new set of participants and experts from the humanitarian, health and development communities. It is the distinct merit of the humanitarian approach that it broadens the set of stakeholders and injects fresh momentum into the disarmament debate.

The second part of the question has a clear answer: adoption of doctrines of no-first-use (NFU). NFU means that the role of nuclear weapons is reduced to one and one only: that of deterring their use by others. Deterrence of conventional forces and extended deterrence would be dropped, and so would threats of use.

Obama's nuclear posture review (NPR) of 2010 stopped short of this. However, having extended unconditional assurances not to use or threaten to use nuclear weapons against non-nuclear-weapon states that comply with their NPT obligations, the NPR added that the United States would work to establish the conditions for a transition to NFU. The nuclear employment strategy of 2013 followed up on it, directing the US Department of Defense to strengthen non-nuclear capabilities and reduce the role of nuclear weapons in deterring non-nuclear attacks (The White House 2013). China has always had an NFU doctrine; India's doctrine is close to it; and in an exchange of letters between Russian and Chinese leaders there is a bilateral NFU commitment between these countries.

If the USA and China – the main actors in contemporary geopolitics – commit and recommit themselves to such doctrines, the UK and India are likely to follow suit, and pressures would mount on the others. If they are not ready to go for universal NFU postures, they may do so in relation to one or more of their NWS peers. A gradual approach to the problem may therefore go a long way towards stripping deterrence of all other functions than that of deterring others from using their weapons. An intriguing disarmament corollary follows: if nobody had them, nobody would need them.

Diluting status gains

The unstated rationale for nuclear weapon acquisition is the status it confers on the possessors. Status ambitions are difficult to pin down because governments are loath to talk about them. There is something illegitimate and even bizarre about seeking prestige through acquisition of the most destructive and indiscriminate of all weapons.

Status played a major role in the British and French decisions to go nuclear, and they got what they wanted: a place at the table (Bundy 1969). France also got the muscle to chart an independent foreign policy. Some decades later, domestic prestige and international status played a role in the Indian government's declaration of the country's nuclear-weapon status.

As Patricia Lewis eloquently explains, status by imitation is quite customary, especially when the referent objects are powerful and few. The desire to be important and unique is a strong driver of human behaviour, and governments are no different from individual human beings in this respect. No wonder, therefore, that the five recognized NWS tried to pull the ladder up behind themselves when they signed the NPT. They have been largely successful, but not quite: the uniqueness has been somewhat watered down by the addition of a few more de facto NWS. Still, status and prestige invite proliferation.

Before it comes to an NWFW – at the springboard to freedom from nuclear weapons if not earlier – a nuclear weapons convention would have to be agreed, presumably superseding the NPT. Such a convention would specify the modalities of an NWFW; the requirements for the elimination of still-existing weapons; the provisions for the elimination and international control of fissile materials and dedicated nuclear infrastructure; and the verification and enforcement requirements. At this point, the difference between nuclear- and non-nuclear-weapon states would be greatly reduced, and with it the status benefits of possessing nuclear weapons. However, states rarely abandon their privileges voluntarily, so some compensatory status remnants may remain.

Once the weapons are gone, advanced nuclear technologies would compete for prestige with sophisticated technologies in other sectors, on a level playing field. Actually, the uniqueness of nuclear technologies has already been deflated considerably. For instance, when the NPT was signed in 1968, the proliferation of enrichment technologies received little attention by the NWS because this was considered too complex for others. By 2016, 15 countries operate enrichment facilities – and they are within reach, technologically and industrially, of many more countries.

Karl Marx noted that the most effective power is the structural one that functions without being actively used. Military force is a case in point, nuclear weapons not least. States have a fine eye for who is more and who is less powerful, and accommodate – consciously or not – to the stronger one. Nuclear weapons represent the highest destructive potential known to humankind, and their status value is particularly precious because they are limited to a few.

It follows that, in principle, there are two ways of diluting the status benefits of nuclear weapons: turning a small number of NWS into many; and reducing the utility of the weapons for national security. The first approach – recommended by a few – would raise the risk of nuclear war, and is here discarded out of hand (Sagan and Waltz 2002). The second brings us back to the utility or futility of nuclear deterrence and can be pursued by puncturing long-lived myths about their utility – such as that they made Japan surrender in 1945, and that they are effective means of blackmail (Wilson 2013) – and by promoting the norm of non-use on humanitarian grounds.

At the springboard

Imagine that the NWS have brought their arsenals down to 100 operational weapons or some similar number compatible with what today is called minimal deterrence: what would give them the courage to eliminate the rest and leap into a world without nuclear arms?

This is hard to foresee, for if and when the powers – big and small – are ready for a serious consideration of the matter, the world will be much different, and it would be presumptuous to claim to know much about it today. However, political order issues aside, some force constellations are known to be more unstable and dangerous than others. A few parameters can therefore be indicated to steer the process away from the greatest risks in the final approaches to zero.

To repeat: we deem it highly unlikely that the NWS would be willing to go for a world of virtual deterrence, where the ready-made nuclear weapons have been eliminated but where reconstitution capabilities are maintained. Why should they go for a form of deterrence with which they are unfamiliar, when they can stay with a form that they know, based on weapons they trust? In practice, a world at or immediately below zero would seem too risky.

Similar concerns exist immediately above zero. At the level of, say, 30 nuclear weapons, the retaliatory capabilities may be in doubt. Some weapons may be destroyed by an attacker, others may be intercepted, and yet others may not function as planned. As a result, first-strike propensities may be too great for comfort. That may lead to surprise attack, hitting an enemy when his guard is down, or to inadvertent escalation when decision-makers begin to think that war can no longer be avoided. Minimum deterrence is a flexible notion, but force levels of one or two hundred operational weapons may have been chosen for good reason.

It would therefore be wise to skip the phases immediately above and immediately below zero, and go directly from minimum deterrence to a world significantly below zero. In a gradualist perspective, the powers may eliminate their weapons when the build-down of reconstitution capabilities has been agreed and has begun, in the expectation that the process will proceed in accordance with the convention that has been adopted. Much as the distance from today's arsenals to minimum deterrence levels is long, the process from no ready-made weapons to no dedicated reconstitution capabilities may also be a time-consuming one that can be achieved only in gradual fashion.

The equity principle

It is hard to imagine an NWFW with different rules for different categories of states. Forty years of discontent with the NPT's division of the world into nuclear and non-nuclear weapon states, and persistent complaints over the slow implementation of Article VI, which was supposed to end it, have led NNWS to insist on equal rules for all. New measures should therefore ensure that capability differences are reduced more and more as the process unfolds.

The NPT was meant to be a regulatory mechanism for non-proliferation, disarmament and peaceful uses all the way to zero. Before approaching that point, the parties may wish to reinterpret some of its provisions, but they will probably see fit to keep the NPT till they come close to the springboard. Then, however, the NPT will no longer be adequate, for it says nothing about what kind of an NWFW to aim at. Therefore, a new convention outlining the ground rules of an NWFW will have to be adopted – its rules informed by the principle of equity, and leading to a world without nuclear weapons where the rights and obligations are the same for all.

Elimination of fissile materials

The importance of fissile material controls was already universally recognized during the NPT negotiations in the 1960s, and they became the central element of NPT safeguards in the early 1970s. The main hurdle on the way to a nuclear device is acquiring weapons-grade materials, so the first requirement in going below zero would be to eliminate, or bring under international control, all stocks of fissile materials dedicated to military use.

Given the vast amounts of fissile materials that exist today, and the time it takes to dispose of plutonium, more steps in this direction need to be taken – the sooner the better [Persbo, Chapter 6]. Uppermost on the international agenda – ever since the 1960s – is a fissile material cut-off treaty (FMCT). Such a treaty should be conceived not only as an arms control measure banning all activities at dedicated military production facilities, but also as a measure limiting the size of existing stocks. The equity principle means that each single step must be designed with a view to reducing the differences on the way to an NWFW with the same rules for all.

So far, limitations and reductions of existing stocks have been an NNWS demand. For the NWS, cut-off has primarily been a non-proliferation measure. However, if they subscribe to an NWFW below zero, that would change. Logically, both categories of states should then take an interest in the vertical as well as the horizontal dimension of the issue. This way, the vision would impact on the negotiability of an FMCT, indicating what a dynamic interactive relationship between vision and measures might be about.

Elimination of nuclear-weapons infrastructure

Faced with the disarmament drive of the early Obama administration days, some nuclear weapon supporters adapted to it by advocating a line of reasoning that has been dubbed anti-nuclear nuclearism: the more advanced the nuclear infrastructure, the further down one may go in operative nuclear-weapons systems (Bond and Parish 2009). The theoretical end-point of that argument is zero operative weapons in return for a comprehensive capability to bring them swiftly back to operative status, perhaps in a timespan not much different from that needed for readying de-mated systems for use. From the perspective of stable nuclear zero, such trade-offs are misguided.

In a world where reconstitution capabilities are maintained, the equity principle means that any state would be free to do the same: an NWFW that allowed current NWS to stay engaged in weapon-oriented activities while prohibiting them for all others would be totally unacceptable. This would be a world of numerous threshold states, translating into another strong argument for going well below zero.

Proliferation resistance

This leaves a set of issues as to how to make peaceful uses of nuclear energy more proliferation-resistant. Today, the promoters of proliferation resistance are mostly suppliers; with some important exceptions, the recipients tend to be naysayers.

Progress has been hampered by the imbalanced implementation of the NPT. Several NNWS have objected to any limitation of Article IV rights as long as the NWS do not do more to meet their disarmament obligations. In this respect, declaratory policies conveying big-power seriousness about an NWFW can be helpful, although this has been a legal obligation under the NPT all along, unequivocally confirmed by the 2000 NPT Review Conference. NNWS therefore hesitate to take anything for granted until words are better supported by facts.

No doubt, deep cuts and measures blocking qualitative developments of nuclear arsenals would create a context more amenable to proliferation-resistance measures. In turn, enhanced proliferation resistance would make it easier for the NWS to continue disarming. In the end, this would make an NWFW more sustainable. Therefore, in any scenario tracing the implications of stable zero to the present, proliferation-resistant modes of nuclear energy are desirable. However, the main driver – concerns about weapons proliferation in a world where nuclear power is proliferating – would seem stronger today and in the foreseeable future than in an NWFW. Today, the incentives for acquiring nuclear capabilities and nuclear weapons are in some cases strong, whereas the mechanisms for enforcing the non-nuclear commitments of the NPT and of nuclear-weapons-free zones are generally recognized as weak. In an NWFW, however, the further below zero one goes, the stronger will be the assurances against re-militarization and the lower the concerns about the shape of the civilian sector.

Verification

International safeguards must also be equitable. NNWS are unlikely to accept another differential deal such as safeguards limited to declared, dedicated facilities in NWS and full-scope safeguards in all the others [Persbo, Chapter 6]. In France, the UK and India, the civilian sectors are in principle safeguarded – in the UK and France by EURATOM/IAEA and in India by the IAEA pursuant to the US–India agreement – but civilian activities are not fully covered in the other NWS.

In a world well below zero, the need for verification will be greatly reduced. The more nuclear weapons are discarded as a means of international security affairs, and the more proliferation-resistant the peaceful applications of nuclear energy become, the less will be the need for verification. If the community of states removes these weapons entirely from the list of options, the function of safeguards will be limited to ensuring that no terrorist organization can get hold of fissile materials.

However, before it comes to that, international safeguards will be of the essence. Fissile materials will need to be accounted for, and the absence of undeclared stockpiles will have to be confirmed. The fuel cycles of the USA and Russia are particularly challenging because they differ greatly from and are much larger than cycles found elsewhere. The cost of disposing of the world's stockpile of weapons-grade plutonium has been estimated at US$24 billion, and it may take one or more decades to verify the initial declarations of these states. Warhead dismantlement and verification should therefore be pursued, the sooner the better, either by verifying the dismantlement of each individual warhead or by verifying the amount of nuclear material being withdrawn [Persbo, Chapter 6].

On the way to the springboard, the need for verification will grow also because the playing field becomes more equal. At low levels of arms, it may be easier for NWS to gain a military advantage and for newcomers to catch up. Verification of a multilateral disarmament agreement, and of NNWS commitments, may therefore have to be stricter than for today's disarmament and non-proliferation deals.

Given the current limitations on transparency in NWS, more comprehensive means of verification should be promoted gradually as new opportunities emerge. Overambitious attempts may backfire and do more harm than good, especially in states in the east and south that emphasize the principles of state sovereignty and non-interference. For instance, universal acceptance of societal verification will be out of the question for some more time, even on the most optimistic of assumptions. For China, secrecy remains a significant part of its nuclear posture.

Deep cuts

Contemplating the next stages of nuclear arms reductions – commonly expected to be US–Russian cuts leading to multilateral talks – a critical question is how to make disarmament a dependable prospect without resorting to a timeline, to which the NWS are opposed. So far, there is no good answer to that. Given the path-dependence of nuclear disarmament, there is something simplistic and artificial about any timeline to zero. The distance from here to there is simply too great to make fixed commitments realistic.

At an advanced stage, however, agreeing on a timeline may become possible. Above, we noted that further cuts can facilitate a shift from antagonistic to cooperative behaviour and that arms control and disarmament can be both catalysts *and* amplifiers of such a change. When approaching the springboard, the confidence that has been built and the cooperative security practices that have developed may facilitate agreement on a timeline for achieving the rest. The fact that the journey to stable zero has become shorter also makes it easier. At this stage, a nuclear weapons convention with a timeline may therefore be realistic.

How deep will US and Russian cuts have to be to engage France, China and the UK in disarmament negotiations? The three have been saying that the superpowers have to come down to their level (to the low hundreds), although in recent years the UK has shown flexibility in this respect. However, if the USA and Russia would agree to cut their forces to three-digit figures while stating their readiness to go for common P-5 ceilings at about the current levels of the UK, France, China, India and Pakistan, that might suffice. Not so if they were to invite the others with proportional reductions in mind, so that the USA and Russia would retain significantly larger arsenals than the others. That idea would be a non-starter.

How can a deep cuts agreement be tied to the vision? The least the USA and Russia can do is to reiterate the objective of an NWFW in the preamble to the agreement. In view of existing undertakings, this is 'free of cost'. Another possibility is to emphasize that, before it comes to elimination, the NWS would have to negotiate a convention defining the modalities of an NWFW and the final steps towards the goal. Yet another option would be to refer to the intermediate aim of multilateral disarmament talks – the deep cuts agreement being a step on the way to the enlargement of the negotiating table. If it takes more than one step to get there, the next US–Russia agreement could contain a declaration of intent to seek further cuts. Taken together, all this means references to the vision, to the need for a convention at an advanced stage of the disarmament process, to the intermediate goal of multilateral disarmament talks, and – before that – a commitment from one step to the next. Achieving one or more of these milestones would convey a seriousness about nuclear disarmament that has been lacking so far.

The Obama administration signalled that the United States is prepared to reduce its deployed strategic nuclear weapons by up to one-third (Jefferson and Kimball 2013). Russia has yet to express an interest in nuclear reductions below

New START levels. Future negotiations ought to encompass sub-strategic weapons as well, for this delicate issue is better dealt with in a comprehensive negotiation than separately. Next in line of importance is China, because of its geopolitical significance. Together, these are the states that most affect the security dynamics in regions of proliferation concern.

The strategic dialogue between the USA and China may develop into arms control and disarmament negotiations between these countries, too. Alexei Arbatov has noted that, for a start, combined limits on land-based ballistic missiles with ranges greater than 500 km might be considered (Arbatov 2014). That would be similar to the way US–Soviet arms control started 50 years ago. A possible side-effect of such a move is that Russia might take a stronger interest in disarmament talks as well.

Collateral measures

When Obama revived the vision of an NWFW, sceptics were concerned that the call was part of a double agenda, the real purpose of which was to sustain and enhance US and Western superiority. The synergies of disarmament and non-proliferation might stop smaller and weaker states from acquiring 'the great equalizer' – nuclear weapons – while the USA could emerge even more superior. At present, no one can match the sophisticated technological capabilities of the USA. Seen this way, nuclear disarmament would not be the hallmark of progressive politics but a conservative goal: change in order to preserve the dominance of the USA and the West.

New programmes may be set in motion to reduce existing imbalances or to make up for the shortfall of nuclear weapons. This is well known from arms control history: compensatory measures have been part and parcel of virtually all agreements, and may flatten the confidence-building effect of disarmament. Sethi's fifth principle – collateral measures to avoid reproduction of the security dilemma – is therefore well taken. So is her emphasis on NOD postures, which may offer a way out of the dilemma.

The principle can best be phrased in terms of common security: building security together with one's opponents and replacing unilateral action with jointly elaborated win–win solutions. This approach is incompatible with striving for superiority and hegemony, so it has failed to gain traction in the USA. Sooner or later, however, ongoing shifts in the international distribution of power may make it more attractive also there, especially in relation to China.

To overcome obstacles posed by unilateral pursuits, future disarmament negotiations may need to go beyond the traditional focus on nuclear weapon systems and incorporate some of the major non-nuclear issues that stand in the way of progress. At present, this applies particularly to high-precision conventional weapons and BMD technologies. They have a profound impact on the willingness of many NWS to engage in disarmament negotiations.

Conventional long-range, high-precision weapons

During the Cold War, arms control limitations centred on delivery vehicles. SORT referred to operationally deployed strategic warheads, but the counting rules referred to delivery vehicles. Those rules became a matter of discussion when the USA made plans for the deployment of conventional warheads on some of its ballistic missiles. New START solved the problem by counting all warheads, conventional or nuclear, against the 1,550 limit: a conventional warhead can be deployed only at the expense of a nuclear one. But Washington was quick to underline that 'New START protects the U.S. ability to develop and deploy a Conventional Prompt Global Strike (CPGS) capability. The Treaty in no way prohibits the United States from building and deploying conventionally armed ballistic missiles' (US Department of State 2010).

CPGS weapons would allow the US to strike targets anywhere on earth in as little as an hour. Conventional warheads on ballistic missiles, hypersonic glide vehicles or other delivery technologies – research and development continues – leave others with the tricky problem of how to deter and defend against conventional strikes. Nuclear deterrence of pinpointed conventional attacks, where the objective is not to conquer another nation but to destroy specific objects may not be credible, and protective measures may be very costly or infeasible. The Russians and the Chinese, while working on similar weapon systems themselves, are obviously concerned about this, and such concerns are by no means confined to them.

Missile defence

Mutual assured destruction is far from being an ideal basis of international security. The risks of breakdown are too great. Moreover, it is counter-intuitive, holding that we are best protected when naked. However, ballistic missile defence makes an untenable situation even worse, for by stimulating competitive acquisitions of offensive and defensive capabilities it obstructs nuclear disarmament.

Ronald Reagan proposed a cooperative US–Soviet missile shield as a hedge, in case someone should try to break out of an NWFW. His idea was theoretically attractive. However, like the Baruch plan for global control of nuclear weapons after the Second World War, the concern was that the technology developer could be left with an advantage. This was how the Soviets saw it in 1946, and this was how they viewed it in Reykjavik 40 years later.

In 1946 the Cold War was brewing; in 1986 it was dying. That year, the successful conclusion of the Stockholm conference on confidence and security-building measures and the Reykjavik summit were the first signs of different times to come. Still, suspicions ran deep in the national security bureaucracies. Moreover, the USA was about to reign supreme in a unipolar world, which reduced its interest in compromises and concerted actions. What appeared impossible then may therefore tell us little about the cooperative ventures that might become realistic if and when the world approaches zero nuclear weapons. The trust that may still be missing during another round of deep US–Russian cuts, and the suspicions that would continue to burden disarmament negotiations well into the multilateral phase, may no longer be there – or they might be there, but in a very different way when the goal is in sight, inviting thinking out of the box. In any event, the unconstrained national development of ballistic missile defence is a major security obstacle to nuclear disarmament, so innovative approaches and in-depth examination of possible solutions are of the essence.

In an NWFW, strict limits on missiles and missile defence may be defined in such a way that national systems would be strong enough to deny ballistic missile aggression by a single actor but not strong enough to avoid saturation by collective action [Müller, Chapter 5]. This would reduce the incentive to break out and leave everybody vulnerable to collective action. Another possibility would be to limit the capabilities to theatre missile defence, excluding those missile defence systems that can easily be plugged together to form a strategic missile defence capability (like advanced SM-3 missiles on Aegis ships in today's technology) [Sauer, Chapter 7]. Proposals have also been made for fully integrated cooperative systems as a hedge against breakout. These are particularly demanding propositions. In a multicentric world, they presuppose such a high level of trust across the board, are technically so complicated and demanding, and remain so different from today's deterrent thinking rooted in self-help that serious political attention must, at best, await an advanced stage of nuclear disarmament.

Sauer's preference is for zero offensive and zero defensive ballistic missiles; his second-best a limitation to theatre missile defence; and his third-best a defensive system shared by all major powers. He concludes that, on the way to an NWFW, missile defence is more a liability than an asset.

Final remarks

Have we made the road map to stable zero unnecessarily complex and difficult? In a sense, yes – for while we have analysed the international parameters of that road map at some length, political leaders will have to reduce the complexity of the issues in order to be able to deal with them. Otherwise, they will be overwhelmed and act on the side of caution, staying where they are rather than making any leap into the unknown.

What that reductionism might look like is not the subject of this discourse, however. Our task has been to examine a range of international issues that are likely to emerge on the way to a world free of nuclear weapons. In so doing, we have started from the vision and worked ourselves back to the present, showing how the vision can be a guide to action. Hence the fundamental importance of getting the vision right, that is, of being as clear as possible about the requirements of stable zero.

We have not paid much attention to the domestic hurdles on the way to an NWFW. Sokov indicates that the biggest obstacles to nuclear disarmament may lie there, in the domestic politics of the NWS. For instance, in the USA there is reluctance, for economic, industrial and political reasons, to subject modern non-nuclear weapons to regulation. These interests are shielded by assertions that the USA should be 'second to none', meaning that its military-technological superiority must be maintained. In Russia, nuclear weapons are invoked to address the concerns of a nationalistic public. Furthermore, if Russia, China and India should succeed in acquiring non-nuclear weapons similar to those of the USA, whatever support there is for nuclear disarmament in the USA may evaporate. All of this comes back to the fundamental warning that unrestricted unilateral development of alternative military tools is likely to undermine nuclear disarmament.

Finally, when complex, difficult problems are to be solved, one single approach is rarely sufficient. Such problems must be approached from many angles and in many ways. This is clearly the case with nuclear disarmament. Arms control; arms reductions; disarmament dividends for human betterment; doctrinal approaches limiting the role of nuclear weapons in international affairs; humanitarian approaches transcending deterrence doctrines; norms of cooperation, restraint and respect for vital interests and for international law; joint search for win–win solutions; and, not to forget, promoting a security culture where the most destructive and indiscriminate of weapons have no place – *all* of these have important roles to play. We must recognize them, not as alternatives but as mutually reinforcing paths to an NWFW.

Given the path-dependence of nuclear disarmament, are we guilty of fruitless speculation? Perhaps, but it is essential to continue discussing the problems and identifying possible solutions. If we can make the road to a world free of nuclear weapons more thinkable, then realization of it becomes more likely.

Notes

1 Square brackets indicate references to chapters in this volume.
2 His reading of world affairs as of 2009, the year his contribution was first published. Later, many NWS have increased their investments in nuclear modernization and expansion.

Bibliography

Arbatov, A. (2014) Engaging China in Nuclear Arms Control. Carnegie Moscow Center. [Online] available from: http://carnegieendowment.org/files/Arbatov_China_nuclear_Eng2014.pdf [accessed 5 February 2016].

Bond, G.D. and Parish, W. (2009) Anti-Nuclear Nuclearism. *Foreign Policy in Focus*. [Online] available from: www.fpif.org/articles/anti-nuclear_nuclearism [accessed 5 February 2016].

Bundy, M. (1969) To Cap the Volcano. *Foreign Affairs*, October.

Deutsch, K.W. (1962) *The Nerves of Government: Models of Political Communication and Control*. New York: Free Press.

Drell, S. and Goodby, J. (2009) *A World Without Nuclear Weapons: End State Issues*. Stanford: Hoover Institution.

ICDSI [International Commission on Security and Disarmament Issues] (1982) *Common Security*. Report by the International Commission on Security and Disarmament Issues, under the chairmanship of Olof Palme. London: Pan.

Jefferson, M. and Kimball, D. (2013) Obama Calls for Deeper Nuclear Cuts. *Arms Control Today*, November. [Online] available from: www.armscontrol.org/act/2013_0708/Obama-Calls-for-Deeper-Nuclear-Cuts [accessed 5 February 2016].

Kissinger, H. (2009) Obama's Foreign Policy Challenge. *Washington Post*, 22 April.

Kuznick, P. (2011). Japan's Nuclear History in Perspective: Eisenhower and Atoms for War and Peace. *Bulletin of the Atomic Scientists*, 13 April.

Møller, B. (1994) Common Security and Non-Offensive Defence as Guidelines for Defence Planning and Arms Control. *The International Journal of Peace Studies*. [Online] available from: www.gmu.edu/academic/ijps/vol. 1_2/Moeller.htm. [accessed 5 February 2016].

Sagan, S.D. and Waltz, K.N. (2002) *The Spread of Nuclear Weapons: A Debate*. New York: W.W. Norton.

Shultz, G., Perry, W.J, Kissinger, H.A. and Nunn, S. (2008) Toward a Nuclear-Free World. *Wall Street Journal*. [Online] available from: http://online.wsj.com/public/article_print/SB12036422673589947.htlm.

Thakur, R. (2013) R2P after Libya and Syria: Engaging Emerging Powers. *The Washington Quarterly*, 36(2): 61–76.

US Department of State (2010) *Fact Sheet*. [Online] available from: www.state.gov/newstart.

The White House (2002) *The National Security Strategy of the United States of America*. [Online] available from: www.state.gov/documents/organization/63562.pdf [accessed 5 February 2016].

The White House (2006) *The National Security Strategy of the United States of America*. [Online] available from: www.state.gov/documents/organization/64884 [accessed 5 February 2016].

The White House (2013) *Fact Sheet: Nuclear Weapons Employment Strategy of the United States*. [Online] available from: www.whitehouse.gov/the-press-office/2013/06/19/fact-sheet [accessed 5 February 2016].

Wikipedia (n.d.) https://en.wikipedia.org/wiki/Russell%25E2%2580%2593Einstein_Manifesto [accessed 5 February 2016].

Wilson, W. (2013) *Five Myths about Nuclear Weapons*. [Online] available from: www.amazon.com/Five-Myths-About-Nuclear-Weapons-ebook/dp/B006R8PGIU [accessed 5 February 2016].

Index

Please note that page numbers relating to Notes will be denoted by the letter 'n' and note number following the note.

ABM Treaty *see* Anti-Ballistic Missile Treaty (ABM Treaty)
Abolishing Nuclear Weapons (Perkovich and Acton) 7
acceptance and tolerance 24–5, 141
Action Plan for a Nuclear Weapon Free and a Non-violent World Order (1988) 24
Acton, James 7
Adelphi papers (International Institute for Strategic Studies) 7
Aegis SM-3 missiles 95, 96
Afghanistan 41; Soviet withdrawal from 62
Air-Sea Battle Concept 118
American Academy of Arts and Sciences 7
Andreasen, Steven 106
anti-ballistic-missile (ABM) systems 11
Anti-Ballistic Missile Treaty (ABM Treaty) 95, 96, 98
arms control 1, 3, 15, 37, 49, 60, 62, 69, 135, 148, 153; conventional 24, 64; and disarmament 60, 61, 78, 112, 115, 129, 138, 142, 151, 152; nuclear 17, 73, 117; US–Soviet 152; verification of arms reductions 78–82; *see also* nuclear disarmament
Asia 2, 3, 16, 17, 18, 128, 133, 134; East Asia 16, 111, 118, 119, 144; South Asia 16, 45, 48, 74, 84, 111, 119; South-East Asia 61; *see also* China; India; Japan; North Korea; Pakistan; South Asia; South Korea; Taiwan
Asian Institute for Policy Studies (Seoul), opinion polls conducted by (2013) 17–18, 27n1

Aspin, Les 57
Austen, Jane 128
Austria 57, 145
'axis of evil' (2002) 35
Axis powers, World War II 18

Badham, John 73
ballistic missile defence (BMD) 18, 27n2, 64, 65, 66, 104, 107, 152; *see also* Anti-Ballistic Missile Treaty (ABM Treaty)
Beckett, Margaret 129
Berlin Wall, fall of 62
bilateral deterrence 16
Bipartisan Strategic Posture Commission, US 98, 107
Bismarck, Otto von 88
Booth, Ken 26
British International Nuclear Disarmament Institute (BRINDI) 129
British Pugwash 129
Brooks, John 127
Brown, Harold 13n2, 36
Browne, Des 92, 129
Bush, George H.W. 101
Bush, George W. 70n1, 95, 96, 99, 101–2, 105
Butler, Lee 36, 65

Canberra Commission 36
Carnegie Conference 129
Carnegie Endowment for International Peace 7
Charter, UN 25, 64, 140, 142
chemical weapons (CW) 19
Chemical Weapons Convention (CWC) 19–20, 47, 49, 85, 92n7, 125, 129

158 *Index*

China 10, 16, 17, 33, 35, 43, 49, 74; denuclearization 12; nuclear disarmament perspective 111–22; and Russia 97, 98, 100, 103; as second-tier nuclear power 116; and United States 20, 152; and Vietnam 34
Clinton, Bill 83, 99
Clinton, Hillary 102, 103
Cold War 1, 15, 16, 31, 34, 37, 69, 114, 118, 134, 139, 143, 153; end of/final phase 15, 50, 61, 70, 74, 123; pre-nuclear and post-nuclear world, comparison 41, 44, 45, 48; *see also* superpowers
collateral measures 49, 141–2, 152–4; simultaneous 24
collective security 58
commitments, uniformity of 140
common security 26, 114, 137, 139, 140, 152; *see also* cooperative security
Comprehensive Test Ban Treaty (CTBT) 48, 143
Concert of Europe 112
concert of powers 62–3, 114
Conference on Disarmament, Geneva 35, 129
Conferences on the Humanitarian Impact of Nuclear Weapons (2013 and 2014) 126
confidence and security-building measures (CSBMs) 138
conventional and political deterrence 63–5
conventional global prompt strike (CGPS) 117, 118, 153
conventional long-range, high-precision weapons 153
Convention on the Prohibition of the Use of Nuclear Weapons (draft resolution) 19, 27n3
Convention with Respect to the Laws and Customs of War on Land (ICRC) 124
cooperative missile defence, possible role of 65–6
cooperative security, pursuing of 58, 139, 140; *see also* common security
counterfactual analysis 30, 31, 37n2
Crimea, Russian annexation (2014) 139
crisis stability 11
cruise missiles 64
Cuban missile crisis 41
Czech Republic 102

Defense and Deterrence Posture Review 46

Delpech, T. 38n5
Democratic People's Republic of Korea (DPRK) *see* North Korea
Department of Defense, US 145
deterrence theory 32, 34, 37, 73, 92n1; *see also* nuclear deterrence
Deutch, John 13n2
Deutsch, Karl 136
disarmament *see* nuclear disarmament
dismantlement 81
DPRK *see* North Korea
Dr Strangelove (Kubrick) 73
Dulles, John Foster 12, 20

East Asia 16, 111, 118, 119, 144
Eastern Europe, democratization of 62
Einstein, Albert 18
equity principle 148–50
European Phased Adaptive Approach (Obama) 95

Ferdinand, Archduke Franz 47
Fermi, Enrico 18
First World War *see* World War I
Fischer, David 86
fissile materials 9, 18, 31, 79, 84; elimination 148–9
Fissile Material Treaty/Fissile Material Cut-Off treaty (FMCT) 84, 85, 148, 149
flexible response 10
FMCT *see* Fissile Material Treaty/Fissile Material Cut-Off treaty (FMCT)
Ford, Christopher 36
'former nuclear powers' 9
Forsberg, Randall 105
forward induction, counterfactual 30
France 12, 35, 116, 146
Frye, A. 106

Gaither Committee 11
Gandi, Rajiv 24
'Gang of Four' 70
Gates, Bill 127
General and Complete Disarmament (GCD) 7
Geneva Conventions (August 1949), Protocol I (1977) 124–5
Geneva Protocol (1925) 124, 125
Gide, André 26–7, 133
Goodby, Jim 136
Goodpaster, A.J. 36, 38n7
Gorbachev, Mikhail 1, 61, 70n2, 101, 112, 116, 133, 138
Graham, B. 99, 101–2

Group of Eight (G-8) Summit, 2007 102

Helsinki Final Act (1975) 141
Hezbollah 34
highly enriched uranium (HEU) 137
Hiroshima 20
Horner, Charles 36, 65
Hungary 62
Hussein, Saddam 9
hydrogen bomb 18

IAEA see International Atomic Energy Agency (IAEA)
Iklé, Fred 105
India 1, 8, 32, 33, 34, 43; and nuclear-weapons-free world (NWFW) 16, 17, 25; and Pakistan 45, 84, 119, 134, 151; verification requirements 84, 89
Indo-Pacific region 114, 118
induction, counterfactual analysis 30
INF (Intermediate-Range Nuclear Forces Treaty), 1987 1, 61, 70n2, 105, 106, 116, 117
information barriers 79, 84, 92n5
Intermediate-Range Nuclear Forces Treaty see INF (Intermediate-Range Nuclear Forces Treaty), 1987
International Atomic Energy Agency (IAEA) 42, 92n9, 113, 142; Secretariat 89; Statute 90; and verification requirements 78, 83, 84, 87, 88, 90, 91
International Committee of the Red Cross (ICRC) 125
International Federation of the Red Cross (IFRC) 125
international humanitarian law (IHL) 124, 125
International Institute for Strategic Studies 7
International Panel on Fissile Materials (IPFM) 82
Iran 12, 35, 113, 126
Iraq 34, 125; botched reporting of nuclear activities (2003) 32
irreversibility 76–7
Irreversibility in Nuclear Disarmament: Practical steps against nuclear rearmament (Cliff) 77
Iskander missiles 98
Israel 10, 34

Japan 16, 20
Jingdong Yuan 136
journals 7

Kampelman, Max 105
Karp, Regina Owen 27
Kissinger, Henry A. 2, 7, 36, 74, 111, 138, 139
Korea see North Korea; South Korea
Kubrick, Stanley 73

Lance short-range nuclear missile 70n2
'latent nuclear powers' 34
Latin America 61
Lavrov, Sergei 101, 103
Lebanon 34
Lebow, Richard Ned 31, 138
Levi, M.A. 70n1
Lewis, Patricia 146
long-range strike options 35

Mamedov, Georgi 101
Mark-41 (MK-41) missile launcher 116
Marx, Karl 146
Medvedev, Dmitry Anatolyevich 102, 103
Mexico 145
Middle East 16, 126; see also Israel; specific Arab countries
Miliband, David 99
minimum deterrence 147
missile defence 153–4; as alternative to nuclear deterrence 95–110; global, in long term 103–4; global, in medium term 98–103; lack of 104–7; scenarios 97–107; 'unilateral' 96, 97–8
missile interceptors 95
Missile Technology Control Regime (MTCR) 105
mobilization bases 8–9
modernization of strategic systems 16
Møller, Bjorn 26
Mueller, John 31, 138
Müller, Harald 21, 74, 95, 100, 112, 113, 116, 117, 120, 123, 124, 127–8, 129, 136, 138, 142
multicentrism 139
multilateralism, nuclear disarmament 88–91, 114
multiple independently targetable re-entry vehicles (MIRV) 10
MX missile basing problem 10, 11

Nagasaki 20, 33
National Security Strategies (2002 and 2006) 143
NATO (North Atlantic Treaty Organization) 45–6, 47, 70n2, 98, 102, 128; missile defence 96

Nelson, Horatio 33
neo-conservatism 61
New START *see under* Strategic Arms Reduction Treaty (START I)
NFU *see* no-first-use (NFU) agreement
'no-cities' 10
no-first-use (NFU) agreement 19, 20, 21, 114, 143, 145
non-discrimination 23
non-first-use-(NFU) policy 114
'non-nuclear' configuration 59
non-nuclear-weapon states (NNWS) 1; verification requirements 77, 78, 87, 88, 90, 150; *see also* nuclear-weapon states (NWS)
non-nuclear world/nuclear-weapons-free world (NWFW) 1, 7–29, 55, 112, 114, 154; acceptance and tolerance 24–5, 141; agreement, main provisions 144; anchoring on principles 140–2; assumptions, contesting 15–21; challenges of building 41–4; inevitability of nuclear rearmament 18–21; keeping dream alive 120–1; and missile defence 103; missile defence, nuclear elimination without or without 96–107; shape of world free of nuclear weapons 44–50; stable *see* stability; verification requirements 75–8; *see also* nuclear disarmament; Schelling, T. C. (on nuclear disarmament)
non-offensive defence (NOD) concept 26, 28n8, 142
Non-Proliferation Treaty (NPT) 1, 2, 7–8, 10, 16, 67, 128, 146; Review and Extension Conference (1995) 120; Review Conference (2015) 57, 111, 116, 120; verification requirements 85, 87, 88, 92
north-east Asia 16
North Korea 1, 12, 35, 48, 113, 126, 128; and missile defence 95, 98; and nuclear-weapons-free world (NWFW) 16, 17, 18; verification requirements 76, 86, 89, 92n2, 92n9; *see also* South Korea
Norway 129, 145
NPT *see* Non-Proliferation Treaty (NPT)
nuclear arms control 17, 73, 117; *see also* arms control; nuclear disarmament
nuclear deterrence: beyond 144–6; Cold War-informed theory 34; continuing belief in contributing to proliferation 126–7; conventional and political 63–5; as default option 56; deterrence theory 73; minimum deterrence 147; missile defence as alternative to 95–110; multipolar, reality of 16; persistence as key obstacle to nuclear disarmament 127–8; remedies 60–9; Schelling on 37n3; as a social relationship 56–8; and verification 123–30; virtual deterrence 55–6, 59–60; *see also* deterrence theory; nuclear disarmament; nuclear rearmament; nuclear weapons; Schelling, T. C. (on nuclear disarmament)
nuclear disarmament 18, 30, 36; Chinese perspective 111–22; cooperative missile defence, possible role of 65–6; and cultural change 55–72; humanitarian approach to 145; multilateralism in 88–91, 114; nuclear deterrence persistence as key obstacle to 127–8; path-dependence 155; security culture without nuclear weapons 66–9, 142–4; transformative function of process 60–2; views of Schelling *see* Schelling, T. C. (on nuclear disarmament); and vision 133–56; *see also* non-nuclear world; nuclear deterrence; nuclear rearmament; nuclear weapons
nuclear dyads 16, 24
Nuclear Non-Proliferation Treaty *see* Non-Proliferation Treaty (NPT)
Nuclear Posture Review, US (2010) 15, 58, 114, 143, 145
'nuclear quiescence' 15
nuclear rearmament: inevitability of 18–21; rearmament parity 22; stability through knowledge of 21–2; *see also* non-nuclear world; nuclear deterrence; nuclear disarmament
'nuclear taboo' *see* 'taboo, nuclear'
nuclear testing 32
Nuclear Threat Initiative (NTI) 7
nuclear weapons: complexes 59; 'credible' arsenals 16; experts 127; and major war 134–5; and nuclear rearmament 18–19; nuclear-weapons infrastructure, elimination 149; security culture without 142–4; shape of world free of 44–50; as social construct 55; tactical 17, 46; US nuclear weapons community 10; verification of non-emergence elsewhere 85–8; warheads 9, 79; *see also* non-nuclear world; nuclear deterrence; nuclear disarmament; nuclear rearmament

Index   161

nuclear-weapons-free world (NWFW) *see* non-nuclear world/nuclear-weapons-free world (NWFW)
nuclear-weapon states (NWS) 1, 2, 16, 34, 50, 128, 145; elimination of nuclear-weapons infrastructure 149; nuclear disarmament and cultural change 57, 58; status gains, diluting 146, 147; verification requirements 75, 79, 85; *see also* non-nuclear-weapon states (NNWS)
Nunn, Sam 2, 7, 36, 74, 111
NWFW (nuclear-weapons-free world) *see* non-nuclear world/nuclear-weapons-free world (NWFW) 14–29
NWS *see* nuclear-weapon states (NWS)

Obama, Barack 2, 7, 25, 36, 44, 50, 111, 114, 129–30, 149, 151–2; European Phased Adaptive Approach 95; and missile defence 96, 99, 102, 103, 106; Nuclear Posture Review (2010) 15, 58, 114, 143, 145; Prague speech 70
O'Hanlon, M.E. 70n1
Organisation for the Prohibition of Chemical Weapons (OPCW) 49, 86
Osirak reactor 34

Pahlavi, Mohammad Reza 34
Pakistan 1, 16, 34, 35, 45, 74, 84, 95, 119, 134, 151
Pareto efficiency 81
Paris Charter 62
Peaceful Nuclear Explosives (PNEs) 8
Perkovich, George 7
Perry, William J. 2, 7, 36, 74, 106, 111
Persbo, Andreas 112, 113, 116, 120, 129
Pinker, Steven 31, 138
Plutonium Management and Disposition Agreement (PMDA) 83, 84
Poland 62, 102
pre-emption 33
pre-nuclear and post-nuclear world, comparison 40–51; challenges of building a nuclear-free world 41–4; Cold War 41, 44, 45, 48; shape of world free of nuclear weapons 44–50
proliferation networks 16
proliferation resistance 149–50
Pugwash Conferences on Science and World Affairs 135
Putin, Vladimir 46, 83, 101, 102, 103
Pyongyang 35

R&D programmes 46

Rasmussen, A. 102
Reagan, Ronald 1, 61, 96, 105, 112, 116, 133, 153
rearmament *see* nuclear rearmament
Red Crescent Societies 125
reductionism 154
remedies, nuclear disarmament: concert of powers 62–3, 114; conventional and political deterrence 63–5; cooperative missile defence, possible role of 65–6; security culture without nuclear weapons 66–9; transformative function of disarmament process 60–2
Responsibility to Protect (R2P) 140, 141
revolution in military affairs (RMA) 49
Reykjavik summit (1986) 1, 61, 133, 139
Rice, Condoleezza 100
Roberts, B. 16
Rocard, Michel 36
Rogozin, Dmitry 100, 102
'rogue' states 97
Ross, Denis 101
Rotblat, Sir Joseph 129
Rühle, Michael 36
rule of law 26, 49, 141
Russell–Einstein Manifesto 135
Russia 10, 15, 16, 27n2, 35, 43, 103; and China 97, 98, 100, 103; Crimea, annexation of (2014) 139; denuclearization 12; military occupation of Syria 47; 'nuclear bravado' 46; and United States *see* United States and Russia/Soviet Union; *see also* Soviet Union, former; superpowers

Saudi Arabia 16
SBX-1 radar 17
Schell, Jonathan 21, 22, 65
Schelling, Thomas C. (on nuclear disarmament) 13n1, 15, 30–9, 40, 41, 42, 59, 135; empirical claims 34–6; flaws in argument 36–7; on impact of existing nuclear arsenals on proliferators objection 35; inconsistency in rationalist assumptions 32–4; no nuclear arms race objection 35; nuclear disarmament discourse 36; wars involving nuclear powers objection 34
Second Nuclear Age, challenges of 114–20
second-tier nuclear powers 116
Second World War *see* World War II
Security Council *see* United Nations Security Council (UNSC)

security culture, without nuclear weapons 66–9, 142–4
self-defense 9
Sestanovich, Stephen 101
Sethi, Manpreet 40, 41, 47, 48, 49, 134, 141, 152
Shultz, George P. 2, 7, 36, 74, 106, 111, 133
Singh, Jasjit 25
Sloss, Leon 106
South Africa 61
South Asia 16, 45, 48, 74, 84, 111, 119
South-East Asia 61
South Korea 16, 17, 18; *see also* North Korea
Soviet Union, former 12, 19, 43; collapse of 74; *see also* Russia
space-based weaponry 64, 138
stability/stable NWFW: acceptance and tolerance 24–5; non-discrimination 23; risks to 16; rule of law 26; simultaneous collateral measures 24; stable nuclear zero 136–7; sustaining 21–6; through anchoring on principles 22–6; through knowledge of rearmament 21–2; verifiability 23, 140–1
Stanley Foundation 7
START I *see* Strategic Arms Reduction Treaty (START I)
status gains, diluting 146–7
Stockholm International Peace Research Institute 36
Strategic Arms Reduction Treaty (START I) 1, 61; New START 98, 103, 111, 116, 120, 152, 153
Strategic Concept 46
Strategic Defense Initiative, US 1
Stützle, W. 62
superpowers 1, 2, 15, 74, 133, 151; and missile defence 101, 102; and nuclear disarmament from Chinese perspective 114, 116; and nuclear-weapons-free world (NWFW) 15, 18; *see also* Cold War; Russia; United States
Switzerland 57
Syria 27n4, 34, 47, 125

'taboo, nuclear' 12, 33, 67, 112, 124, 137, 143, 144; non-nuclear world/nuclear-weapons-free world (NWFW) 17, 19, 20; nuclear disarmament and cultural change 56, 59, 67, 68, 70
tactical nuclear weapons 17, 46
Taiwan 16

Tannenwald, Nina 67
Tertrais, Bruno 36
Third Special Session on Disarmament (1988), UN 24
Thränert, Oliver 104
Treaty on Conventional Armed Forces in Europe (CFE) 24
Treaty on the Non-Proliferation of Nuclear Weapons 35
Trilateral Initiative 42, 83–4
Turkey 16

Ukraine 45, 111, 116, 133
United Kingdom 35, 86, 146; denuclearization 12; 'National Nuclear Centre of Excellence' proposed by 129; as second-tier nuclear power 116
United Nations General Assembly (UNGA) 68; Resolution 70/48 126
United Nations Office for Disarmament Affairs 69
United Nations Security Council (UNSC) 49, 64, 89, 120, 133, 139, 142
United States 8–9, 38n5, 43, 77, 129, 154–5; Bipartisan Strategic Posture Commission 98, 107; Department of Defense 145; nuclear alliances with 123; Nuclear Posture Review (2010) 15, 58, 114, 143, 145; Strategic Defense Initiative 1; tactical nuclear weapons 17, 46; *see also* Bush, George H.W.; Bush, George W.; Clinton, Bill; Clinton, Hillary; Obama, Barack; Reagan, Ronald; superpowers
United States and Russia/Soviet Union 96; cuts 151–2; and non-nuclear world 20, 24; and nuclear disarmament from Chinese perspective 111, 116, 120; pre-nuclear and post-nuclear world, comparison 43, 45, 49, 50; US–Russian Joint Declaration 102; and verification requirements 83, 84; *see also* Russia; Soviet Union, former; United States
unity of action by international community 20, 23
USF-22 stealth fighter jets 17
USS *John S. McCain* 17
USSR *see* Soviet Union, former
Uzumcu, A. 86

verification 31, 113, 150; arms reductions 78–82; and nuclear deterrence 123–30; requirements 73–94; that disarmed remain disarmed 78, 82–5; that nuclear

weapons do not emerge elsewhere 85–8; verifiability 23, 140–1; world without nuclear weapons 48, 75–8
VERTIC (Verification, Research, Training and Information Centre, London) viii, 77, 129; VERTIC-VCDNP programme 48
Vienna Conference (2014) 126
Vienna symposium on Stable Zero 37n1
Vietnam 41; and China 34
virtual deterrence 55–6, 59–60
vision, and disarmament policy 133–56; conceptual requirements 139–40; as guide to action 144; international political order requirements 137–9; nuclear weapons and major war 134–5; stable nuclear zero 136–7; *see also* non-nuclear world/nuclear-weapons-free world (NWFW); nuclear disarmament
vulnerability 11

Walker, William 36
Wall Street Journal 7, 8
Waltz, Kenneth 128
war: Cold War *see* Cold War; First World War *see* World War I; major war, and nuclear weapons 134–5; nuclear power objection, involving 34; Second World War *see* World War II
WarGames (Badham) 73, 74
Warsaw Treaty 61
Weapons of Mass Destruction Commission 36
Wheeler, N.J. 26
World Nuclear Association 76
World War I 41, 43, 47; Battle of Ypres 124
World War II 10, 18, 41, 43, 47
A World Without Nuclear Weapons? (Schelling) 7–13, 14

Yeltsin, Boris 101

Taylor & Francis eBooks

Helping you to choose the right eBooks for your Library

Add Routledge titles to your library's digital collection today. Taylor and Francis ebooks contains over 50,000 titles in the Humanities, Social Sciences, Behavioural Sciences, Built Environment and Law.

Choose from a range of subject packages or create your own!

Benefits for you
- Free MARC records
- COUNTER-compliant usage statistics
- Flexible purchase and pricing options
- All titles DRM-free.

REQUEST YOUR FREE INSTITUTIONAL TRIAL TODAY

Free Trials Available
We offer free trials to qualifying academic, corporate and government customers.

Benefits for your user
- Off-site, anytime access via Athens or referring URL
- Print or copy pages or chapters
- Full content search
- Bookmark, highlight and annotate text
- Access to thousands of pages of quality research at the click of a button.

eCollections – Choose from over 30 subject eCollections, including:

Archaeology	Language Learning
Architecture	Law
Asian Studies	Literature
Business & Management	Media & Communication
Classical Studies	Middle East Studies
Construction	Music
Creative & Media Arts	Philosophy
Criminology & Criminal Justice	Planning
Economics	Politics
Education	Psychology & Mental Health
Energy	Religion
Engineering	Security
English Language & Linguistics	Social Work
Environment & Sustainability	Sociology
Geography	Sport
Health Studies	Theatre & Performance
History	Tourism, Hospitality & Events

For more information, pricing enquiries or to order a free trial, please contact your local sales team:
www.tandfebooks.com/page/sales

 | The home of Routledge books

www.tandfebooks.com

Printed in the United States
By Bookmasters